MID SUSSEX CHURCH WALKS

30 Walks to 90 Churches

Diana Pé

Published by ***PP (Pé Publishing)***
Email: Tonype@onetel.com

ISBN 0-954-36902-5

Cover: Audrey Stevens

Maps: Stephen Good

Photographs: Diana Pé

Printed by: Downland Print Services Ltd, 2006

Preface

All the walks in this book can be found in Ordnance Survey Explorer Maps 121, 122, 134 and 135. In the rare cases where the walk overlaps onto two Explorer maps, I have also cited the OS Landranger Maps (197 and 198). The relevant map or maps are given at the start of each walk. It is a good idea to bring them along to supplement the maps drawn by Stephen Good.

In several walks we pass a little way on a long distance footpath. A list of these paths, some quite famous, together with their mileages is at the back of this book, page 156.

Whilst on the subject of mileage, I must apologise to those walkers who believe that the metric system should be used exclusively. Others wish to hold to miles and yards. I find I favour both. So, whilst shorter distances are given in metres, I do occasionally slip into miles, or even half miles! – Sorry! The length of each walk is also in miles.

I have written this book as a sequel to my first publication: 'West Sussex Church Walks'. Not expecting such joy further east, I made my next books in Dorset and Cornwall. I have now returned to Sussex and have come to appreciate and love this part of the county. The Weald is not dramatic, but is beautiful like an English water colour. It was once impenetrable and still retains a secret charm. The Downs, as portrayed by Esther Meynell (see the first paragraph of my introduction), are magnificent. The rivers form part of the rich history of Mid Sussex. You too will come under the spell of this lovely part of the county – you may already be there!

Acknowledgments

My thanks for their help in the preparation of this book go to John Avenell, Dennis Clarke, Stephen Good, Dr T.T. Hlaing, Gabrielle Ma, Windy Leung, Robert Pe, Tony Pe, Doreen Peskett, Kathleen Ramsay, Daphne Reeve, Karen Standing, Audrey Stevens and Peggy Synge.

My gratitude also goes to those generous ramblers belonging to Brighton and Hove 200th, Horsham and Billingshurst Ramblers and West Sussex Ramblers Association. They have checked the walks thoroughly and offered some valuable suggestions. Many of their ideas are woven into these walks and one or two pitfalls have been avoided!

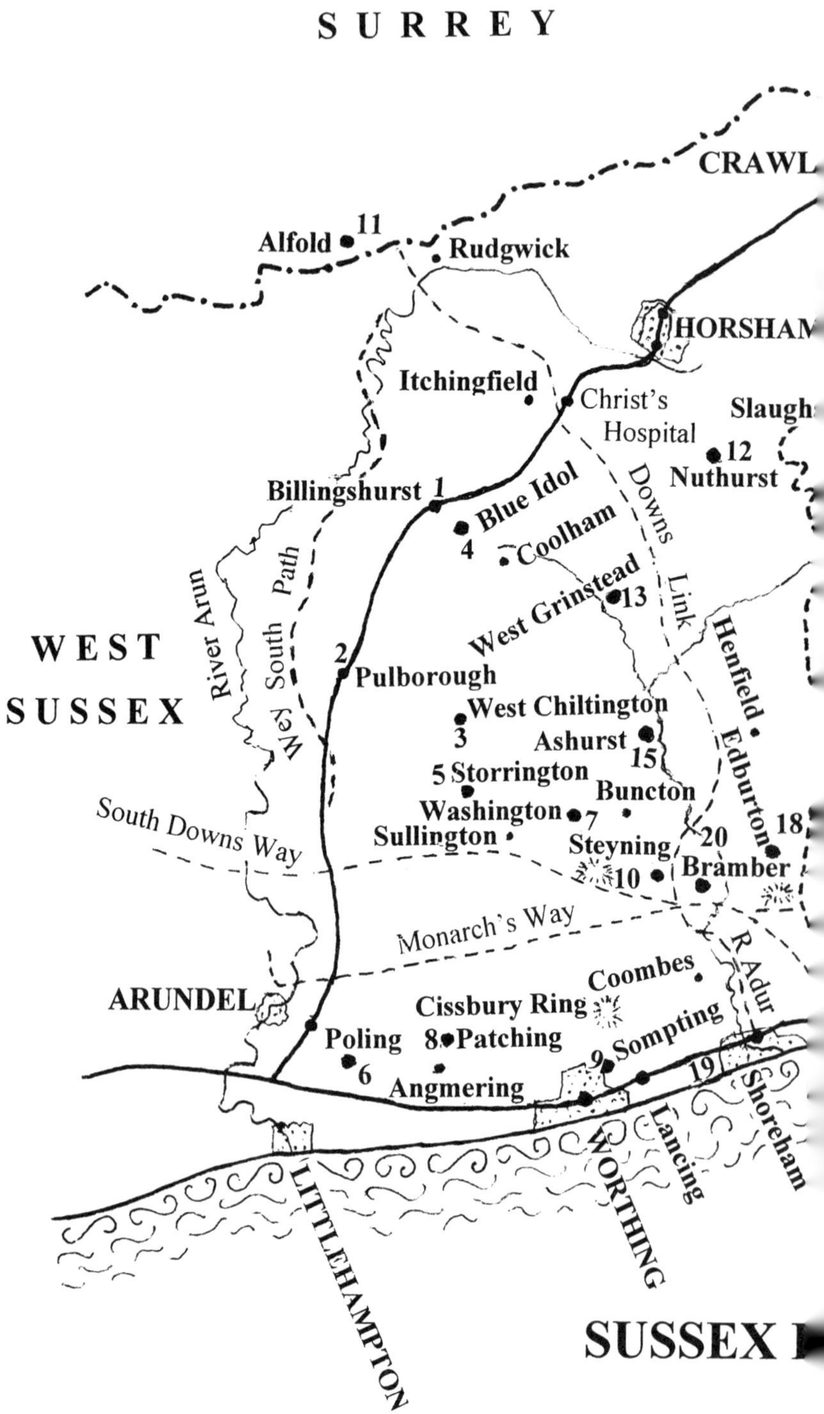
SURREY
CRAWL
Alfold 11
Rudgwick
HORSHAM
Itchingfield
Christ's Hospital
Slaugh
12 Nuthurst
Billingshurst 1
Blue Idol
4
Coolham
Downs Link
West Grinstead 13
River Arun
Wey South Path
WEST SUSSEX
2 Pulborough
West Chiltington
3
Ashurst 15
Henfield
Edburton
5 Storrington
Buncton
Washington 7
Sullington
South Downs Way
Steyning
20
18
10
Bramber
Monarch's Way
R Adur
Coombes
ARUNDEL
Cissbury Ring
Poling 6
8 Patching
9 Sompting
19
Angmering
WORTHING
Lancing
Shoreham
LITTLEHAMPTON
SUSSEX

Present Boundary
KENT
EAST GRINSTEAD
Worth
Worth Way
22
Kingscote
Railways
Footpaths
Worth Abbey
Bluebell Railway
W. Hoathly
ASHDOWN
FOREST
Ardingly
21
Horsted Keynes
lefield
ckfield
24
Lindfield
VARDS
ATH
Sheffield Park
Wivelsfield
25
Ouse
River
EAST
SUSSEX
Plumpton Green
17
Jack & Jill Windmills
Cooksbridge
29
Hamsey
Ditchling Beacon
LEWES
26
30
Glyndebourne
27
Kingston
Glynde
South Downs Way
16
Southease
28
BRIGHTON
Seaford

TION MAP

The Downs separate the Weald in the north from the coast. The huge forest, the Weald once stretched from Kent to Hampshire. Now there are fragments where the wanderer may sometimes capture the secret spirit of Pan. The chalk Downs have withstood intrusion through past centuries. The Wealden forest and a reputation for the worst roads in England discouraged overland travellers to Sussex.

Rivers have pushed through the Weald and the Downs, finding their way to the sea. The River Arun in the west, the Adur in the middle and the Ouse to the east all stay within the county and flow from north to south.

For Saxons, local stone was the main building material. Downland churches were built of flint with some chalk and Roman brick. Sandstone was used in the Weald. Ironstone was popular.

Some fine Norman churches have survived from the 12th century. Great monastic houses with magnificent churches were to be the pattern for similar buildings in Sussex.

Diana Pé and her walking companion, Doreen Peskett are residents in West Sussex. They have ventured further into the vast county of Sussex and found delight in the 'whale-backed' Downs, the forest of the Weald, the waterways and long distance footpaths and cycle ways. Here is a guide to the countryside, the historic towns and villages and the many varied old churches of Sussex.

Published by PP ISBN 0-954-36902-5

Also available from the same author:

ISBN 0-9543690-0-9

ISBN 1-85058-720-5

ISBN 0-954-36901-7

INTRODUCTION... Writers in Sussex

"...there is an incomparable magic in the Downs that lie in the middle of the range, between west and east – there they seem to turn, and shed their woods, like a cloak slipping off their shoulders, and become most truly typical of all that is meant by the South Downs. The colour changes, becomes less green, has a paler tinge, as though a little moonshine has mixed with the light of day".

If justification were needed for a book of walks in Mid Sussex, these words of Esther Meynell, written in 1945, surely express it perfectly. Following in the footsteps of other writers on Sussex: Rudyard Kipling, W.H. Hudson, Charles Vince, H. J. Massingham, and the poet, Hillaire Belloc, Esther Meynell expresses a true love of the county. Another lady writer, Margaret Fairless Barber, who wrote under the pseudonym 'Michael Fairless' was famous before the First World War for her account of Sussex folk and her own premature journey towards death in 'the Roadmender'. Whilst convalescing from illness, she chatted with country people on the Henley Road near her home. She died aged 32 in 1909. She is buried in Ashurst. (Ashurst to Henley, Walk 15).

'I am back in my own place very near my road - the white gate lies within my distant vision; near the lean grey Downs which keep watch and ward between the country and the sea; very near, nay in the lap of Mother Earth, for as I write I am lying on a green carpet, powdered yellow and white with sun`s own flowers; overhead a great sycamore where bees toil and sing; and the sighing shimmering poplars golden grey against the blue.'

Hillaire Belloc worked in his home in Shipley (Walk 4) and is buried at the Catholic Church, West Grinstead (Walk 13).

'I will build a house with deep thatch
to shelter me from the cold
And there shall the Sussex songs be sung
And the story of Sussex told.'

From 'The South Country' by Hilaire Belloc.

Virginia Woolf's home, Monk`s House, Rodmell is now a National Trust Property and we can visit it in Walk 27.

The Downs and The Weald

The South Downs dominate Sussex, *"Our blunt, bow-headed, whale-backed Downs"*, described by Rudyard Kipling in his poem, "Sussex". They separate the Weald in the north from the coast. The huge forest, the Weald once stretched from Kent to Hampshire. Now there are fragments of woodland where a wanderer may sometimes capture the secret spirit of Pan. The chalk Downs have withstood intrusion through past centuries. The Wealden forest and a reputation for the worst roads in England discouraged overland travellers to Sussex. Rivers have pushed through the Weald and the Downs, finding their way to the sea. The River Arun in the west, the Adur in the middle and the Ouse in the east, all stay within the county and flow from north to south. Usually they flow gently through quiet meadows where cattle graze and reed birds warble but they have a formidable force and do not welcome bathers. Their floods, too, when they occur, are dramatic. In the past rivers offered a way through the impregnable Downs. To prevent invasion from Europe, castles were built to guard the rivers. Arundel Castle overlooks the Arun, Bramber Castle the Adur and Lewes Castle the Ouse. The Downs are the basis of many walks in this book and they form a backdrop to others. The natural fortresses, Chanctonbury and Cissbury are part of our way. In **Walks 7 and 10** we look up to the famous 'Chanctonbury Ring', an Iron Age fort where beech trees, planted in 1760, lasted until the Great Storm of 1987 blew them down. In **Walk 9** we cross the largest earthwork in Sussex, Cissbury. 4000 years ago Neolithic (late Stone Age) man dug out the flint here; flint and wood were his only materials. The ditch and rampart were built later. Romans also occupied Cissbury. When they left in mid- 4th century, Sussex became more isolated. Then the Saxon pirates came in 5th century. They murdered, pillaged and destroyed. Cissa, an early Saxon leader is believed to have seized Cissbury. Eventually the Saxons settled down to clearing the forest and cultivating the fields. The downland was kept for grazing sheep.

Another large earthwork, Devil`s Dyke is a long angular enclosure, a natural cleft in the Downs. According to legend, the Devil was jealous of the many churches in Sussex and tried to blight the Downs here. **Walk 18** takes us up to the Iron Age hillfort where Devil`s Dyke Hotel stands. We then follow the South Downs Way, a long distance Stone Age path east-west across the Downs. The steep escarpment on this section takes us to Edburton Hill with the remains of a motte and bailey castle. North of here we come to Iron Age Fort, Wolstonbury Hill in **Walk 17.** Further east, **Walk 20** starts on the South Downs Way at Ditchling Beacon. Fires were lit here to announce news of the Armada. Yet further east we come to Mount Caburn, a contour fort, following the shape of the hill.

There are no mountains in the Downs. 'Mount Caburn' is now a Nature Reserve. On these hills the rambler is in his element. There is little to disturb his peaceful appreciation of the magnificent views, the whirling birds, the skylarks soaring in the spring. Orchids and cowslips appear then on some slopes. He will be lucky to find the precious, vivid blue rampion and the even scarcer white rampion. Other downland flowers include milkwort, violet, vetch and centaury. Later in the year he will find scabious, harebells and dwarf thistle. Wild thyme and marjoram offer sweet sharp scents. Bushes that grow on exposed slopes are short and bent by the wind. Hawthorn, gorse, the wayfaring tree and occasional juniper survive the winds.

To the north of the Downs we tread woodland paths and venture into the medieval deer parks of the High Weald. Rudyard Kipling, in his poem 'Puck`s Song' remembers that this part of Sussex did open up to rural industry, iron smelting, lime burning, forestry in the Tudor period:

'Out of the Weald, the secret Weald,
Men sent in ancient years
The horse-shoes red at Flodden Field
The arrows at Poitiers'

The Saxons knew the Forest of the Weald as 'Andreaswald'. It took time for Christianity to penetrate the thick forest. St Wilfrid introduced this new religion 681-686 A.D. It spread so successfully, the county earned the name, 'Selig Sussex' – 'Holy Sussex'. Saxon Lords, who built churches, gave their names to the parish: Lyminster was Lullingminster meaning 'the church of Lulla'. Princess Eadburh, grand daughter of King Alfred gave her name to Edburton. Warminghurst means 'the people of Wyrma'. Telscombe or Titelscumb means 'Titel`s valley.

The first churches were wooden. King Alfred the Great (871-899) encouraged the building of Christian churches. Priories and monasteries were established throughout the county. They provided education, medical and social help. Alfred`s successors continued the work and stone churches were built during the reign of Edward the Peaceable (959-975). Some of these have survived to this day. Saxon churches tend to be rectangular with high walls and tall, narrow doorways. Arches are round-headed. Some two-light windows can be seen at Worth (Walk 22) and Sompting (Walk 9). The method of laying stones horizontally and vertically, 'long and short work' is used in Sompting, Worth and Sullington (Walk 5). A pilaster strip was used in Sompting and Worth. Local stone was the main building material. Downland churches were built of flint with some chalk and Roman brick, where available. Sandstone was used in the Weald. Ironstone was popular.

Worth is a handsome example of a Saxon church. Unusually large, it may have had links with royalty. Sompting has an impressive Saxon tower rising above the A27. The shape of Clayton church (Walk17) and the chancel arch are Saxon. Some doors and windows in Poling and Lyminster (Walk 6) are Saxon. Sullington (Walk 5) has a church tower with typical Saxon 'long and short' work. Wivelsfield (Walk 25) and Slaugham (Walk 14) have ancient doorways that are probably Saxon. Traces of Saxon work can also be found in the churches of Old Shoreham (Walk 19), Coombes (Walk 10), and St John under the Castle, Lewes. The town of Lewes (Walk 26) held one of Alfred`s Fortresses. The ramparts and lanes that still exist may be of Saxon origin.

The Normans

After defeating Harold in 1066, William the Conqueror was determined to exercise firm control over England. He was particularly hard on Sussex, punishing the people for their support of Harold. He and his followers enlisted the support of the Norman religious leaders who preached loyalty and submission. Saxons, already deeply religious, were to be suitably impressed by the grandeur of Norman architecture. Great monastic houses with magnificent churches in Normandy were to be a pattern for similar buildings in Sussex. William`s followers welcomed the acquisition of land in Sussex. Its proximity to the Norman coast enabled them to keep an eye on estates on both sides of the channel. William de Warenne presided in Lewes. He and his wife Gundrada were responsible for 39 churches in Sussex including Cuckfield, Slaugham and Ditchling. He summoned monks from Cluny. They built a great Cluniac Priory and church in Lewes. William de Braose ruled in Bramber. In 1080 a Benedictine Priory was founded in Bramber then moved to Beeding. (Walk 20). Roger de Mongomery established Arundel as a new centre of Norman power. The nunnery at Lyminster was given to the Convent of Almenèches.

Norman churches were larger with massive walls. Their walls were wide rather than tall. Often the church was in the shape of a cross. A tower in the centre had transepts on either side, forming the Norman 'crossing'. The chancel sometimes had a curved or apsidal end. Windows tended to be splayed internally. The Normans impressed the people with their technical and artistic skill.

Some fine Norman churches have survived from early 12th century to this day. Old Shoreham, St Nicolas (Walk 19) is an adaptation of an existing Saxon church. Low arches and lavish decoration were brought into the nave. Steyning Church (Walk 10) was developed with greater freedom. The Normans could knock down the wooden Saxon church. Monks from the Abbey of Fécamp built a high crossing. One of the high arches from this period has survived. The chancel arch with fine carvings is also Norman. New Shoreham, St Mary de Haura (Walk 19) has its crossing intact. The tower walls are thick, the arches simple. The grandeur is severe and unadorned. The beauty of Caen stone has greater impact. Other Norman churches include Bramber (Walk 20), Itchingfield (Walk 1), Stopham (Walk 2), Iford (Walk 27), started soon after the Conquest. The nave was built first, followed by the central tower and the chancel. There were no transepts. Tower arches are round and sturdy.

The Knights Templar built several Norman churches. They were a body of fighting monks, founded in 1119 to defend the Holy Sepulchre and protect pilgrims on their way to Jerusalem. These powerful knights owned a house in Bramber where St Mary`s House now stands (Walks 10 and 20). They built Washington Church, later much renovated (Walk 7), part of Sompting (Walk 9) and a massive church in Shipley (Walk 4). Shipley has a central tower and no transepts. The chancel is high, as are the tower arches. This Norman church is unusual in having double splayed windows.

Three churches near the River Ouse have unique round towers; they are St Michael in Lewes (Walk 26), Southease and Piddinghoe (Walk 28).

Late Norman or Transitional churches were more ambitious with soaring arches, tall pillars, rib vaulting and exuberant carving. From 1150 onwards the designers let rip with ornamentation: dog-tooth, zigzag, scallops, foliage, rosettes, rolls were carved into the stone. Aisles were often added to the naves of parish churches, usually on the south side making the building asymmetrical. A chapel might stand at the east end of the aisle. These aisles tended to be narrow with nave roofs sloping down to a low outer wall. Most aisles were later changed or replaced but their arcades survive, see West Chiltington (Walk 3). This period brought a variety of piers and pillars. Some chancels were rebuilt. At New Shoreham, the aisles, choir and vaulting are late Norman. The tower of this church has a lower stage in early and an upper stage in late Norman style. In

Steyning the nave was skillfully transformed with aisles, four arcaded bays and clerestory windows.

Among the smaller churches with late Norman features are Lewes, St Anne (Walk 26) and Rodmell (Walk 27). They have similar south arcades added to churches that formerly did not have aisles. St Anne`s is larger with taller pillars. Lyminster has a spacious Transitional north aisle with a four-bay arcade added to the Saxon church.

The Early English style of architecture followed in around 1150 and lasted into the 13th century. Gothic or pointed arches now prevailed. The tendency was for thinner walls, wider openings, higher arches. A chancel arch would have maximum span. Many new chancels were built with a triplet of lancet windows in the east end. Naves were more open. Arcades opened to wider aisles. Decoration was more restrained. Transepts in the form of chapels were sometimes added. Towers tended to be at the west end.

In Sussex many ordinary parish churches have Early English work. Thakeham (Walk 3) has an Early English chancel and a south chapel of the same period added to the Norman nave. Little Warminghurst also on this walk is mainly Early English. Open naves with Early English arcades and wide aisles can be found at Findon (Walk 8) and Ashurst (Walk 15). Clapham (Walk 8) has a Transitional north arcade and an Early English south arcade. Ditchling (Walk 29) has an Early English chancel. Edburton (Walk 18) is nearly all Early English with many lancet windows. Chancel windows in Stopham (Walk 2) are Early English. The north chapel, added late in the period, was once a chantry of St Katherine. West Grinstead (Walk 13) has slender pillars, if a little short, of that period. Telscombe (Walk 28), Botolphs (Walk 20) and Rodmell (Walk 27) all have fine west towers of that period.

Wealth in Sussex declined in the 13th century, putting a limit on church building in the next centuries. **The Decorated Period** (1260 - 1360) held to the Gothic style with geometrical tracery in windows. Few churches in Sussex favour this style. Four churches are essentially Decorated; they are Ardingly (Walk 21), Lindfield (Walk 24), Rudgwick (Walk 11) and Nuthurst with many later changes (Walk 12). Bolney, Slaugham (Walk 14) and Kingston (Walk 27) have Dec. work. Warminghurst has a Dec. east window.

The Perpendicular Period (1360 – 1485) is characterised by some of the finest towers, straight lines and windows with mullions. In Sussex it can be found more in the Weald. The forest here was beginning to open to human activity. Poynings (Walk 18) and Pulborough nave and porch (Walk 2) and St Thomas a Becket, Lewes (Walk 26) are Perpendicular. Towers of this period include Bolney (Walk 14), Henfield (Walk 15) and Hamsey (Walk 30). The tower of Wivelsfield (Walk 25) is Decorated in the lower and Perpendicular in the upper part. West Grinstead has a Perpendicular porch. Itchingfield (Walk 1) has a Belfrey of this period and Decorated windows. Lindfield (Walk 24) and Pyecombe (Walk 17) have some Perpendicular windows.

The Tudor Period (1485 to 1585) has few church buildings. Twineham (Walk 14) is the exception and Washington can claim to have a Tudor tower. The south arcade of Cowfold Church (Walk 13) has the depressed arches of this period.

In England, the religious institutions had acquired donated land. By 16th century they owned 40% of the land. Henry V111 came to the throne in 1509 and soon set about seizing the land and breaking up the monasteries. **The Dissolution**, as his vandalism is called, caused the country to loose great monastic buildings. The magnificent Priory and Church of Lewes were destroyed. This monarch created a new subservient nobility by distributing the stolen land to his favoured followers. The new owners were more interested in the land than in the buildings and these were allowed to decay.

The Palladians (1710-1760) favoured a restrained Classical form. One church in Sussex is a late example of this style. It is St Mary The Virgin, Glynde (Walk 26).

The Walks Today

We saunter beside rivers and cross remote footbridges. Seaside walks are scarce, thanks to twentieth century conurbations. We come close to the sea in Shoreham. In this, Walk 19 there is an option to venture into suburbia to see Portslade Church. Walk 16 is a stroll through the historic ways of Brighton, including the sea front.

On clear days there are wonderful glimpses of the sea from the neighbouring Downs. Often towns are hidden and you can admire the view as it was before we humans sprawled along the coast.

Today, major trunk roads, A29, A24, A23 slice north-south through Sussex, whilst the A27 carries the coastal traffic. Most of the walks in this book stay within the slices of the countryside that somehow retain the fragile character of the county. Occasionally I have found an underpass or a suitable bridge to enable the walk to follow the legitimate course of the footpath. Usually, I have avoided crossing these highways where the relentless traffic would mow down anything or anyone in its way. Planners in most cases have ignored the footpaths that used to cross the ground where the highways pass.

Oh for the halcyon days of M. Fairless and 'The Roadmender' when the author could sit by the roadside and watch the world go by!

For illustrations of different styles of church architecture, see the introduction to 'West Sussex Church Walks' by the same author.

Contents

Let the train take the strain on walks 1, 2, 16, 19, 25, 26, 18 and 30
Walks 23 and 26 each include a section across a golf course

5 Walks Near Brighton

5 Walks Near Haywards Heath

5 Walks Near Lewes

5 Walks
Near Billingshurst

Walk 1: Billingshurst to Itchingfield

From a country town you cross meadows and woodland to approach Itchingfield on the remote paths taken by monks from the medieval Sele Priory. Return along roads through a private estate and back across fields after resting in a quiet arboretum.

Starting Point: The free Library Car Park behind Budgens, High Street, Billingshurst.
Map: OS Explorer 134 (A compass might be useful on this walk) **GR**087259
Distance: 10 Miles **Terrain:** Fairly flat, small hills, muddy in places

***Note 1:** from Itchingfield it is just over 1 mile to Christ`s Hospital Station.You can take the train back from here to Billingshurst if you wish to shorten the walk. Follow the map and walk on roads from Itchingfield Primary School, marked* in the Walk below.*
***Note 2:** Add ½ mile to visit the pub at Barns Green. Otherwise, bring a picnic!*

The Churches

St Mary`s Parish Church, Billingshurst stands on a commanding site above the Roman road, Stane Street. Some pretty cottages climb up the short slope to the church and more cottages line the path behind. The outlook for Billingas tribe who settled on this *Hyrst* or wooded hill can only be imagined. Today the church has a tall imposing 15th century spire, 120 feet high and octagonal. It is covered in wooden shingles. The heavy tower was built in the early 13th century and the south aisle dates from 1280. An archway leads to the oldest part of the church, the Lady Chapel (1230). The north aisle was added in 1430. The nave has a handsome 16th century wagon roof with bosses carved to depict the arms of some local families. The porch is also 16th century. The glass in the aisles and in the east window is worth attention. In 1866, during a church restoration, some medieval glass was found and set in a window in the south aisle. The eight bells really do give a melodious sound. From the distance when I first heard them, I initially thought a band was playing!

The Parish Church of St Nicholas, Itchingfield has a secret past. The settlement of Ecci`s tribe, the Echingas deep in the forest was not discovered and is not mentioned in Domesday. In 1240 it was known as 'Hechengefeld'. The name has undergone many changes. In 1541 'Hedge and Fylde' appears in the Horsham parish register! From 1730 onwards it was 'Itchingfield'. The structure of the church has also changed over the years. You would have entered the first Norman building of 1125 through the west door for no tower existed then. The north and west walls of the nave are Norman. Some windows in the north of the nave and chancel are Norman. The tower, built of solid wood has survived from the 14th century. In 1865 a shingled spire was added. The chancel was rebuilt in 1713 and again in 1866. The south aisle was added in 1865 and the 15th century window from the chancel was fixed in the south wall. In 1889 the church seats were

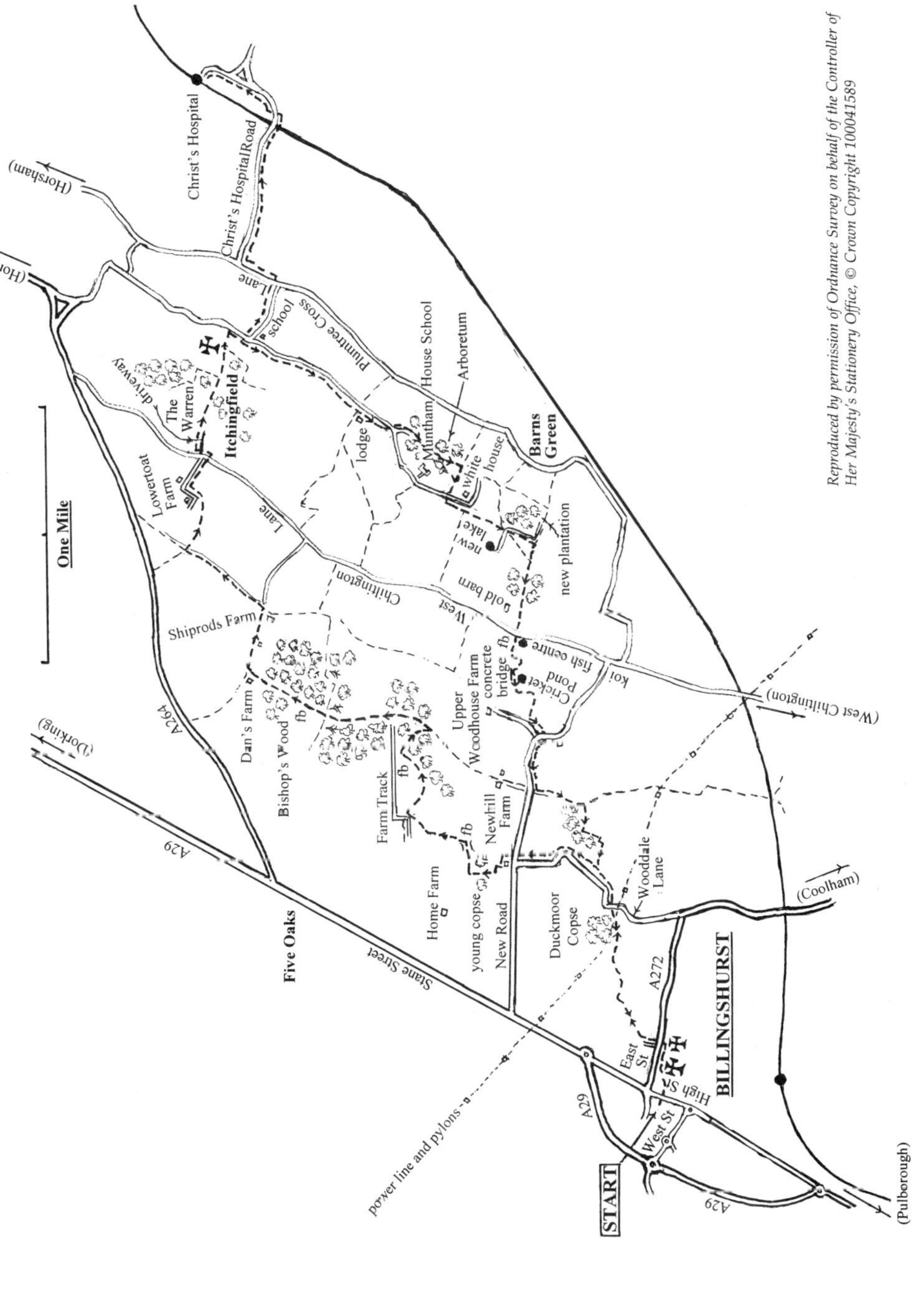
One Mile
(Horsham)
(Horsham)
Christ's Hospital
Christ's Hospital Road
Lane
school
Plumtree Cross
Muntham House School
Arboretum
white house
Barns Green
driveway
The Warren
Itchingfield
Lowertoat Farm
lodge
Lane
new lake
new plantation
old barn
West Chiltington
Shiprods Farm
fish centre
koi
Cricket Pond
fb
concrete bridge
Upper Woodhouse Farm
(West Chiltington)
(Dorking)
A264
Dan's Farm
Bishop's Wood
fb
Farm Track
fb
Newhill Farm
fb
Home Farm
young copse
New Road
Duckmoor Copse
Wooddale Lane
(Coolham)
A29
Five Oaks
Stane Street
A272
BILLINGSHURST
East St
High St
West St
A29
START
power line and pylons
A29
(Pulborough)

declared 'free'. Hitherto local parishioners owned and handed down their seats. For a list of owners and occupiers and for much more of interest see the church guide.

The Priest`s House, standing small and alone in the grassy churchyard has survived from medieval times. What is this little house built of wood, clay, wattle and daub with Horsham slabs on the roof? – It was first built to house the monk who rode from Sele Priory near Bramber to take the services here and collect the tithes. It was later used as an almshouse.

The Walk

Cross Billingshurst High Street to climb steps to the church opposite. Face the porch in front of the tower and take the path on the left. It passes between the church and some old cottages and leads to the A272. Continue on course along the pavement. In 50 metres you reach the Catholic Church and cross the main road with care to the footpath opposite.

The footpath follows a short road with a few select houses. At the end, avoid the path straight on and turn right into a footpath through an alleyway. You have left the town behind. You make an abrupt descent of a hill covered in bracken and scrub. Many off-shoots of the main path may lead you astray so head northeast. In 75 metres you come to crosspaths. Go straight on down to a T-junction at the valley bottom. Turn right along a woodland path leading to open fields.

Just outside of the wood, avoid the path sharp left. Cross the small field diagonally left. Then take the path along the left hand field boundary heading due east. In the next large field follow the boundary on the right. You enter Duckmoor Copse on a track passing under cables.

You reach Wooddale Lane and turn left. Walk along the lane for half a mile, passing a pond and a couple of houses. At a T-junction with New Road, cross to the footpath opposite. This goes behind the garden of a house on the left then follows the field boundary north. Continue on route through a young copse and out the other side. Turn right, following the field boundary on the left. In 250 metres turn left to cross a footbridge with metal gates at both ends. You are again heading north. Now the field boundary is on your right.

In 500 metres you reach a farm track. Turn right away from the farm track and enter a large sloping field with a view to woodland. Head for a stile in the far left corner. Cross a footbridge and emerge to another field. Hug the woodland on the right. In 300 metres at the way marker, turn right into the wood. Cross a new footbridge over a sunken stream. The path ahead through the wood is clearly defined. In 300 metres you reach a wider path, a bridleway at a T-junction and turn left. Again you are heading north, this time through woodland with glimpses to the field on the right.

In 400 metres you reach an opening and pass a boggy nature reserve on the left. You then enter Bishop's Wood, cross another footbridge and continue on course through deep woodland. Avoid crosspaths and keep straight on.

After 1 kilometre of woodland, you emerge to a gently sloping field. Walk up to the cottage opposite, Dan Farm. Pass this on your left and you come to a cross track. Turn right and follow the track past widely separated cottages, 'Three Chimneys' and 'Shiprods'. Shiprods Farm is nearby on the right. At crosspaths turn left and north on a wide path with a narrow strip of tarmac along the centre. Pass the odd farm cottage and horse paddocks. Just after two houses facing each other on either side of the track, you come to crosspaths. Turn right here and follow the field boundary on the right. In the next field cross diagonally left to Lower Toat Farm. Walk up the access road and turn right.

At West Chiltington Lane turn left and immediately right into a driveway. There is a narrow path on the left, flanked by rose bushes sharing the driveway to a house. Keep the roses on your right and your path leads to a wide, sloping field, 'the Warren', typical weald country. Follow the slightly raised path down to woodland and keep straight on over a footbridge. Avoid a path in the wood to the left Cross another footbridge. Suddenly you reach an opening below a long Norman church. This is Itchingfield.

From Itchingfield Church carry on towards the road and turn right. In 100 metres the road bends left. **This is where the weary walker can head for Christ`s Hospital Station. (See above).*

For the full walk, go straight on along a track, passing the primary school on the left. Follow this wide track southwest for nearly a mile when you reach the entrance gates to Muntham House School. The <u>track</u> curves right here.

You go through the gates and veer left on a path that passes through the grounds of Muntham House School, sometimes through woods and sometimes on the edge of the sports fields. You have a view to the school building on the right. When you reach **crossways**, turn left and enter Julia and Emma`s arboretum, a sheltered arbour with seats and fine views to Barns Green below and the distant Downs beyond.

Thirsty walkers can head down to the pub in Barns Green and come back again.

Leave the arboretum and return to the **crossways**. Go straight on towards a detached house. Pass the house on your left and Muntham House School on your right. You come to the <u>track</u> you left earlier and turn left.

Just past a half- white house on the left, the track bends to the left but you take another way. There is a multiple fingerpost on the right. Turn into the field on the right and you have a view over a new lake below. Follow the hedge on the left, passing the lake away to the right. Go through a farm gate onto the wide new track, built for the lake. Keep on course along this track. There is a wood on the left. In 100 metres turn right and head due west through a newly planted screen of trees. In the next field hug the strip of woodland on the right. At the end go through woodland to an open field and pass a large disintegrating barn on the right. Cross yet another field to emerge at a tarmac road. This is West Chiltington Lane.

Cross the road to a footbridge and stile opposite. (Here the OS map should be discarded for half a mile as it has not caught up with the present course of the path). As you enter the field you pass a bungalow and see the buildings of a koi fish centre beyond on the left. Follow the boundary of your field on the left for 150 metres then turn left into the next field. Turn right and walk up the edge of the

field (even though the finger post directs you diagonally left). Head for a large pond, known locally as the cricket pond. Cross over a flat, concrete bridge and turn left, passing the pond on your left. Make for a field boundary and go through. Turn right, hugging the hedge on your right. In 200 metres you reach the access road to Upper Woodhouse Farm, seen on the right.

Turn left to walk away from the farm along the access road. In 100 metres you are back in New Road. Turn right and walk for 350 metres along New Road. Just past Newhill Farm on the right, turn left at a gate with an ancient sign, 'Priors Farm'. Here is a neglected bridleway. In fact there are three farm gates to negociate before you can stride out along this hedge-lined track, heading south. The hedge thickens into woodland.

In 350 metres pass a strip of woodland on the right. Immediately turn right at a stile into a rough, remote meadow. The ground underfoot here is bumpy where cattle have trod when it was wet. You have to hug the woodland on the right. At the field corner turn left with another wood on your right. Follow the field boundary as it bends to the right. Turn right at a footpath on the right. Cross a footbridge into a narrow path bounded by barbed wire on one side and a hedge covered ditch on the other. The space allowed walkers reflects a niggardly attitude!

You escape the strait jacket of this path to arrive on the familiar Wooddale Lane. Turn left then right into Duckmoor Copse. Retrace your steps back to the valley bottom. Turn left up through the scrub land. Note that the clearer path is just past the finger post. At cross paths go straight on along the elevated path to Billingshurst.

Walk 2: Pulborough to Pallingham Bridge and Stopham

This walk is never far from the River Arun, an important waterway from Roman times. Wey-South Path nearby follows an old canal intended to link London with Portsmouth. Toat monument dominates landscape to the north of this walk. It is an octagonal tower on a hill, built in memory of a tea merchant, Samuel Drinkald.

Starting Point 1: Stopham Bridge, a lane opposite the Garden Centre on A283 west of Pulborough. **GR**032183
Starting Point 2: Pulborough Station **GR**043186
Distance: 7 Miles **Terrain**: Flat with some gentle hills
Maps: OS Explorer 121 and 134 **or** OS Landranger 197
Warning: The river crossing at Pallingham Quay can be very muddy in wet weather.
Local Information: Pallingham once had a wharf when the river was wider here. In 1650 there was a loading quay for barges carrying timber for the rebuilding of Arundel Castle. Later, Arun Navigation Company had docks here to repair and build barges. The last barge was blown up by its own cargo of gunpowder in 1864. Stopham had a wooden bridge in 1309. In 1403 it was replaced by the bridge we cross on our walk. A 1986 bridge was built for traffic along A283 and we pedestrians enjoy the old bridge!

The Churches

Pulborough Parish Church, St Mary (manned by volunteers the first Saturday of the month, 10 a.m. to 12 noon and 2 to 4 p.m.). The church stands on a high slope, probably a Roman base. It overlooks the river plain at the confluence of the Rivers Rother and Arun. A Roman Station stood beside Stane Street near the Rother. In Domesday 1086 two churches are mentioned in 'Poleberge'. No signs remain of the Saxon church which must have stood here. The present lofty building consists of nave, tower, two aisles and a chancel with the Onley chapel. The chancel has some 13th century windows and a 14th century sedilia. The south window dates from the 15th century when the church was enlarged. The nave and chancel are out of line. The chancel arch is Early English. Pevsner describes the church as 'good Perpendicular'. It is built of local stone with Horsham slabs in the roof. In 16th century the tomb of John Onley filled the chapel bearing his name. The rector, John Austin demolished this tomb and had one made for himself and his wife. The next occupant was a 4-barrell organ until 1947. Then a grand new organ was installed near the tower. The chapel regained its space and was restored by J. Comper to its present charming beauty.

Stopham, St Mary The Blessed Virgin: Nineteen inhabitants are mentioned in Domesday: Ralph, Robert, Torquil and 16 villeins. The church was built some time around 1066. A small, blocked window in the north wall of the chancel, the shapely

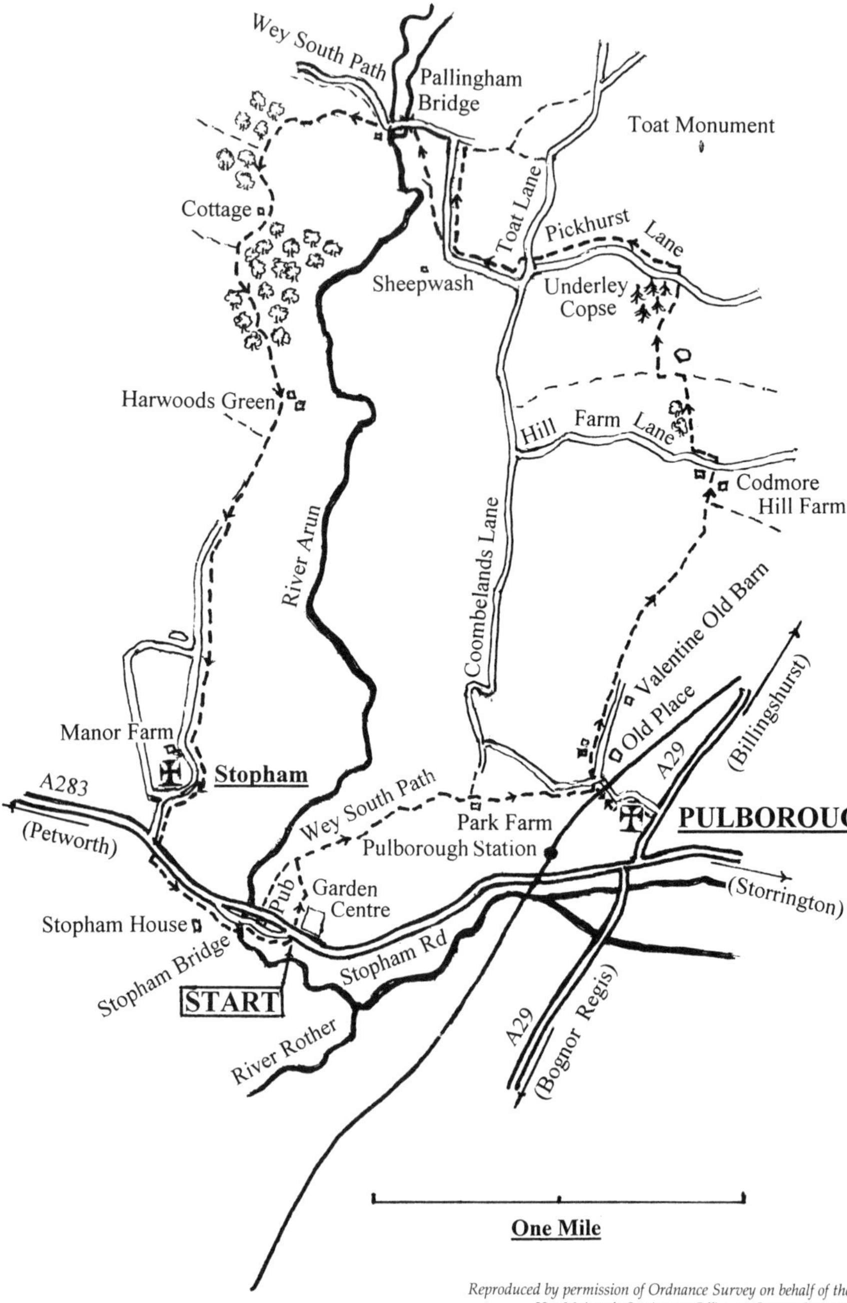

Wey South Path
Pallingham Bridge
Toat Monument
Cottage
Toat Lane
Pickhurst Lane
Sheepwash
Underley Copse
Harwoods Green
Hill Farm Lane
Codmore Hill Farm
River Arun
Coombelands Lane
Valentine Old Barn
Old Place
A29
(Billingshurst)
Manor Farm
Stopham
A283
(Petworth)
Wey South Path
Park Farm
PULBOROUGH
Pulborough Station
Pub
Garden Centre
(Storrington)
Stopham House
Stopham Bridge
Stopham Rd
START
River Rother
A29
(Bognor Regis)
One Mile

south doorway and the original high arches above the north and south doorways are of this period. The chancel arch and parts of the tower are Norman. The other windows in the chancel are Early English. Two local families who came over with William the Conqueror and have stayed ever since are commemorated in the church. They are the Barttelot family from the Manor and the de Stopham family from Stopham House.

The Walk

(From Pulborough Station go along Stopham Road to join the walk.)

From the lane leading down to Stopham Bridge, cross the main road, A283 to the garden centre opposite. Take the track on the left uphill beside the walled edge of gardens. In 150 metres, leave the gardens behind and keep on route through a field.

At a T-junction of paths at the top you join the Wey-South Path. Turn right and follow the sandy ridge northeast, offering views to the Downs on the right and down to the nearby River Arun on the left. Keep the fringe of trees on your left and follow footpath signs. In ½ a mile come down to Park Farm. Wey-South Path goes down the sunken drive to the left. You take a different route. Cross to the path over a field with a view to Pulborough Church ahead.

At Coombelands Lane turn right, go past houses and note a private track on the left. Just after the bridge over the railway line, you reach the church.

From Pulborough Church retrace your steps over the bridge and turn right at the noted track, now on your right. Here a footpath follows the drive, passing Old Place on the right and quaint cottages on the left.

Old Place Mill, a working water mill from c1500 to c1900, is now a private house.

Carry on heading north along the track and through gates to Valentine Old Barn. Go past the converted barn and uphill beside trees on the left. After rough ground you come up to a wide, open field. Follow the hedge on the left until it peters out. Veer to the right across the field along a wide swathe of grass towards a large notice. Keep to the left of a finger post and maintain your direction. A notice warns you to beware of galloping horses. Cross two gallops and one tarmac drive.

Make for the large Hill Barn ahead. Walk through the farmyard to Hill Farm Lane.

Turn left to walk along Hill Farm Lane past the half-timbered farmhouse. In 100 metres turn right at a footpath sign. Slide down a steep sharp slope towards ponds and lakes in lowland. Pass a copse on your left. It contains a pond. You are heading for a new lake. Before reaching the lake turn left at a T-junction. Follow the enclosed path for 100 metres. The path continues west but you turn right into a field. Follow the hedge on the right to a larger copse with the name 'Underley'. Follow the edge of the copse on your left until you reach the tarmac Pickhurst Lane.

Turn left and walk along this quiet wooded lane to a T-junction, Pickhurst Corner.

The road to the left is Coombelands Lane and leads back to Pulborough.

Turn left then immediately right to join Wey-South Path. The sign 'Pickhurst' is on one side of the entrance and 'Sheepwash' on the other. Enter an immaculate yard and make for the concrete road ahead leading to the house called 'Sheepwash', hiding behind gates and trees. Follow the track to the right and in 100 metres you have a choice:

Route A. *Keep straight on along the track you come to a T-junction. Turn left to walk along this other track and cross the overgrown canal before reaching the river.*

Route B. Veer left on Wey-South Path, you cross a sloping field with views to the far side of the river. Follow the hedge on the left, passing a house screened by trees. Turn left and follow the boundary of the garden. There is a steep narrow path down to a little water meadow. Cross diagonally left to join the track from the alternative route. Turn left.

At Pallingham Quay a rough footbridge crosses the little river. Then a picturesque humped-back bridge crosses a backwater. When you reach the other side, say goodbye to Wey South Path as it takes the track to the right. Instead, head towards the large house on the left. Pass this house on your left and climb away from the river. Follow the hedge on the left for 50 metres then cross a little plank footbridge to go over a horse gallop. Do not be tempted up this gallop. Instead, cross a stile into the next field.

Turn right and hug the hedge on the right. The path climbs gently up to woodland and curves to the left. Avoid the footpath to the right. In another 150 metres, enter the wood and bear left. Cross a woodland track and climb more steeply up past a pretty cottage on the right. Join the rough access track to this cottage and keep on course.

At the top follow the curve of the track to the left and down through daffodil woods for ½ mile to Harwoods Green. Pass two cottages on the left. They have a lovely view across the river to Toat Monument and we can share their view. Continue down past a fine old brick farmhouse and curve to the right.

You now have to climb a little, passing woodland on your right. The tarmac lane comes to meet you and lead you mainly downhill for another ½ mile. On the way you pass a pond on the right in the valley and avoid the lane to the right. There is then a gentle hill past Manor Farm. Curve right to Stopham Church.

Go past Stopham Church on your right, passing cottages on the left overlooking the Green. At a T-junction turn left. This road leads down to the A283. Cross with care to the pavement opposite and turn left. Pass Stopham House on the right and cross the river, now much wider. Take time to linger on the medieval bridge. Pevsner need not have worried; this is still an idyllic spot. Return on the lane past the nearby pub and up to Starting Point 1.

Stopham

Walk 3: West Chiltington, Thakeham, Warminghurst

Avoiding nearby conurbations, head for the fields, quiet woodland and villages that have stood up to modern development and retained fascinating churches.

Starting Point: West Chiltington Church (parking at the front or in the car park).
Map: OS Explorer 121 **GR**091184
Distance: 6 Miles **Terrain:** Gently undulating, one muddy lane.

The Churches

West Chiltington, St Mary and the street leading to it, form the most attractive part of this otherwise dull village. It is a Norman church with a Transitional arcade to the south aisle. The main entrance has the original Norman doorway, with some modern repairs. The 13th century porch may be the oldest in Sussex. The octagonal font is also 13th century. The west window of the south aisle is original Norman. Other windows are 14th century. There is a central tower and the spire was added in 1602. There is a very long squint to the chancel. The church is famous for its mural paintings, 12th century at the end of the south aisle and 13th - 14th century on either side the nave. One puzzle in the south aisle murals is the inclusion of a medalion with a rope cross. A similar design of cross can be found in Fishbourne Roman palace and in the Roman catacombs in Salzburg.

West Chiltington

Thakeham, St Mary`s is a cruciform church with Norman nave, Early English chancel and Perpendicular tower. One Norman window is in the north wall of the nave. The north transept was originally the site of the tower. This is now on the west side. The wooden south porch is also late Perpendicular.

Warminghurst, The Holy Sepulchre is mentioned in Domesday. The name means 'the high wood of Wyrma`s people'. Over the years the number of people has diminished and the church is now cared for by the Churches Conservation Trust. Pevsner describes it as 'A noble remote church…the inside is magical'. It is a simple sandstone Early English church. The roof covers nave and chancel in one stretch. A pine screen with semi-circular arches was installed between the nave and chancel around 1700. The arms of Queen Anne are above the screen. 18th century

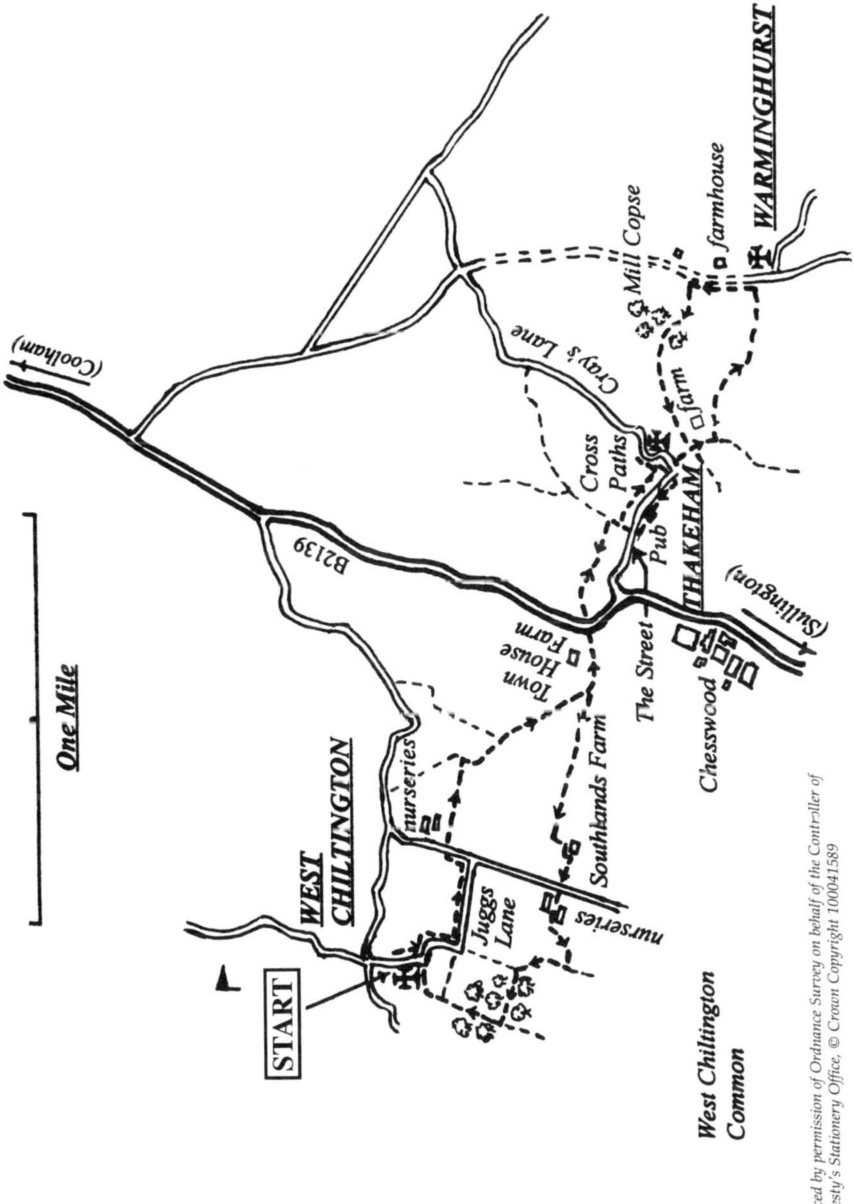
One Mile
(Coolham)
B2139
Cray's Lane
Mill Copse
farmhouse
WARMINGHURST
farm
Cross Paths
Pub
THAKEHAM
(Sullington)
Town House Farm
The Street
Chesswood
WEST CHILTINGTON
nurseries
Southlands Farm
Juggs Lane
nurseries
START
West Chiltington Common

pine box pews are still in place. The three-light east window is Decorated. Among the monuments is one of Edward Shelley, his wife, their 7 sons and 3 daughters. Percy Bysse Shelley is a descendant of this family. The house of William Penn, the Quaker (See Walk 4) once stood just south of the church. He drafted the first constitution for Pennsylvania when he lived at Warminghurst Park.

The Walk

At West Chiltington walk down Church Street, passing a pub in a corner on the right. At the bottom you reach crossways. Avoid the track to Churchfield Farm straight on. Turn left up leafy Juggs Lane. At the top you reach a junction with Southland Lane. Turn left and in 75 metres turn right up a track signposted to Ploughboys Rest. Pass houses with small holdings. The track becomes a narrow enclosed footpath. You soon escape from it to fields. You are at a path T-junction and turn right along the edge of the field.

Follow the path as it veers left along a ridge past a row of trees. Looking south you have a view over fields and woods to the Downs. Do not be tempted down a track to the left. Up ahead is the less picturesque silo of Town House Farm. Below on the right is a large mushroom farm. The path curves around the wooded edge of the hidden reservoir of Town House Farm. **Note for the return walk** a path on the right joining us here. Avoid the second path on the right that leads down to the mushroom farm. Our path enters the farmyard on the left then turns right taking the concrete drive down to B2139.

Cross the road (take care) diagonally left and climb up steps to a stile into an elevated field. Follow the well marked path to the next field. Go through a small patch of woodland then hug the hedge on the right separating us from the back gardens of houses. At the field corner on the right go through trees to **cross paths**. Turn right then immediately left to walk down a private driveway serving houses and passing the back of the village school.

Facing you at the bottom you come to the delightful black and white Church Cottages. Thakeham Church with its big tower is up on the left.

Thakeham

From Thakeham Church walk back past Church Cottages on your left and the driveway that brought you here on the right. You come to a T-junction in the village.

The pub is up The Street on your right. We shall be walking up here later but you may want to seize the opportunity for refreshments now.

At the T-junction turn left and go through a farm gate with the notice, "Footpath Only"! Go through to a past century where cattle graze beside ancient farm buildings and an unmade road ahead leads to Warminghurst, caught in a peaceful time warp. You come first to the mellow farmhouse, Warminghurst Farm. The church, behind trees to the right stands on the corner of Park Lane and Rectory Lane.

From Warminghurst Church retrace your steps as far as the farmhouse, ignore the track that brought you here, and continue down the no through road. This tree covered lane sinks into mud. Walkers have scrambled up the bank on the left but in 200 metres have to scramble down again to get access to the footpath. Follow this waymarked path to the left and climb gratefully out of the sunken lane. You are now heading back west.

Hug the hedge on the left and enjoy extensive views over the countryside to the right. You enter a lovely little bluebell wood, Mill Copse and follow the narrow, worn path down to well drained marsh land. Turn left out of the wood to cross a secluded glen where I met a fox head on. In the far right corner of this glen you cross a bridge over a stream. In the next field you keep on route to follow a slight ridge and enter a strip of woodland. Go through the farm gate to look over a familiar farm down to the left. You pass it to return to the unmade road.

Turn right to re-enter the world at Thakeham. Go up The Street, passing the pub on your left and other handsome cottages as you climb for about 250 metres. Turn right to climb steps to a path to familiar **cross paths.** Turn left and return across the field behind back gardens and down to the main road, B2139. Cross to the concrete of Town House Farm and follow your path back past the wooded screen, now on your right.

Take the noted footpath that forks to the left. Cross flat fields on a westerly course to Southlands Farm. Go on the muddy way past a cottage, cross a concrete farmyard and turn left to join a driveway heading west. Cross Southlands Lane. There are two entrances to old nurseries opposite. A finger post under a dark tree points to the left entrance.

Head for a large greenhouse which you pass on your left. Another finger post, attached to a building, also points to the left and across a field corner. Go through the hedge to a T-junction of paths. Turn right up to a strip of woodland. Turn left to another junction of paths. Keep straight on along the edge of a paddock. At the corner of the paddock, avoid the horse trail to the right. Instead, go straight on over a stile through the hedge and turn immediately right.

Follow the hedge, now on your right up through small fields on the edge of West Chiltington. Avoid the first footpath to the right. Keep on course on an enclosed way down and up to crosspaths. Turn right here for West Chiltington Church.

Warminghurst

Walk 4: The Blue Idol, the Quaker Meeting House near Coolham to Shipley

This walk is so flat part of it was used as an airfield during the war. D-Day veterans remember it well. Other delights include welcome pubs and the biggest working windmill in Sussex. Some road walking cannot be avoided.

Starting Point: Oldhouse Lane, signposted to the Blue Idol, off A272 west of Coolham
Map: OS Explorer 134 **Distance:** 7 Miles **Terrain:** Flat **GR**107231
Local Information: Shipley Windmill (1879), once owned by Hilaire Belloc, is open most Sundays, Easter to October.

The Churches

The Blue Idol Quaker Meeting House is in a delightful black and white farmhouse dating 1600. It reflects the simple religious reverence of a sincere people. How did it acquire its incongruous name? –A blue ceramic figure was found in the empty or 'idle' house that became known as 'The Blue Idol'. William Penn used to walk here from his home, Warminghurst Place. He established a Quaker meeting house here in 1681 after returning from America where he founded the state of Pennsylvania.

St Mary The Virgin, Shipley shares the banks of the River Adur with a white windmill, complete with sweeps. Both have seen barges from Shoreham tie up here. The church is centuries older than the windmill. In 12th century Knights Templar, an order of fighting monks, replaced the Saxon building with a large solid stone church. The tall narrow south door still has Saxon proportions. The Knights built a Norman church with central tower and no aisles. The west door with zigzag carving and carved capitals also the arches of the chancel are Norman work. The south porch was added in 14th century. The north aisle was rebuilt in 1893. The tower was repaired and strengthened 1983-4. Six of the stained glass windows are by C.E. Kempe. A window in the south wall depicts Shipley windmill. John Ireland the composer is buried in the churchyard and his plaque is on the south wall of the church.

The Walk

Note: 1. A public path diversion order has been made to try to settle a route through Barnhouse Farm. I have given two alternative routes. When you come to this point, if the Barnhouse way is open, you should be able to cut across to the **road route**, following the map. In all, we walk about 2 miles along lanes.

2. Near Coolham I have had to include about 400 metres along the verge of B2139.

From the car park, continue south along Oldhouse Lane on foot, passing the Meeting House on your left. In 500 metres you pass the handsome buildings of

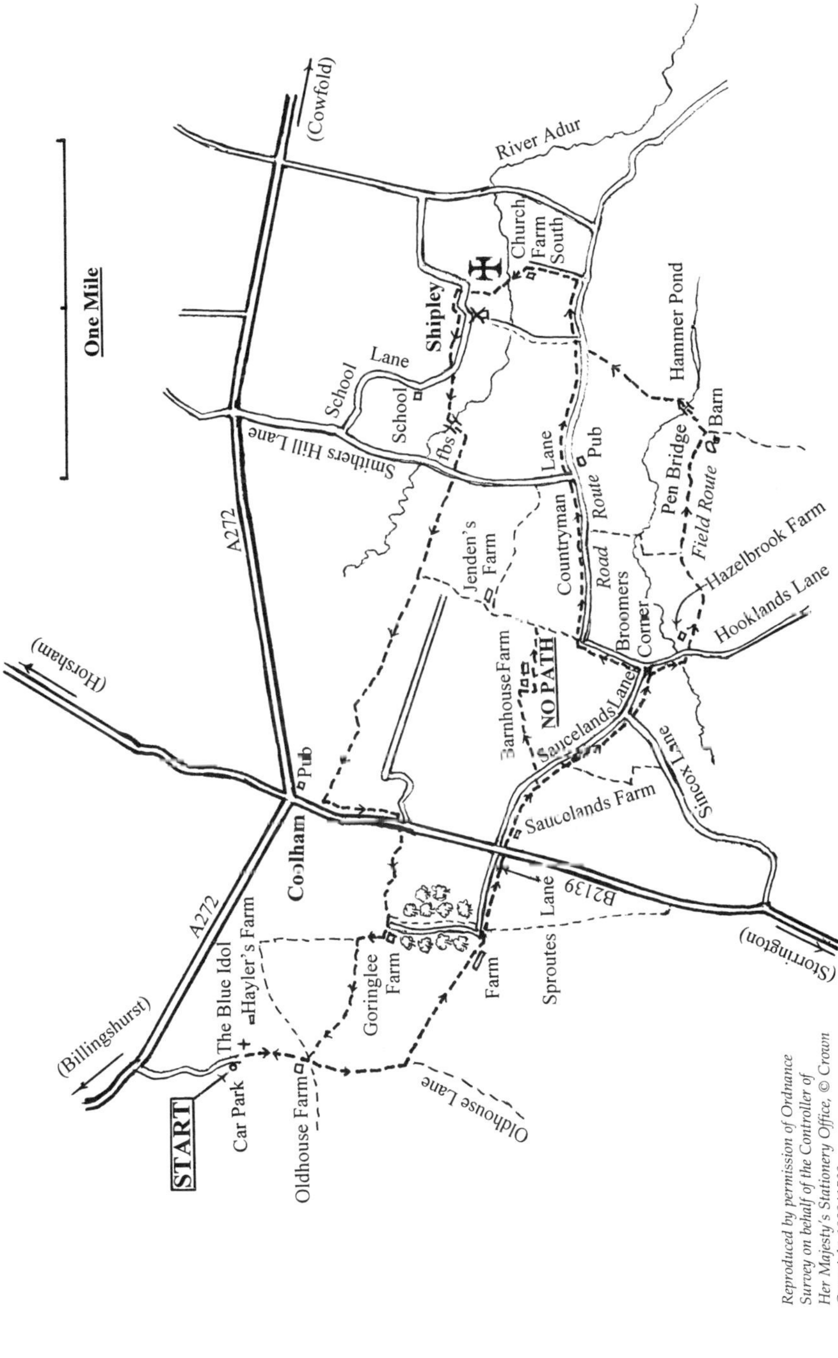
One Mile
(Cowfold)
River Adur
Church Farm South
Shipley
School Lane
School
fbs
Smithers Hill Lane
A272
Hammer Pond
Pen Bridge
Barn
Field Route
Road Route
Pub
Countryman Lane
Jenden's Farm
Hazelbrook Farm
Hooklands Lane
Broomers Corner
Barnhouse Farm
NO PATH
Saucelands Lane
Sincox Lane
Saucelands Farm
(Horsham)
Pub
Coolham
B2139
Lane
Sproutes Lane
Farm
Goringlee Farm
Hayler's Farm
The Blue Idol
(Billingshurst)
(Storrington)
START
Car Park
Oldhouse Farm
Oldhouse Lane

Oldhouse Farm on your right and a footpath on your left. Keep walking south and enter woodland on a narrow footpath. In 250 metres turn left. You can see two parallel gates ahead. You leave the woods, go through the gates into a wide flat open field. Make for the large barn ahead hugging the hedge on the left. In September it bears a crop of luscious sloes.

Keep the barn and other farm buildings on your right and keep straight on heading east on the concrete road. This becomes a tarmac road, Sproutes Lane. Cross with care the B2139 to Saucelands Lane opposite. On the left is a sign indicating the wartime airfield.

Walk along Saucelands Lane for 300 metres. After a bend in the lane, you come to a track on the left signposted to Barnhouse Farm.

This footpath is on the 'Unavailable Paths List' of West Sussex County Council. Apparently the diversion will be referred to the Secretary of State. Among the cluster of buildings here is a beautiful house in herringbone brick with a Horsham stone roof built in 1500. If the diversion is settled, you should be able to walk through to a T-junction with a bridleway, turn right and reach the **bend** below, joining the Road route.

Shipley

Road route (including a pub): Walk to the end of Saucelands Lane, avoiding a road, Sincox Lane on the right. You reach a T-junction at Broomers Corner and turn left. In 300 metres you reach a **bend.** Head east along the lane to a junction and a pub on the right. Keep on past the pub and along Countryman Lane for 1 kilometre. Avoid a footpath on the left, a green lane on the right (where the field route joins) and a bridleway on the left.

Field Route *(Muddy in places and slightly longer): Walk to the end of Saucelands Lane, avoiding the road, Sincox Lane on the right. You reach a T-junction at Broomers Corner and turn right into Hooklands Lane where you pass some delightful old white cottages on the right. In 200 metres just past Hazelbrook Farm, turn left into a footpath where gates and stiles impede the way through pens for sheep, hens and, turkey fowl. If you make it over the last stile, you come to a wide, flat field. The surface is dry even though reeds abound. In 400* *metres, avoid the path to the left. Continue east with the hedge on your left and a distant view to the Downs on your right.*

In one kilometre from Hazelbrook Farm, the path curves right into bushes and crosses the little Pen Bridge to a pond and a barn. From here, resume your course to the nearby green lane. Turn left at this T-junction and pick your way through the churned mud. The lane is hedged and there is no escape! Fortunately the surface improves as you proceed northeast and in ½ mile you reach the tarmac of Countryman Lane. Turn right and avoid the bridleway opposite. You have now joined the 'road route' and take the next track left.

Both Routes Pass Honeypool cottage on the right. There is a view to Shipley Windmill on the left. Turn left at a gate with the notice 'Church Farm South'. Here is a driveway leading to cottages and the River Adur. Cross footbridges to another century. Ahead is a water meadow below the lovely old church and the white windmill of Shipley.

From Shipley Church continue up the path to the village. Just past the red phone box, turn left into School Lane to pass the windmill on your left. In another 200 metres at a bend in the road, turn left into a footpath. Cross a small field diagonally left below a large school house on the right. Enter a hedge- lined track and turn left. The path takes you over wooden footbridges and follows the field boundary on the right. In 150 metres take a right fork into a farm track. Cross tarmac Smithers Hill Lane to the bridleway opposite. This path is enclosed at first with thick hedges. The hedges give way to open fields. You are heading northwest for over a mile to Coolham. Along part of the way, a spaced row of little trees is dedicated to individual airmen. Plaques give their names and the dates of their deaths. Continue to the B2139 at Coolham. *There is a pub to the right.*

Turn left and walk with care along the narrow verge of this road. In 400 metres at Farley Cottage on the left, cross the road to the footpath opposite. Hug the field boundary on the right for two fields. Then make for Goringlee Farm ahead. Avoid the path on the left and keep straight on through the farmyard. Just before the last building turn right to leave the farm by an enclosed track. In 25 metres turn left into an idyllic little valley. Take the path that follows the stream down on the left for 500 metres. After the second field you leave the valley at a copse in the right hand corner. Cross a little field to Oldhouse Farm. Here you are back on the original track. Turn right for the Blue Idol.

The Blue Idol

Walk 5: Storrington to Sullington

This walk is a world away from Storrington`s busy shopping street with constant through traffic. Here are Victorian monasteries, idyllic pastures, heavenly hills and wild Downs.

Starting Point: Monastery Lane, named after the monastery at the top, built in 1902.
Either the car park near the petrol station at the roundabout **GR**085144
Or the verge half way up the lane **GR**084143
Map: OS Explorer 121 **Distance:** 5 or 6 miles **Terrain:** Hilly

The Churches

Storrington

The Parish Church of St Mary, Storrington stands in an elevated part of the town. A church is recorded in 'Estorchetone' in Domesday and it may well have stood on this site. The old names suggest that there was a stork colony here. The present large imposing building is a far cry from those days. The north aisle and Lady Chapel formed an early church, possibly 11th century. The church was enlarged in 13th century. A new nave and chancel were built and a tower added. The church spire did much damage when it was struck by lightning in 1731. The whole tower collapsed and the roof of the nave was broken in 1745. It took 9 years to raise the money for repairs. More changes were made in 1876 when the chancel was extended and the south aisle added. The 21st century has made a charming contribution; when you enter from the porch you are automatically greeted by soft music.

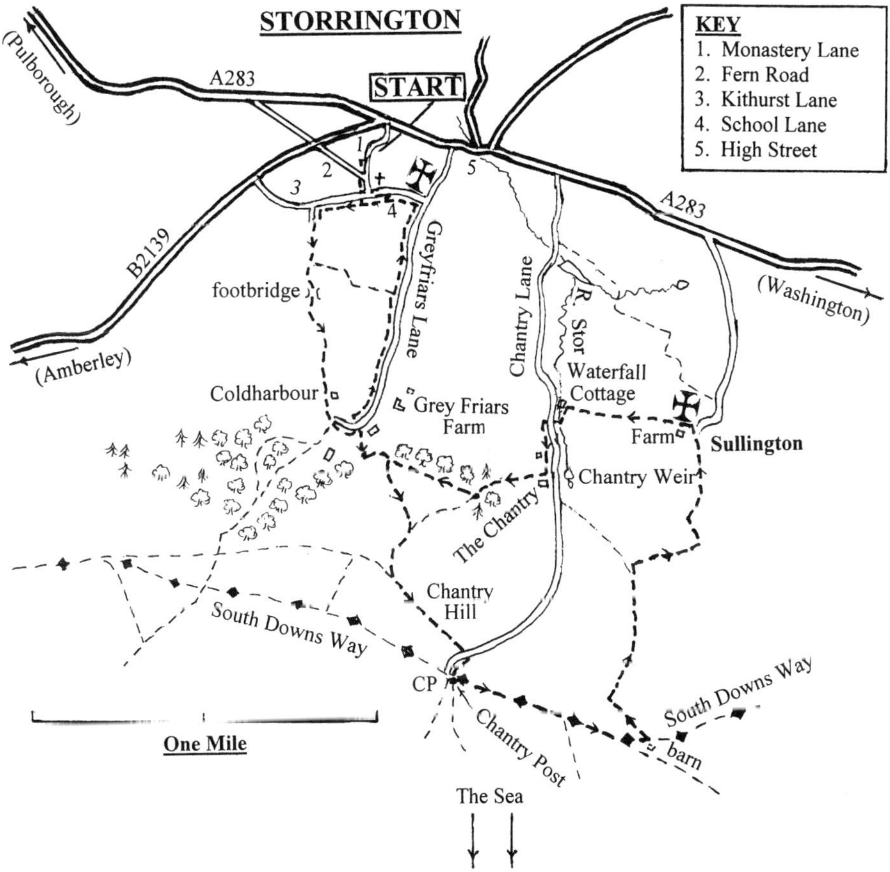
STORRINGTON
START
A283
(Pulborough)
B2139
(Amberley)
(Washington)
KEY
1. Monastery Lane
2. Fern Road
3. Kithurst Lane
4. School Lane
5. High Street
footbridge
Greyfriars Lane
Chantry Lane
R. Stor
Waterfall Cottage
Coldharbour
Grey Friars Farm
Farm
Sullington
Chantry Weir
The Chantry
Chantry Hill
South Downs Way
CP
Chantry Post
barn
One Mile
The Sea

The Roman Catholic Monastery and Church were established here with the help of the Duke of Norfolk. In 1880 the French Government closed some monasteries. White Canons came from the abbey at Frigolet in the Rhone Valley and found refuge here. Their church was founded in 1902 but most of the monks returned to France when restrictions were lifted during the First World War.

St Mary's Church, Sullington stands on an ancient site. The name may mean 'the hamlet of Sula's or Sulja's people'. The narrow nave of the church suggests Saxon proportions. At the base of the tower, Saxon stones are set 'long and short'. The tower is Norman. The main body of the church is Early English, with the exception of the Decorated east window. The 'Mary' window is more recent. The north aisle was once a chantry, founded by Richard, Earl of Arundel in 1389. Entrance to the church is through the tower. A knight skilfully carved in marble lies on your left. This little corner of Sussex, church, farm, manor and tithe barn is not quite idyllic. A farming industry is here and corrugated buildings jostle the church as tractors turn in the yard.

Sullington

The Walk

Go up Monastery Lane to crossroads. The Catholic Church is on your left and the cemetery straight ahead. Turn right along Kithurst Lane. At the end you join a track curving left. Do not go far! A footpath sign is on your left. Take this narrow path down to fields. A stream joins you at the bottom. Cross the stream on a footbridge and escape to the fields. Cross diagonally left to find a grass platform heading due south to the Downs. Pass a delightful cottage, 'Coldharbour' and continue on its driveway to a junction of paths.

It is possible to go straight up a steep wooded way to the top of the Downs. I prefer to turn left along the track to Greyfriars Farm. Turn sharp right just before you reach the farm onto a path leading more gently to the top. It starts in woodland and soon curves up to open downland. A row of trees below will form a canopy later on our return walk. Behind, the view of Storrington offers a wealth of ecclesiastical buildings. As you climb gently up to Chantry Hill, you can look across steep valleys to pink chalk pits.

Near the top at a T-junction, the path curves left and you follow another grassy platform. It leads unexpectedly to a car track, Chantry Lane. Turn right up this lane to the Chantry Post with a handsome new signpost above the car park. Turn left and follow the Washington direction along the South Downs Way heading east. You soon emerge to an open track across fields. The distant sea sparkles over to your right. You are in the midst of downland. In half a mile pass a barn on your right then turn left almost immediately onto a farm track.

This track curves all the way down to Sullington Church, a mile away. On a fine day it is well worth following the parallel path up on the left. Avoid the first right turn leading to the farm track again. Instead, carry on into a bumpy remote part of the Downs. You come down to and ignore a path to the left. At this junction you return to the farm track down on your right. Turn left down the track, concrete towards the bottom, until you reach the quagmire of the farm at Sullington. The unspoilt little church is opposite.

To return to Storrington, turn left taking the track between corrugated farm buildings and the church. Go past two houses and enter the field with the shapely Downs above on your left. Keep to the hedge on your right for 500 metres. The hedge gives way to a wire fence. At a copse turn left to walk downhill on a muddy path. At the bottom is a little field where you turn right, passing Waterfall Cottage on the right. There was once a fulling mill here, harnessing the waters of the tiny River Stor.

Go down to the gate into Chantry Lane and turn left. There really is a waterfall on the left. Continue up the lane for 250 metres to the magnificent ponds and garden of Chantry Weir. Turn right here onto a driveway through farm buildings, known as the Chantry. Keep straight on heading southwest across a field to crossways near a copse. Avoid the track to the right and continue up to the copse. This is a delightful elevated stroll through the line of trees we saw earlier. To the right we look down to the apparently ancient pile, Greyfriars. In fact it was built as recently as 1890.

After half a mile in this woodland, you reach a familiar track and turn right to Grey Friars Farm. The track becomes a road, Greyfriars Lane. Ignore the path on the left back to Coldharbour. Instead keep straight on down the lane back to Storrington. The Parish Church dominates this lane as you enter the town.

Turn left in front of the church. This is School Lane. Ahead is the Monastery. Turn right after the Roman Catholic Church and walk back down Monastery Lane.

5 Walks
Near Worthing

Walk 6: A. Poling to Angmering
B. Poling to Lyminster

Mainly a flat walk on the coastal plain, this walk is a miracle of rural peace amongst an area of heavy traffic and urban sprawl. Part B of this walk uses the same track both ways

Starting Point: three choices beside the no through road to Poling:
Beside the seat **GR**047053
At a small layby **GR**046048
At T-junction **GR**046047
Map: OS Explorer 121 **Distances:** circular to Angmering under 5 miles
Poling to Lyminster and back 2 miles
Terrain: Flat
Local Information: Mondays, Wednesdays and Fridays coffee and biscuits are served in the Vestry Hall, Angmering. Shops, pubs and a restaurant are also nearby.

The Churches

St Nicholas, Poling. This venerable building from the ancient village of Palyinge shares a peaceful oasis with birds and sheep. Its nave is the size of the original Saxon church here. There is still a small Saxon window high up in the north wall of the nave. It is between the two trefoil head windows. The piers and arches of the nave are Transition Norman. The tower was added in 1420. Not far away, at the north end of Poling Street, are the remains of St John`s Priory, once the domain of the Knights Templar.

Also beside the north end of Poling Street, near the Priory a new large milestone has inscriptions including a poem by J. M. Inglis:

Not Poling - Paling
Previous to a church`s tower
Brackish water stained the mire
A tiny hamlet perched on staves
Not Poling – Paling lapped by waves

Where do they sleep the ancient folk?
Who ploughed with oxen, glazed a pot
We who have settled close to bones
Rekindle to re-enact their souls.

St Margaret`s Church, Angmering. This large, handsome building is a blend of old and relatively new. The original 12th century church was enlarged and rebuilt in Early English style in 1853 thanks to the generosity of local landowner, William Gratwicke. The chancel arch and archway to the porch belong to the original church. The tower has cheques of flint and stone. The convent of Syon House, Isleworth was responsible for building the tower in 1507.

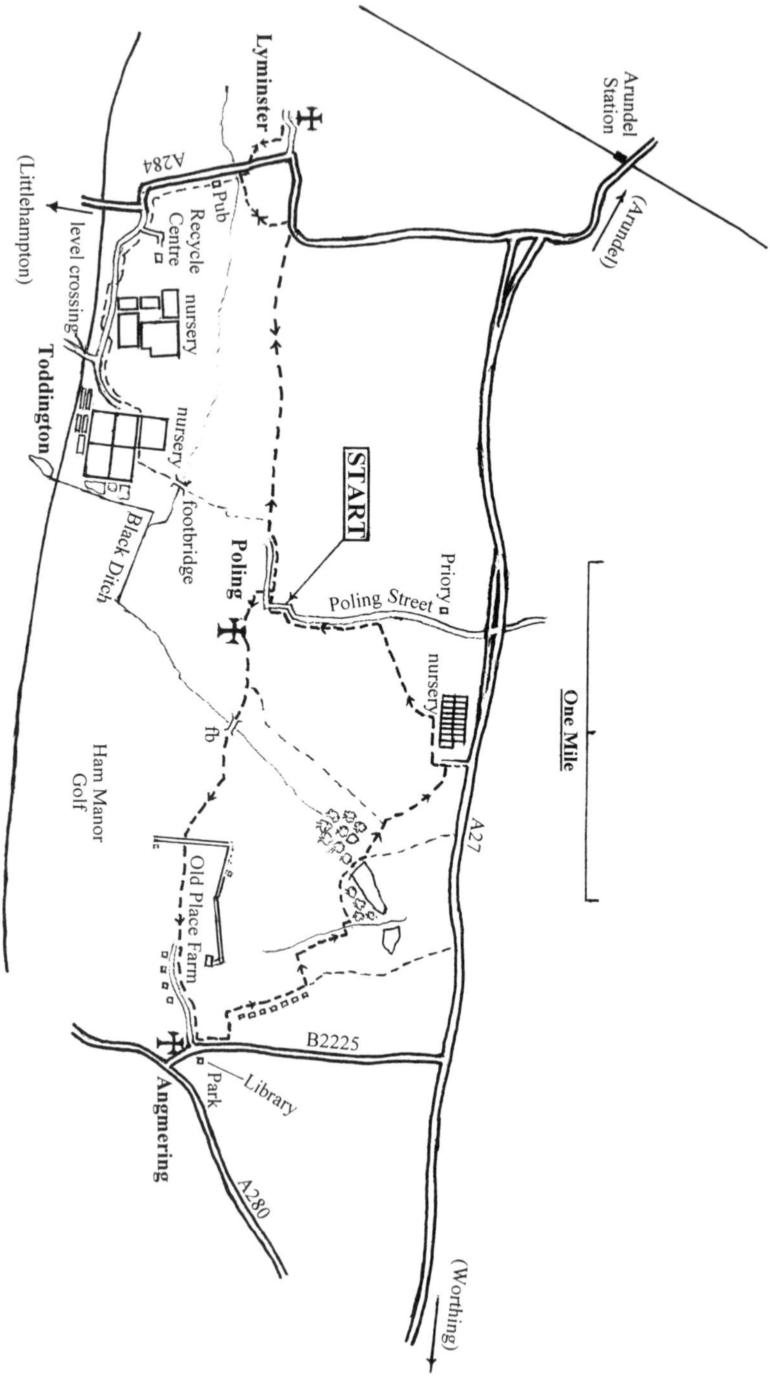
Arundel Station
(Arundel)
Lyminster
A284
(Littlehampton)
Pub
Recycle Centre
level crossing
nursery
Toddington
nursery
footbridge
START
Black Ditch
Poling
Priory
Poling Street
nursery
One Mile
fb
Ham Manor Golf
A27
Old Place Farm
B2225
Library
Park
Angmering
A280
(Worthing)

St Nicholas Church once stood just across the road in East Angmering. The foundations of this small Saxon church are buried under the turf in the little park behind the library. The church was closed in 1593 and demolished. Only a small heap of stones remains.

St Mary Magdalene, Lyminster stands on the site of a Saxon Benedictine Nunnery at 'Lullyngminster'. This tall, narrow building with thick walls reveals its Saxon origins. The arch of a blocked door on the south side of the nave and the head of a window above the west pillar on the north side are Saxon. The Normans added the north aisle in 1170 and the font of Sussex marble dates from this period. The lower part of the tower is early 13th century and the bell chamber is 15th century. The north porch was added in 15th century. There are some beautiful windows, in particular the two lancets and the circular window in the nave of circa 1260. Outside the churchyard on the north side there is a pool, Nucker Hole on the path towards Arundel. The name 'Nucker', derived from the Anglo-Saxon 'Nicor' meaning 'sea-monster', confirms the local legend that a dragon once ravaged the countryside hereabouts.

Angmering

The Walk

Part A - Poling to Angmering

Go along Poling Street to the T-junction and telephone booth. Turn right and walk for about 50 metres to the footpath signposted to Poling Church. It is a tarmac walkway. At the end, turn left and pass the Manor on the left.

Go through the churchyard, heading east with the church on your right. Pass a horse exercise yard on the right then cross to a muddy farm track on the left and continue east. You leave this track for open fields. Avoid the path to the left leading to woodland. Instead, veer slightly to the right where there is a bit of hedge. Keep this on your right. Cross a generous wooden footbridge and keep on along the clearly defined footpath over flat, treeless fields. You are on a well-drained plain, once the estuary of the River Arun.

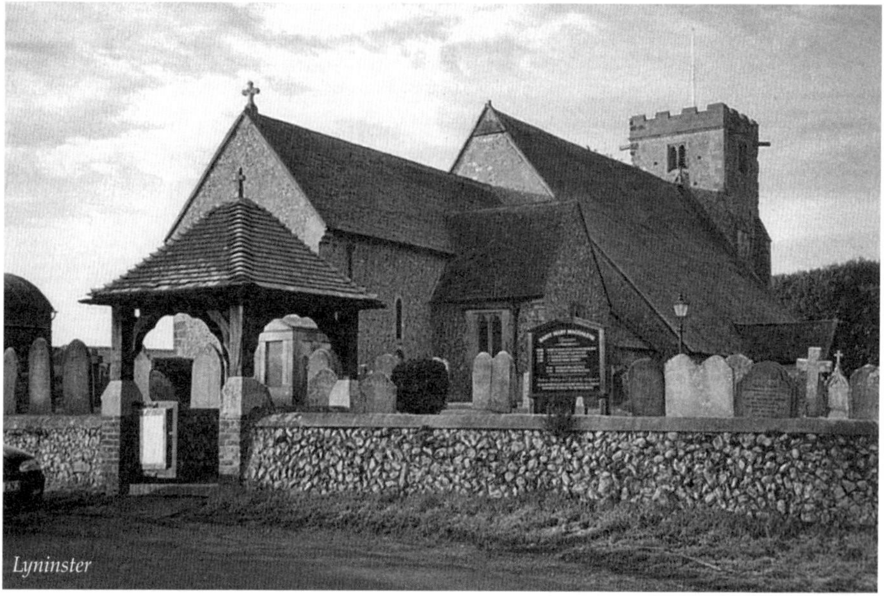

Lyninster

Cut across a straight farm way and head for Angmering along an enclosed track. You can see the tower of Poling Church behind and Angmering Church in front. In about 1 mile from Poling, you come to a residential road on the edge of Angmering and veer left. Old Place Farm is over to the left and detached houses are on your right. This road, the Thatchway curves to the right towards the village and takes you to St Margaret's Church.

Enter the churchyard on your left. After visiting the church leave by the lych gate. A car park is down on your right and the Vestry Hall nearby. The library is across the main road. Behind the library is the little park with the scant remains of St Nicholas Church.

Part A - Angmering to Poling

Cross back to St Margaret's and turn right, heading north. Walk on the pavement beside the B2225 Arundel Road. Pass a grassy play area then a school, both on the left. Avoid a footpath also on the left. In about 250 metres at a postbox, turn left into a small housing estate. You are on Bewley Road. At the end of the road after the last house, turn right onto a footpath.

Follow the enclosed path behind back gardens with fields on your left. In about 100 metres, just before playing fields, turn left away from the main path. In 150 metres turn right to join a track towards Steyne Wood. Just before you reach the wood leave the track and veer left. Enter the wood and walk along the southern

Poling

edge for 100 metres. The path turns right into the wood and passes next to Decoy Pond, quite a sizeable lake.

After passing Decoy Pond, you come to a wide, grassy track with a cottage ahead. You have to leave this track immediately and strike out onto the path on the left. Cross the field diagonally left towards a narrow strip of woodland. Go through a gap to scrubland with a choice of paths. Turn right into a new plantation. There is a stream in the hedge on your right. You have to leave this hedge and follow the overgrown, unpromising little footpath on the left. It leads uphill through the scrub to a flat field.

Make for the houses on the other side of the field. Go between houses to their access road and turn left. This is a dead end for cars. Do not be deterred by the big wire gates on the right. They lock away the large windowless sheds of a mushroom farm. Go through the gap beside the gates and follow the high wire fence on the right. A tall leylandii hedge is on the left. At the fence corner you have to turn left to cross a stile into a field. Walk diagonally right towards a farm gate. Go through to an open track leading back to Poling Street. Turn left when you get there.

Part B - Poling to Lyminster and back

Go along Poling Street to the T-junction and telephone booth as above and turn right. Pass the footpath to the church on the left. Continue through the hamlet past the few bungalows and houses old and new. At the end of the street keep straight on along the track which serves as a footpath to Lyminster. In 200 metres avoid the path on the left and plod on along our westward track.

In a mile you reach A284 at Lyminster. Cross to the pavement opposite and turn left. In 250 metres there is a signpost to Lyminster Church. Turn right into Church Road.

Retrace your steps to Poling.

Walk 7: Washington to Buncton

From a picturesque downland village, surrounded by busy roads, make for the lower slopes of the Downs. Discover a simple solitary church. Have tea or lunch at rustic tearooms and return across farmland and past a gigantic sandpit.

Starting Point: Opposite the pub, on Washington Bostal, a continuation of London Rd to the east of A24 **GR**123129
Map: OS Explorer 121 **Terrain:** Undulating **Distance:** 6 Miles

The Churches

Washington, St Mary: The Church stands on a hill on the site of a tiny Norman church. Pretty cottages have since climbed up to dwell in the lee of the church. The first recorded vicar is Bovo in 1174. The early church was linked to the Priory of Sele at Beeding, see Walk 20. Transport to and from Sele was on foot or horses. Never could they have foreseen the speeding traffic of the A24, now below the church. A narrow bridge links the church with the Downs to the west. Knights Templar built a larger church with a tower. Later the tower was incorporated as a lean-to to a new Tudor tower. In 1865 the church was again dismantled and rebuilt. Only the tower was spared.

All Saints, Buncton is one of many isolated churches in West Sussex. Avoid a visit at Halloween. Only then is the church closed to keep out crazy black magic vandals.The basic shape of this Norman church has changed little since it was built, 1066- 1200. It consists of nave and chancel, both tall for so small a church. Small Norman windows are high in the nave. Saxon influence is in the tall doors north and south of the nave. In the north wall above a scaffolding hole is a wall painting, fleur de lys. The east end of the chancel, including the Decorated window, is 14th century. Ornate blocked arches on the outer walls of the chancel have been inserted in 14th century. They probably came from Sele Priory, see Walk 20.

The Walk

With your back to the pub turn right and walk up the road. Just past a gate in the hedge on the left you will find a footpath. Turn left here into a field. Cross diagonally right, go over a footbridge and take the enclosed path uphill. Pass a cottage down on the left. Cross a concrete farm track into another field. Veer right uphill to a corner of the field. In the next field at a T-junction, turn left to follow the main path heading east below the Downs.

Pass Tilleys Farm on the left and keep on course for 350 metres then veer right towards the Downs. Resume an easterly course through undulating woodland for one mile. At crossways you pass a flint cottage on the right and turn left down Chanctonbury Ring Road. Go downhill for nearly 1 mile to the main Washington Road, A283.

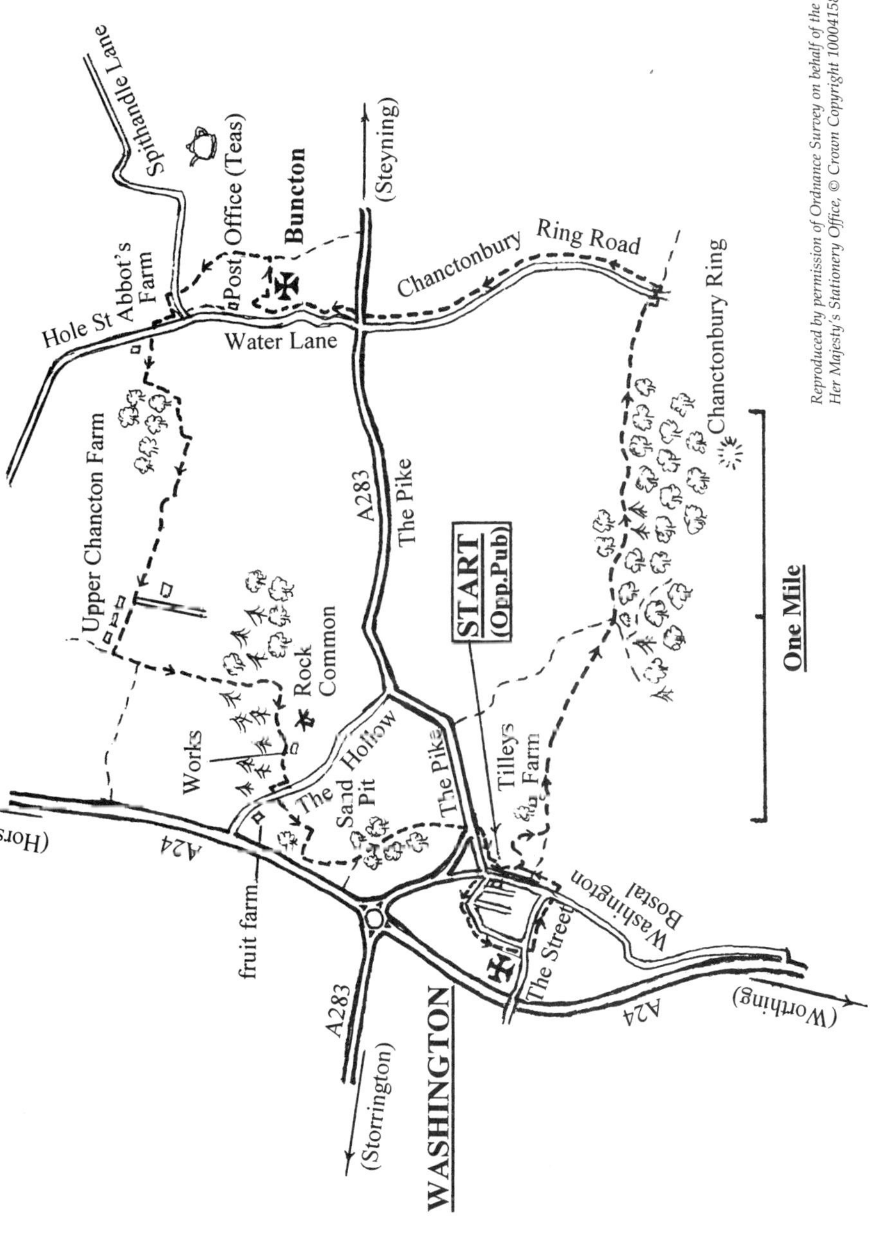
Spithandle Lane
Post Office (Teas)
Buncton
(Steyning)
Hole St
Abbot's Farm
Water Lane
Chanctonbury Ring Road
Chanctonbury Ring
Chanctonbury
Upper Chancton Farm
A283
The Pike
START
(Opp.Pub)
Rock Common
Works
The Hollow
The Sand Pit
The Pike
Tilleys Farm
One Mile
(Horsham)
A24
fruit farm
Washington Bostal
The Street
A283
(Storrington)
WASHINGTON
A24
(Worthing)

Cross with care to Water Lane opposite. Follow the path as it keeps changing sides on the lane for 300 metres then stop at the church board on the right. Here a steep path leads down then up through woodland to Buncton Church. From the church, pass the cross high on the east end and go through a gap in the hedge to a footpath. Continue east through open fields with the Downs in view on the right. In 100 metres turn left and follow the path to a ruin. Here cross the field diagonally left to cottages on Spithandle Lane. Turn left and walk downhill back to Water Lane. Turn left to the nearby post office and the unexpected joy of tearooms that you share with chickens, ducks and geese.

Buncton

Go back along Water Lane, passing Spithandle Lane on the right. Water Lane becomes Hole Street here. In 150 metres you reach some cottages at Abbot`s Farm. Just before the garden of a cottage on the left, turn into a footpath heading west. The path heads up to a corner at the edge of woodland. Turn left and hug the wood then the hedge here on the right. The Downs are ahead. As woodland peters out, look for a fingerpost on the right. It directs you to the right side of the hedge heading west. This is the public right of way. Some walkers have chosen the farm track on the left side with downland views. Both ways lead up to Upper Chancton Farm where you are greeted, first by caravans, then by the old farm buildings and finally, if you are lucky, a pot bellied pig.

Go through the farmyard and turn left at the open fields at the top. Ahead you

can see the windmill without sails on Rock Common. Avoid the path to the right and head for the newly landscaped mound of rubbish below the windmill. Enter a screen of trees and follow the narrow path as it passes the northern edge of the mound. Eventually, you reach a big sandpit. **Take care to keep out of the way of lorries!** Go through a works entrance to a tarmac lane, The Hollow.

Across the lane, 2 feet above the ground, there is a puzzling arrow pointing to the left. Ignore this and turn right then immediately left beside a fruit farm and orchard. This is another narrow footpath around the edge of a huge sandpit. At its southern end you get a chance to view it. Meanwhile, follow the path as it bends to the right. The high banks at the edge of the sandpit are on your left. Go down through a screen of trees and turn left. A stream joins you in this screen of woodland and hems you on the right. The bank edge of the pit is still on your left. Avoid the path to the right over a footbridge. Keep straight on past a caravan site on the right. You then come up to an open field. Cross the field to a farm gate in the hedge opposite. *In wet weather it may be wise to keep to the left hand side of the field before heading for the farm gate to avoid the bog in the middle!*

You are back on the A283. Turn right and cross with care to the road opposite. This is a slip road, 'the Pike' leading down into Washington Bostal and London Road.

To visit Washington Church, cross to School Lane and walk up to the recreation ground and village hall. Keep climbing on School Lane until you reach a T-junction at the top, the Street. The church is on your right.

Walk 8: Patching, Findon and Clapham

Delightful villages in the Downs stand peacefully above and apart from the South Coast conurbations. They hold their link with the past and skylarks still soar in the spring sky. Some of our paths follow Monarch`s Way (More on this Way at the end of the book).

Starting Point: The top of the Street, a continuation of France Lane, Patching.
GR088068 **Map:** OS Explorer 121 **Distance:** 7 miles **Terrain:** Quite hilly

The Churches

Patching, St John the Divine. Perhaps from medieval times successive Archbishops of Canterbury have climbed to this same church from their episcopal palace in Tarring, for they have held 'Patchinges' since 948. Patching was a chapel to the mother church of Tarring. To find Tarring, you have to go down to Worthing town. Patching is still a small downland village and the church has not changed so very much since the building of 1200 in Early English style. It has the lancet windows of that period. The barn-like roof is original. There may once have been a north aisle to the tower. The church may have been built to fit the tower. The nave is not in line with the chancel. There have been several Victorian restorations and a pulpit with carved panels. The octagonal font is 15th century.

St John the Baptist, Findon was parted from the village in 1930 when the A24 bypass was built. The church and manor house, Findon Place stand in rural quiet on the west side of the road. The church is mentioned in Domesday 1086 when there was probably a Saxon building here. A Norman church replaced it around 1120. There is a rare 12th century sanctus bell above the pulpit. A large aisle with chancel chapel were added in 13th century. An unusual later addition was the single span roof over nave and aisle. The tower is early 13th century. The chancel, north and south chapels are Early English with some Perpendicular windows. The south chapel, used as a vestry, has a fine window, a memorial to John Lyall. Restoration work of 1867 cost £2408, a tidy sum. There are some handsome William Morris tiles behind the pulpit.

The Church of the Blessed Virgin Mary, Clapham stands up at the northeast end of the village with woodland and fields for company. It was built at the end of the 12th century, replacing a Norman church. A bit of Norman work is in the northwest wall of the nave. The arcades and tower are 13th century. In the belfry are three bells, possibly dating 1350 to 1360 and the oldest in the country. The north arcade is Transition Norman and the south arcade Early English. Victorian restorations have kept the church in a good state of repair. The architect Sir Gilbert Scott was interested in English Gothic and lancet windows abound. Behind the altar there are William Morris tiles depicting archangels with a surround of vine and grapes. The guardians of this church today make a valiant effort to keep it open to visitors despite the attention of thieves and vandals.

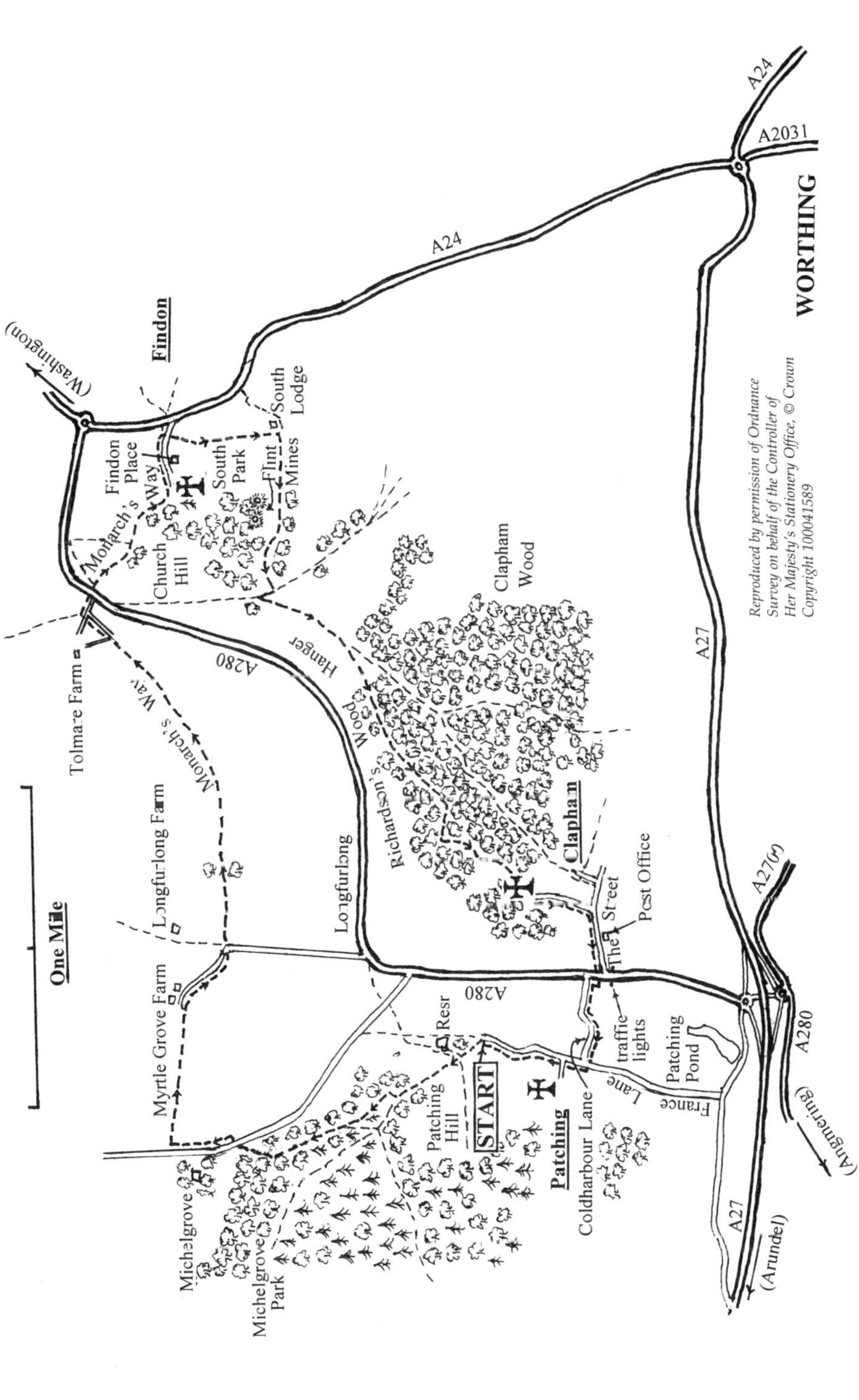
(Washington)
Findon
A24
A24
A2031
WORTHING
South Lodge
South Park
Flint Mines
Findon Place
Monarch's Way
Church Hill
Clapham Wood
Hanger
A280
Tolmare Farm
Monarch's Way
Longfurlong Farm
Longfurlong
Richardson's Wood
Clapham
Post Office
The Street
A27
One Mile
Myrtle Grove Farm
A280
Resr
traffic lights
Patching Pond
A27
A280
Patching Hill
START
Patching
Coldharbour Lane
France Lane
(Angmering)
Michelgrove
Michelgrove Park
A27
(Arundel)
Reproduced by permission of Ordnance Survey on behalf of the Controller of Her Majesty's Stationery Office, © Crown Copyright 100041589

Patching

The Walk

Continue up to the Downs and veer left on a wide grassy track, heading for Patching Hill. Pass a small reservoir down on the right and keep straight on at cross-paths. Admire the view over Longfurlong on the right but avoid the tracks leading that way. Instead, you approach a glade with majestic trees and enter the woodland of Angmering Estate.

Clapham

Go straight on along the right hand of parallel paths. In 75 metres turn right on a path leading along the edge of the wood where you enjoy glorious views across parkland to the Downs. In 200 metres you join the main track, Monarch's Way approaching from the left. Go down to the lane at Michelgrove.

At the lane turn left, passing Michelgrove cottages then the house on the left. The ancient manor house, home of the Shelleys for 300 years, no longer exists. A Mr. Walker bought the estate in 1800 and changed the house to Regency style. In 1828 the house was again sold to the Duke of Norfolk who demolished it.

After a high wall on the right, turn right to a bridleway and head due east on this fenced way. In half a mile you come down to Myrtle Grove Farm and follow the way markers through the farmyard, now holding several small business enterprises. Do not be tempted to the sheds but go past a mower repair outfit and depart along the farm access road.

In 200 metres you reach a lane. Turn left here then immediately right and step out across wide fields. A long hill or hanger looms ahead to the right. Our path through the first field leads down to a line of trees and a timber dump. Go through to the next field where the path is well defined up to an enclosed track. You are heading northeast, still on Monarch's Way.

You are approaching A280 at a recent section of road. In 19th century, finding that Michelgrove was absorbing their fortune, the Walker boys tried operating a coach to and from London. They built the road, 'Longfurlong' for the passage of their coach. Their new road runs below the looming hanger. Later in this walk, our way back is along the top of this hanger.

Kathleen Ramsay (left) and Diana Pé

Pass Tolmare Farm down on the left and start the gentle climb up the track towards the main road, Longfurlong. In 200 metres turn right at a concrete track and pass a small unofficial car park on the right. Pause at the main road and look across to the other side. There are two paths opposite, about 20 metres apart. Avoid the main stony track on the right. Pick your moment and cross to the little path on the left.

Follow the grassy downland path up then down towards a playing field below. Stay well above the field and turn right heading southeast. Keep in this direction with the hill on your right. In 500 metres you reach Findon Church, ensconced in woodland.

Findon

From Findon Church, continue on Monarch's Way, passing Findon Place. (The last Lord of the Manor died in 1945). Turn right just before you reach the A24. An enclosed path leads through South Park for 450 metres. After South Lodge turn right at a T-junction.

You climb through woodland for half a mile, passing old flint mines near the top. You then escape to open downland. Turn right on the main track then almost immediately left. Follow the path along the top of the hanger above Longfurlong Road, A280. You can look down across the woods, fields and farms you passed earlier. Further off the masts of Bignor Hill stand out.

In half a mile fork right towards Richardsons Wood. The path is well defined here. For about a mile it passes through five delightful patches of pastureland. After the third patch, you re-enter the wood and turn left. At the fourth patch you cross the field half-way then veer right into more woodland. At the fifth and final meadow, you keep straight on to enter the churchyard of Clapham Church.

Go through the churchyard to the main entrance and turn left. Go down the wooded track to the village lane. Turn right and walk past cottages, including the old post office. Then pass the prefab home of today's post office and village shop. You come down to the A280. The church spire of Patching can guide you here. First, Traffic lights on the left enable pedestrians to make a safe crossing. On the other side, turn right and walk beside the Longfurlong for a short way to a tarmac lane flanked by houses. This is Coldharbour Lane and leads back up to Patching. When you reach the Street, turn right and visit Patching Church on your way back to the car park.

Walk 9: Sompting to Cissbury Ring *(Short Walk)* and to Findon *(Long Walk)*

A magnificent walk across downland to Cissbury Ring, one of the great prehistoric landmarks of Sussex. The walk can be extended to follow the Monarch`s Way to Findon, where Church Hill has Stone Age flint mines. Enjoy distant views to the sea and famous features including Chanctonbury. See the Introduction for more details.

Starting Point: Sompting Church **GR**162055
Map: OS Explorer 121 **Terrain:** Hilly and exposed in places
Distances: 7 Miles or 14 Miles (Add 1 mile for an optional tour of Cissbury ramparts)

Note: Findon Church is also included in Walk 8. Refer to that walk to read a description of Findon Church. There is no walk to Broadwater Church, described below. Sadly it is in a suburb of Worthing.

The Churches

Sompting Parish Church stands almost alone in the rising Downs. The village of Sompting is south across A27. The church tower, with stone pilaster strips on each wall, is a monument to Saxon architecture. The spire or Rhenish helm is the only one in England. There are others in West Germany. This spire gives evidence of pre-Conquest links. Small Saxon windows are high in the tower. Inside are original timbers and there is a fine Saxon tower arch. You enter the church through the south porch and realise immediately that here is a huge, historic shrine. Knights Templar built the south transept as a private chapel in 1180. It is spacious and solid, a church in its own right. The north transept is also a church with chapels for the Templars. The 12th century nave and chancel are on the site of the original church, mentioned in Domesday in 1086. It has no chancel arch. In 1324 the Knights of St John or the Hospitaller took over the church. We owe St John's Ambulance to them.

Broadwater Parish Church stands on clay that was once under the sea. When a Saxon church was built at 'Bradwatre', no doubt the sea could be seen or heard nearby. Now a congested suburb of Worthing jostles the church. The remains of a doorway on the south side of the chancel could be Saxon. The late Norman church consisted of nave, chancel and tower. Norman ornamentation in the form of chevrons is still in the eastern tower arch. The western tower arch was reset in pointed style in 14th century. There is a tablet on the floor to John White the surgeon who looked after convicts in the 1797 fleet to Australia. He kept them in good health. The nave was given Perpendicular windows in 15th Century. The transepts were built in 12th century and the walls straightened in 1855 by an experimental method of Charles Hide. Chapels in the transepts were removed in 1826. There is a blocked Norman window in the gable of the north transept. The

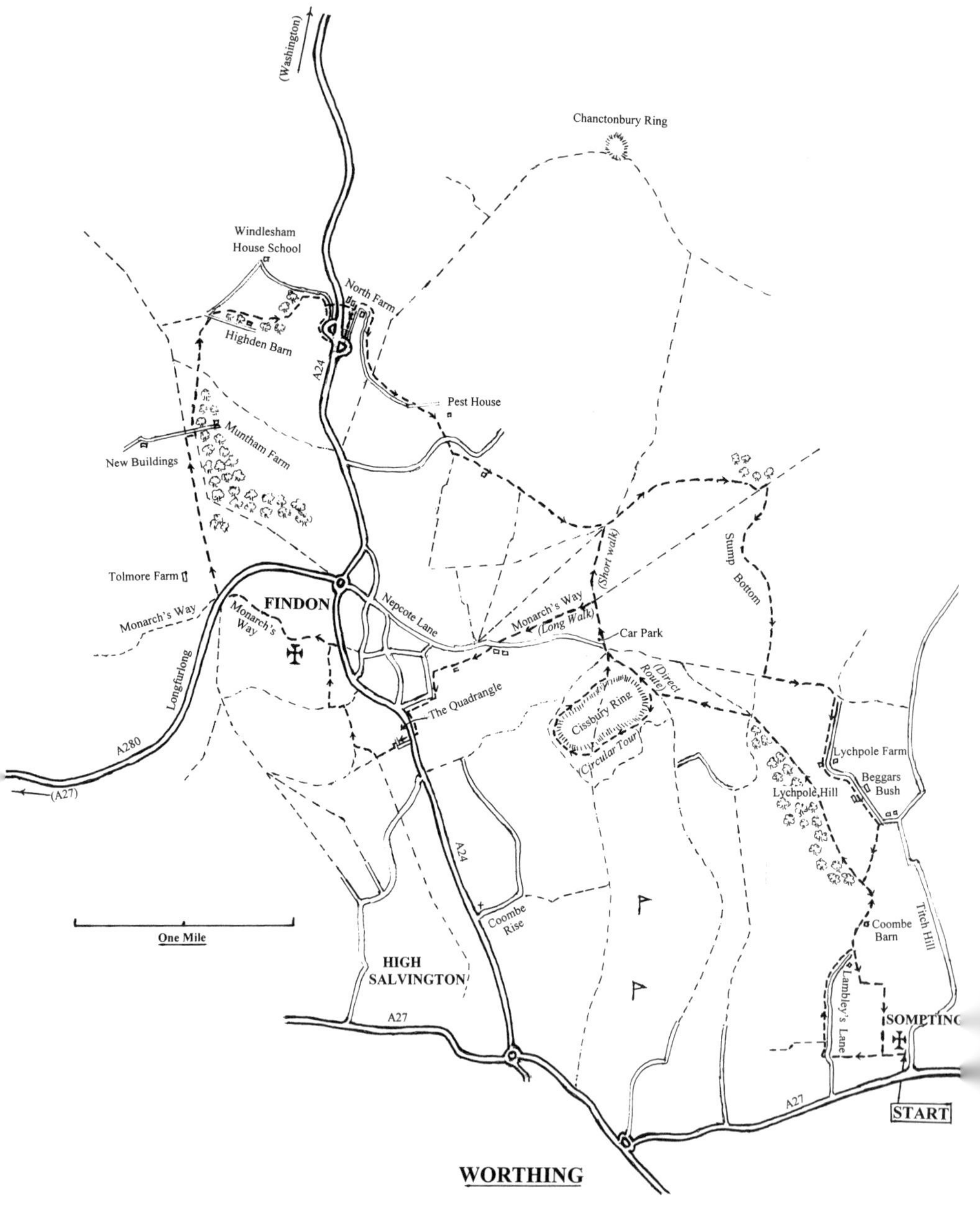
(Washington)
Chanctonbury Ring
Windlesham
House School
North Farm
Highden Barn
A24
Pest House
Muntham Farm
New Buildings
Stump Bottom
(Short walk)
Tolmore Farm
FINDON
Nepcote Lane
Monarch's Way
(Long Walk)
Car Park
Monarch's Way
Monarch's Way
Longfurlong
The Quadrangle
(Direct Route)
Cissbury Ring
(Circular Tour)
A280
(A27)
Lychpole Farm
Beggars Bush
Lychpole Hill
A24
Coombe Rise
One Mile
Coombe Barn
Titch Hill
HIGH
SALVINGTON
Lambley's Lane
A27
SOMPTING
A27
START
WORTHING

chancel has a 15th century screen. Set in the floor near the screen is a Sussex marble slab, an altar before Queen Elizabeth 1 banned them.

The Walk

Sompting to Cissbury Ring.

Just below Sompting Church Car Park, take the footpath west with occasional views over Worthing to the sea on the left. Ignore the first path on the right and keep heading west for under ½ mile to a concrete farm track, Lambleys Lane. Turn right and follow the concrete track uphill for 500 metres to farm buildings, Lambleys Barn. Go through the gate. Avoid the private track to the left and take the bridle way as it forks right, passing horse paddocks then a copse. A view opens to Beggars Bush and the Downs. Go down past Coombe Barn on the right. Climb up above the track with its surface of chippings and walk parallel to it. The track leads down to a double farm gate.

Cissbury

On the left of this double gate is the entrance to a wide valley. We follow the valley northwest with Lychpole Hill on our left. There is a distinctive fringe of trees along the top of the hill. In one mile we reach National Trust land at the base of Cissbury Ring. Go through two wooden gates. Fork left after the second gate with the sign 'National Trust' and climb fairly steeply through scrub for 500 metres. At the open space near the top, there is a wide track along an uncultivated swathe to the right, leading straight down to the **car park**. It is on the north side of Cissbury.

If you wish to explore Cissbury Ring, ignore this swathe and continue on the climb, left then right up onto the ramparts. Turn left and take a clockwise tour until you see the car park on the left below. Take a path down the slope to this ***car park*** *on the north side.*

At Cissbury Ring Car Park pass the access road on your left and keep straight on heading north on an enclosed bridleway. In 350 metres the Monarch`s Way crosses our track. This is the moment for decisions.

For the long walk, *follow the instructions below under the heading, 'Along the Monarch`s Way to Findon and Highden'.*

To Return to Sompting, cross Monarch`s Way and continue north on the track for another 450 metres to the next crossing and fork right.

*Head northeast on a quiet bridle way. As you descend there are views of bare downs and distant sea. In one kilometre fork right and go down into a small copse in 'No Man`s Land'. When you emerge from the copse, do not go up the hill

Sompting

ahead. Instead, turn right into a track with, at present, the misleading notice 'Private Road, Farm Access Only'. 30 metres along this track, a finger post confirms that you are on a right of way. It wends its way south through Stump Bottom with sparse hedges and rounded slopes.

In one mile at a T-junction, turn left and walk up to cross paths. Turn right to go past a wide metal farm gate and down the farm track to the flint buildings of Lychpole Farm. Veer left through the farm and join a concrete track to Beggars Bush where you have to walk between less attractive great sheds.

At the next junction turn right to follow the track southwards. Go through a gate into familiar downland with Lychpole Hill in sight. Follow the chippings of the track as it climbs up past Coombe Barn. In another 150 metres, at the copse, turn left onto a footpath that leads up over the brow of the hill and into a narrow path through bushes. Turn left into an open field and enjoy the wide view over Sompting to the sea. At the field corner turn right, descend to the familiar path below. Turn left for the church.

Along Monarch`s Way to Findon and Highden.

From the car park at Cissbury Ring you have already headed north to the decision point. Turn left and follow Monarch`s Way southwest down to rejoin the road to Nepcote Green. Leave Monarch`s Way here to cross the Green diagonally left passing a conservation barn on the left. At Nepcote Lane turn left and walk between the cottages of old Findon. The lane bends to the right and leads down to the A24.

Turn left and walk along the pavement beside the A24 as far as a nearby island in the road. Cross here to houses at the Quadrangle. Go along the short road to a T-junction and turn left. In a few yards you come to a fence with an opening into an alley. Turn right and walk up through the alley to horse paddocks.

In 200 metres turn right into an enclosed track leading to Roger`s Farm. At the farm head north on the concrete track for 350 metres to a junction. Turn left to walk up a track for 50 metres, then right, passing South Lodge on the corner. Continue on a northerly course through South Park. Unfortunately the track is still enclosed but we have a view of Findon Place and Church on our left until walls and hedges confine us.

Eventually, at a T-junction go through a kissing gate and turn left into the lane up to Findon Church. We have rejoined Monarch`s Way. Pass the large house,

Findon Place, an 18th century building next to the church. After visiting Findon Church, continue northwest along Monarch`s Way on the edge of woodland. Chanctonbury Ring can be seen away to the right. On our left we are under the lee of Church Hill. After a gradual climb, a cricket field comes into view ahead. Avoid the path to the right and continue up to the top of the hill bearing left over the brow so that you come down to the A280, known as Longfurlong.

Cross A280 to a rough yard. Tolmare Farm is indicated. Go through the yard. The main track, Monarch`s Way leads down to the left. Ignore this and keep straight on along an elevated bridle way, heading northeast. Pass Tolmare Farm down on the left and a little tree topped hill on the right. There are extensive views over downland.

Ignore the first path to the right. Continue for another 350 metres to cross tracks. Avoid a farm road that leads to New Buildings down on the left. Turn right to the nearby entrance to Muntham Farm. Do not enter. Turn left to join a bridle way that runs parallel to that we have just left. Follow the edge of a copse on the right. In 450 metres go through the hedge on the right. Continue on course on a new path. At the next junction turn right towards nearby Highden Barn.

Do not go down to the barn but turn left onto the concrete drive. This drive leads eventually to Windlesham House School; it is not for us. Immediately after a copse turn right and eastwards. There is a field on our left and the copse on our right. In 150 metres, veer right to enter the copse. Continue eastward into and out of the copse again. Finally emerge to a field above the A24. Hug the copse on the left and then turn right down to another Windlesham House School driveway and then the road. The official route of the footpath is straight across the busy A24.

Instead of risking this road crossing, pedestrians have turned right to walk on the driveway towards the nearby bridge over the A24, taking care of the occasional vehicle on the slip roads on either side. They cross the bridge, keeping to the left and come down to a farm track on the other side. They turn left here away from the slip road and make for farm buildings that house small businesses. At the T-junction with the main track they rejoin the public footpath and turn right. Climb uphill on the track. It veers to the right and passes the same farm buildings down below. The track winds up to a junction. Keep straight on along our track, heading southeast.

In 500 metres the track goes downhill through trees and towards a Pest House. Before reaching the house and at a low point, go through a little gate on the right. Climb up through a field overlooking the house down on the left. Cross a tarmac road to the path opposite and keep on course to a cross track. Turn left into an enclosed track and head southeast for the next one kilometre. On the way, pass a farmhouse on the right and a bridleway on the right. Come out onto the Downs, go straight on at a junction of bridleways. At the nearby second junction, again go straight on but veer left and northeast on this quiet track.

We have now joined the short walk and follow the instructions above: * "Head northeast....", the second paragraph under the heading **'To Return to Sompting'**.

Walk 10: Steyning to Coombes

This walk from the lovely old town of Steyning takes you along the River Adur to St Mary's House, a medieval home for monks. Cross riverside fields and lanes to the rural idyll of Coombes then climb to open downland and descend into Steyning again.

Starting Point: The large car park opposite Steyning Parish Church **GR**179112
Maps: Explorer 122 also crossing onto Explorer 121, Landranger 198
Distance: 9 miles **Terrain:** flat then hilly
Local Information: You walk past St Mary's House just outside Steyning. If you wish to visit this beautiful 15th century thatched cottage, you will have to come in the afternoon on Thursday, Sunday or Bank Holiday Monday when it is open. Otherwise you can peer at it from the gate. (Phone 01903 816205)

Churches

St Andrew`s Church Steyning is according to Pevsner: "Late Norman, virile and inventive; certainly the best in Sussex and among the best in England" and very different now from the original Saxon building. In 8th century St Cuthman, the founder ended his journey here from Chidham Church (See Walk 5, *West Sussex Church Walks*). The vehicle carrying his mother broke down at Steyning and he built a small wooden church here. St Cuthman was buried in the church and his shrine drew many pilgrims. Prosperity came to Steyning with navigation of the nearby River Adur. Steyning harbour attracted the attention of Saxon kings and then the Normans. The Abbot of Fécamp established a College of Canons here even before the Conquest. In 1100 Norman monks replaced the wooden building with a large stone cruciform church dedicated to St Andrew. The present grand chancel arch would have been under the first tower. The chancel arches are the oldest part of the building today. Anglo-Saxon carvings are on the capitals of the chancel aisles. The nave was built 50 years later. It has solid pillars and Norman arches. Each arch and capital has individual carving: chevron, foliage, rosettes and dog tooth. The inner doorway is also Norman and has chevron carving. The 15th century door itself swings on its original hinges and still has a sanctuary ring. Any renegade who reached the church and held the ring was safe from his pursuers in medieval times. The font with a bowl of Purbeck marble is Norman. 13th century storms changed the shape of the Sussex coast. The River Arun silted up and Steyning lost its harbour. The Crown took over from Fécamp in 1461. Windows in the aisles were enlarged during this century but the east part of the church started to decay. In 1602 the crossing tower, transepts and chancel were demolished and a west tower was added. This tower is faced with Caen stone and knapped flint in a chequer board pattern. In 18th century the chancel was rebuilt in Gothic style. In 1863 the east window was inserted. St Cuthman is remembered in a window designed by Ann Goodman in 1983.

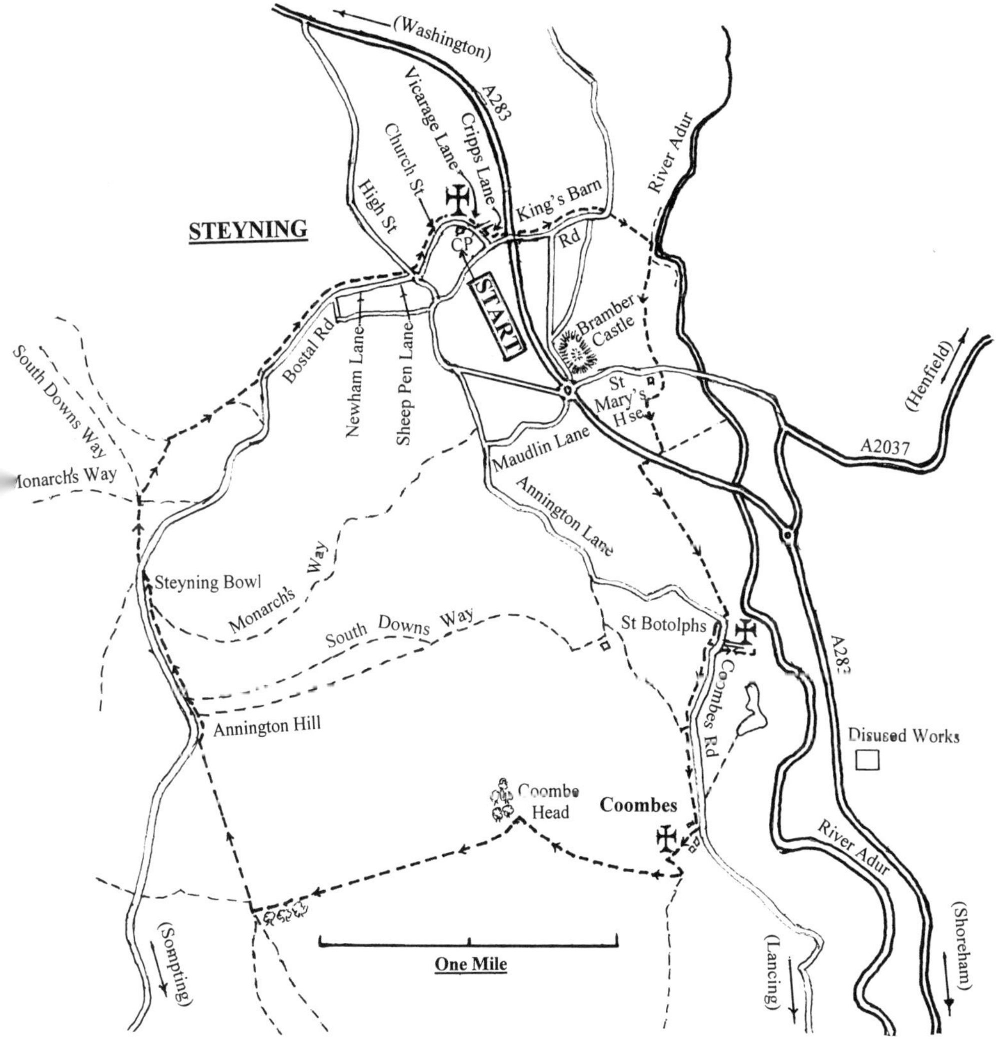
(Washington)
A283
Vicarage Lane
Cripps Lane
Church St
High St
King's Barn
Rd
STEYNING
CP
START
River Adur
Bramber
Castle
Bostal Rd
Newham Lane
Sheep Pen Lane
St
Mary's
H'se
(Henfield)
A2037
South Downs Way
Monarch's Way
Maudlin Lane
Annington Lane
Steyning Bowl
Monarch's Way
South Downs Way
St Botolphs
A283
Coombes Rd
Annington Hill
Disused Works
Coombe Head
Coombes
River Adur
One Mile
(Sompting)
(Lancing)
(Shoreham)

Coombes

The Parish Church, Coombes is part of the Downs where it has lain for almost 900 years. It was once the centre of the medieval village of Cumbe. Little remains of the village, but the villagers have left their messages on the walls of the church. There are 12th century pious paintings: scenes of the Nativity on the north and south walls and Christ in Majesty above the chancel arch. There is a humorous painting on the side of the chancel arch: a man grimacing as he bends under the weight of the masonry. Changes have been made to the church over the ages. The Saxon nave has been widened. Windows in the nave were altered in 14th century. The chancel was enlarged at the same time and the walls aligned with those of the nave to form a rectangular building. The south doorway and chancel arch (2ft 6ins thick) remain intact from the early Norman church. Between the two 15th century windows south in the chancel is an 11th century door. The porch and east window are 16th century. Horsham slabs are on the roof. The bellcote is 18th century.

The Walk

First, enter Steyning Church from Vicarage Lane. When you leave the church, turn left to walk along Vicarage Lane and turn right into Cripps Lane. Take the bridge over the Bypass and you are in the quiet residential King`s Barn Road. Go gently downhill on the pavement, passing individual houses and avoiding side roads. At the bottom, the road bends left and you take the footpath on the right leading down to the River Adur at a footbridge.

Do not cross the bridge. Stay on this side of the river and walk along a raised bank as far as the next field. Turn right away from the river on a well-defined path heading south for 500 metres. Bramber Castle is up on the right. When you see some white houses on the left you have reached The Street and cross to St Mary's House opposite.

Continue south on the footpath past the entrance to St Mary`s House. Pass a small estate of mobile homes and turn right at the corner. A field is on your left and mobile homes on your right. The path curves left into the field and onto the main road, A2037. Cross with care to the footpath opposite where you join the Downs Link, a fairly long distant cycle track. (Details of this track are at the end if this book).

Follow the Downs Link southeast for 500 metres. The river is away to your left and a hedge is beside you on the right. At a junction with the South Downs Way, turn right away from the river and through to Annington - Coombes Road.

Turn left, pass St Botolph's Church on the left (see Walk 20). In another half mile you reach the hamlet of Coombes and turn right up the short road through cottages and the farm to the Church.

From Coombes churchyard go through the gate on a path leading uphill through a copse to downland. As soon as you are up out of the trees, turn right, go through a farm gate and turn left. Follow the field boundary on the left. Climb steadily up towards the copse, Coombehead Wood, almost the only feature on these bare, open downs. Veer left here, still following the boundary on the left. Pylons rise up from Winding Bottom, below right. Ahead is another patch of woodland. Pass this on your left and you come up to cross tracks. You have now climbed for one and a half miles from Coombes Church.

Steyning

Turn right to follow the high, enclosed track northwest for half a mile. You reach the tarmac road that rides the Downs to Steyning ahead. The South Downs Way joins us from the right. Do not walk on the road. Keep straight on through a gate to follow this long distance footpath parallel to the road. In 500 metres Monarch`s Way another long distance path joins us from the right. Continue north for 100 metres then cross the road and continue up to cross ways. Over to the right colourful hang gliders float over dizzy heights when the wind permits. (Both ways are described at the end of this book).

Do not take the path to the right. You also say goodbye to the Monarch`s Way as it heads left and to the South Downs Way ahead. Instead, take the little path half right, signposted to Steyning. In 250 metres at a T-junction you have a wide view of Steyning and the countryside below. Turn right here on the bridleway down Steyning Round Hill. In 250 metres leave the bridleway as it curves to the right. You go straight down on a footpath that enters a fringe of woodland and emerges to Newham Lane at the edge of Steyning.

Newham Lane continues downhill through a housing estate until it reaches the old town and narrows to enter Sheep Pen Lane. Keep going in the same direction passing White Horse Inn on the left. Cross the High Street to the historical delights of Church Street. *For details of the succession of lovely ancient buildings here, read "Steyning An Historic Walk Around The Town" available locally.* They include Brotherhood Hall and Saxon Cottage.

At the end of Church Street, turn right at the library into Vicarage Lane where the Parish Church of St Andrew stands magnificently over the place below.

5 Walks
Near Horsham

Walk 11: Alfold to Rudgwick

We have slipped into Surrey to start this walk following part of the Sussex Border Path, much of it through bluebell woods. Views open to the North and South Downs.(Details of the long distance paths are at the end of this book).

Starting Point: Rosemary Lane, behind Alfold Church.
Map: OS Explorer 134 **GR**037341
Distance: 9 Miles **Terrain:** Mainly flat, may be muddy in places.
Local Information: Apart from the pub at Alfold and one at Rudgwick, you pass near the pub at Bucks Green on the return walk. Rudgwick also has a post office and shop.
Note: A compass may be useful in woodland. At the time of writing, restoration of ponds in the wood at Monkton Hook has churned up the ground but I was able to get through.

The Churches

Alfold Church, St Nicholas was a remote Wealden church consisting of just nave and chancel in Norman times. The village now stands just inside the Surrey border. Its name derives from the Saxon, "Aldfold" meaning "enclosure for animals". The large Norman font of 1080 has carvings on the side of arches over Maltese crosses. There is a staple for fastening the lid to prevent the theft of water for black magic in Medieval times. Additions to the church were made in 1200 with a south aisle and rounded pillars. This is intact but the north aisle of 1280 burnt down in 16th century. In 1842, on discovering the original arches under plaster, the rector Rev. R. Sparkes had this aisle rebuilt. He also had the north porch moved from beside the tower to its present place. Ancient oak pillars support the bell tower. A recent addition in 2000 of three bells means there are now 6 bells in the belfry. The roof timbers for this church date from 14th century, a tribute to the Wealden oaks. The chancel east window was formed in1321. In the chancel south wall is a Perpendicular window. There is a 15th century arch on the north side. The single slab of Sussex marble, found under the chancel floor by Rev. R. Sparkes, has been reinstated as the communion table. It lay hidden to protect it from Cromwell's men.

The Church of the Holy Trinity, Rudgwick stands at the northern upper end of the village. Here is a ridge at the border of Sussex. In fact the Saxon name, 'hrycg wic' means 'ridge farm'. In 1260 Alard the Fleming from the manor of Pulborough was granted permission to hold a fair at Rudgwick. A fair would bring affluence to the village. The handsome west tower was built at that time. The whole of the rest of the church is 14th century with huge wooden roof beams. The north aisle has a separate roof running parallel with the nave. There are many two light 14th century windows. Those of this aisle are remarkable for their finely carved heads.

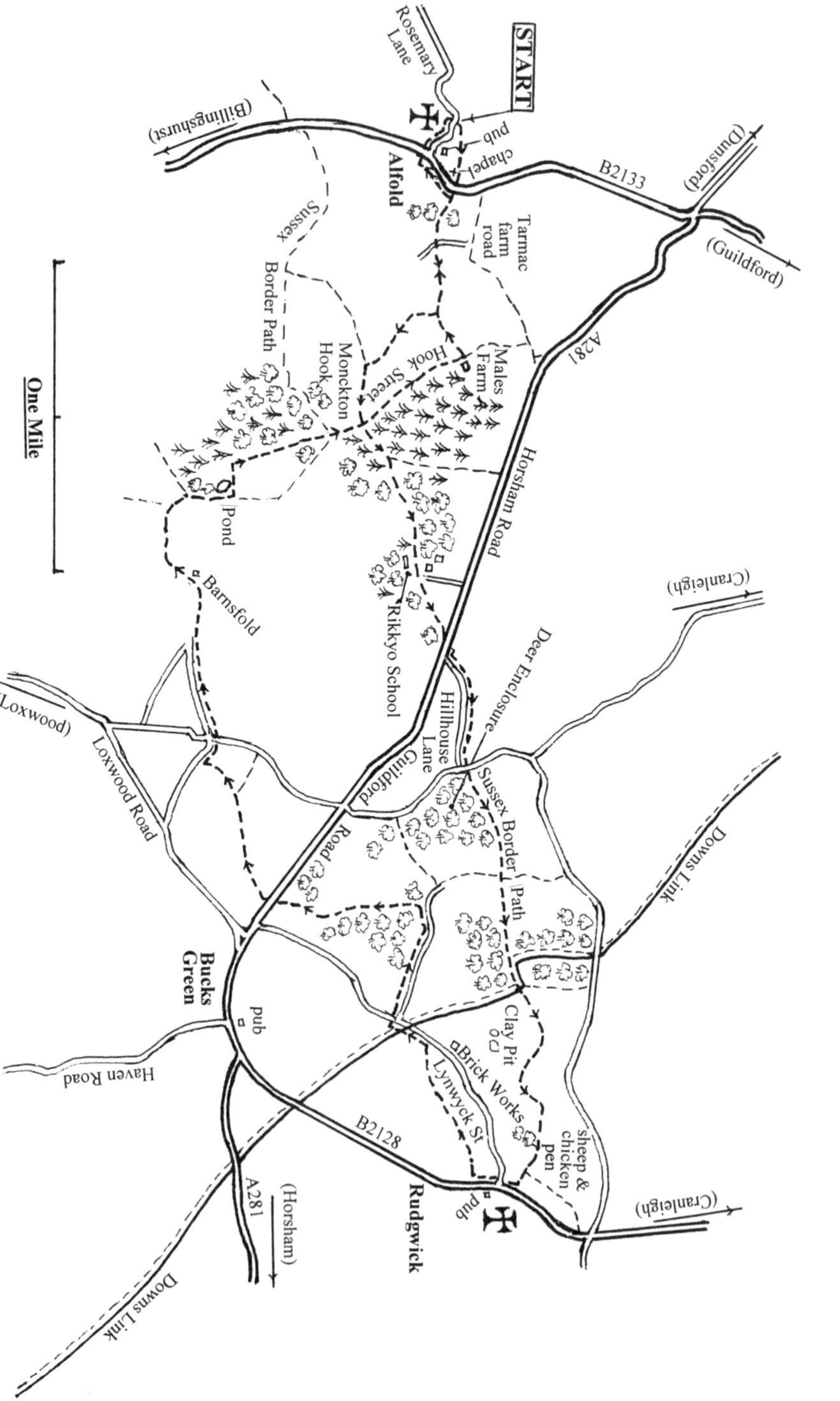
START
Rosemary Lane
pub
chapel
Alfold
(Billingshurst)
B2133
(Dunsford)
(Guildford)
Tarmac farm road
Sussex Border Path
A281
Males Farm
Hook Street
Monckton Hook
Horsham Road
Pond
One Mile
Barnsfold
Rikkyo School
(Cranleigh)
Deer Enclosure
Hillhouse Lane
(Loxwood)
Loxwood Road
Guildford Road
Sussex Border Path
Downs Link
Bucks Green
pub
Haven Road
Clay Pit
Brick Works
Lynwyck St
sheep & chicken pen
B2128
Rudgwick
pub
(Cranleigh)
(Horsham)
A281
Downs Link

The arcade has octagonal pillars and three arches with varied tracery. Similar mouldings are in the tower arch. The chancel has a piscina in the south wall and an aumbrey in the north wall. The square font of Sussex marble with round headed panels is late Norman, 12th century. Outside, the variety of stones make a beautiful, mellow building. Many stones probably came from an earlier church on this site.

The Walk

Take the footpath opposite Alfold Church car park. Fork right to walk along the narrow enclosed path behind the village. This leads to Alfold Chapel on the main road, B2133. Cross diagonally right to another enclosed footpath. This twists to the left behind a garden pond, passes through a copse then a small field. You come to a tempting tarmac road. It is not for us! Instead cross to the field ahead. Cross diagonally left passing a strip of trees on the right. Keep on course across the wider field. At the field boundary avoid the path straight on.

Turn right and follow the boundary on the left through three fields. After a sharpish bend, you come to a T-junction. Turn left here then immediately right, following arrows on the post. Cross this field diagonally right towards woodland. *(You may have to go round the edge of the field).* You reach woodland at **Monckton Hook** where I once heard nightingales.

Just inside the wood you are at crossways. Avoid the byway on the left, Hook Street but remember it for the return walk. Avoid the byway to the right, the westward going Sussex Border Path. Take the bridleway half left facing you. It has low posts. If you search the posts you should find a badge indicating "Sussex Border Path". Head northeast on this path through the wood.

In 250 metres cross a junction of forestry tracks to the rough path opposite into more woodland. This is still Sussex Border Path and keeps on course. It leads mainly on the edge of the wood. In 500 metres you reach Rikkyo School with many buildings and spacious grounds. When you reach the main driveway, keep straight on to follow the edge of a playing field on the left.

You come down to the Horsham to Guildford road, A281. Cross diagonally right to Hillhouse Lane. This "hill" is a mere bump on the generally flat land. At the end of the lane you come to Knowle Lane and cross to the footpath opposite. It is hemmed by high fences and passes through a deer enclosure in woodland. You come out thankfully to a delightful grassy slope with views over wealdland to the South Downs and to the north a glimpse of the North Downs. Continue northeast up to woodland, passing a telephone mast on the left.

250 metres into the wood, another long distance path, Downs Link joins us from the left. *Downs Link follows the course of the old railway line. Here it has come up from the tunnel, now a haven for bats.* In 100 metres Downs Link departs to the right. Avoid this right turn and also the track on the left. Instead continue northeast across a small field, still on the Sussex Border Path. Pass the edge of the wood on the right. Climb out to a view over a clay pit down on the right.

Alfold

Follow the path as it curves into further woodland, passing a chicken and sheep enclosure on the left. Go down into the wooded valley and climb up to the edge of Rudgwick. Once again, a narrow enclosed path on your left takes you to the village. You are on the ridge of 'Ridgick', as it once was called. Turn right for the church and pub.

To return from Rudgwick to Alfold cross the street B2128 to the pub car park.

Follow the footpath on the left of the car park. Go down an enclosed alley heading southwest. Continue on route through a copse then across fields. In half a mile you reach Lynwyck Street. There is a large brick works on the right, still in operation. Turn left and admire the brickwork in the local cottages. The road takes you over the bridge across the old railway line, converted to a long distance footpath. Once again we cross Downs Link.

Continue on the road for another 50 metres and turn right. There is a fork of paths here. Take the left fork and follow a firm hardcore track with some brick chippings in it. It crosses a concrete track and itself becomes concrete. In 450 metres the track turns right. You should leave the track here. Turn left and south into a field. Keep on course through woodland then walk on the edge of the wood, now on your left. In 450 metres the woodland drops away and you cross a field going down to the left where a short track takes you up to the A281. **Bucks Green can be seen to your left.**

Cross the A281 to the footpath opposite heading west across fields for half a mile. Midway you reach a finger post. At this point you change from left to right of the hedge. In 350 metres you veer left down to a tarmac lane and turn right.

Keep straight on at crossroads, following the no through road. It leads to a beautiful black and white cottage. Pass this on your left then in 300 metres pass the lone cottage, Barnsfold on the right Your track becomes a grassy lane and reaches woodland in 100 metres. Before you enter the wood, you will see a notice on the right forbidding you to walk in the field. Instead you take the muddy track at the edge of the wood with glimpses to the forbidden field on the right. Ignore two bridle ways to the left and take the footpath on the right to walk north with the field still beside you.

This path takes you past a pond on the left. There are ornamental trees here as in a park.

After the pond turn left past its northern banks. Ignore the path on the right. At a T-junction turn right onto a pleasant firm woodland track heading northwest. In 500 metres you join the Sussex Border Path and continue north for 200 metres until you reach the familiar cross tracks at **Monckton Hook**. Avoid the Sussex Border Path off to the right. You took this on your outward walk.

The path outside the wood on the left is the one that brought you here on the outward walk. This time we shall take the track that continues our route northwest, Hook Street. It follows the edge of the wood and in ½ mile comes to Males Farm where you turn left. Cross a field to a copse. Here on the left is the path we took earlier. We avoid it now and keep straight on, retracing our steps to Alfold. Turn left at the main road and walk through the little village to the church.

Walk 12: Nuthurst to Horsham

From a peaceful village take quiet paths through fields and woods to the edge of Horsham, guided by the church spire. Wander in the old town. Return via Denne Park, Pedlars Way and Sedgwick House, scene of Alice Liddell`s honeymoon.

Starting Point: Nuthurst Street, outside the church or near the pub. **GR**193262 or 3
For permission to park at the Black Horse, Nuthurst, phone 01403 891272
Map: OS Explorer 134 **Distance:** 9 Miles **Terrain:** Undulating, muddy in places.

The Churches

St Andrew`s, Nuthurst is the parish church for six hamlets. It stands on the site of an earlier building, probably Saxon. Outside, in the chancel north wall, there is an ancient window from this early church. Inside, in the baptistry, the font of Purbeck marble may be Saxon. In the 14th century a new church was built in Decorated style. This basic building can still be appreciated despite the many later changes. On entry the visitor notices a complete absence of pillars. In 1857 the nave was lengthened and a tall shingled spire was added to replace the short plain one. In 1907 the chancel gained a marble floor and oak wall panelling. In 1946-7 more restoration work was undertaken. In particular the three light Decorated east window has stained glass fitted in 1949 making a striking effect. St Andrew is depicted forcefully as missionary and sailor. The tracery above has pre-Reformation glass showing Christ in Majesty and angels bearing incense. Another interesting window by Thomas Denny (1994) is in the north wall of the nave. It is in remembrance of Alexander Moschini who died aged 16. The intricate, mainly blue design rewards careful study. The west window, added when the Victorians enlarged the church, catches the setting sun. It is a memorial to the two sons of John and Frances McCarogcher. The windows in the south wall of the chancel are also associated with the McCarogcher family. The most puzzling assortment of glass is in the 'Jigsaw Window'. The story that villagers made this assembly of glass at the 1660 Restoration is belied by the inclusion of some Victorian glass.

Nuthurst

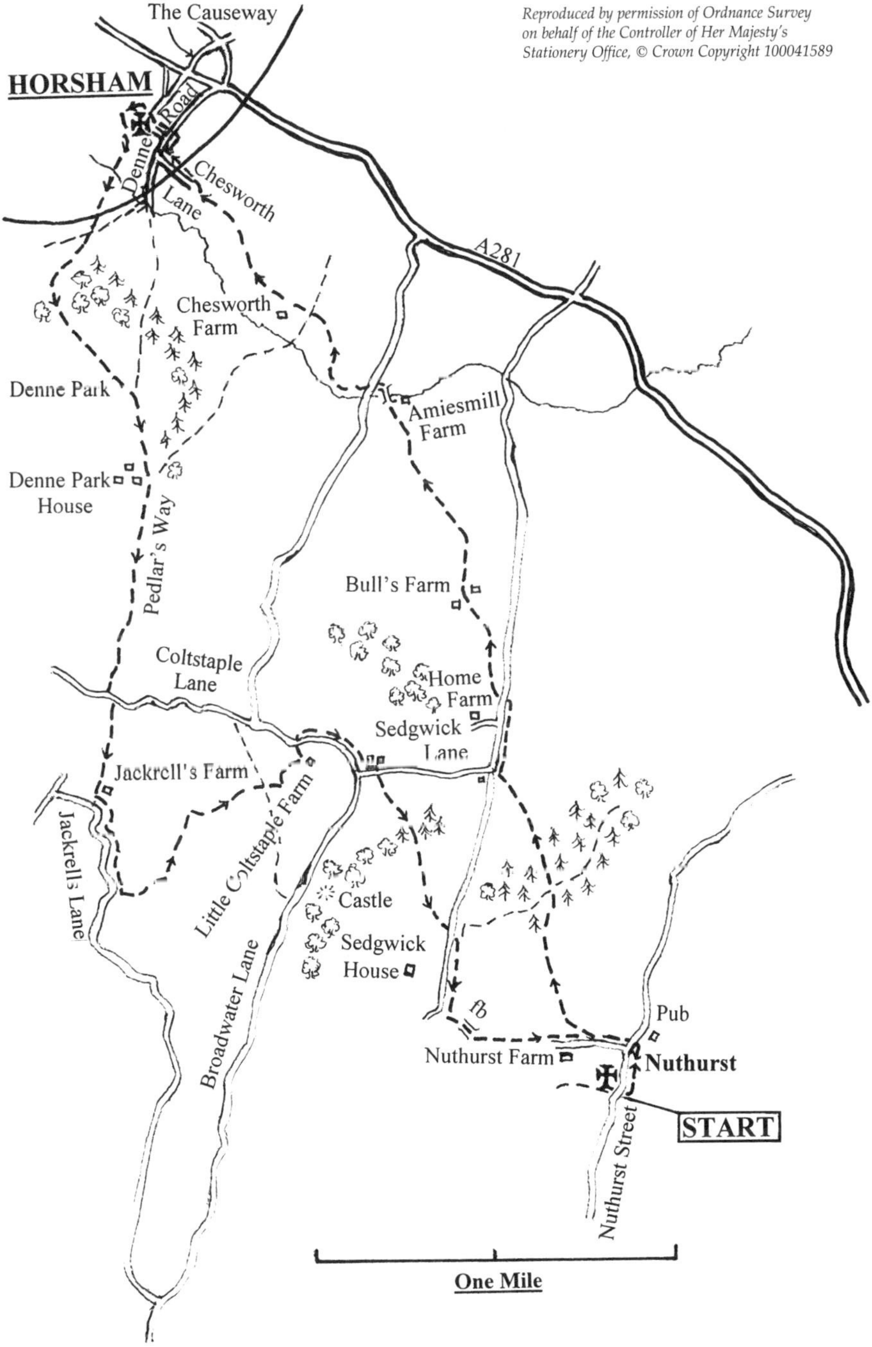

The Causeway
HORSHAM
Denne Road
Chesworth Lane
A281
Chesworth Farm
Denne Park
Amiesmill Farm
Denne Park House
Pedlar's Way
Bull's Farm
Coltstaple Lane
Home Farm
Sedgwick Lane
Jackrell's Farm
Jackrells Lane
Little Coltstaple Farm
Castle
Sedgwick House
Broadwater Lane
Pub
Nuthurst Farm
Nuthurst
START
Nuthurst Street
One Mile

Horsham Parish Church of St Mary the Virgin stands near the main medieval north –south road over the River Arun. This road and waterway would have been essential amenities when the church was built here in 1247. Evidence of an even earlier building has been found in the north west of the nave and the base of the tower. The yellow sandstone tower supports a spire covered in shingles. This tall slender broach spire has a twist to the southeast. Later work on the church includes raising the roof in 13th century, rebuilding the chancel arcades in 14th century, adding the porch in 14th and 15th centuries. At the same time the generous addition of chapels to the north, east and south sides has allowed private prayer and contemplation. Many windows were changed to Perpendicular style in 15th century. Through all these changes, the core is still medieval. The chancel and the nave are the same width. There is a continuity of bays: five in the nave and three in the chancel. The magnificent east window was installed in 1865. It is the work of the London firm of O`Connor, following the design of the window that was there in 15th century. West windows of both the south aisle and the north aisle have rich colours in the glass by Heaton and Co. The Victorian architect, S.S. Teulon presented a fine rose window to the Holy Trinity chapel. There is much more of interest in this fine church that manages grandeur, comfort and warmth.

Horsham

The Walk

Walk north along Nuthurst Street to the nearby pub and turn left. Take the footpath opposite the pub. It follows a track between houses then fields. In 100 metres, just past the large house 'Fox Hollow', turn right and leave the track to cross an open field. Go uphill diagonally left then follow the field boundary on the left, passing through several farm gates. Climb steadily for 400 metres up to woodland. Swing to the right here then continue uphill hugging the strip of wood on the left.

Enter the wood, climb up to cross a woodland track and reach a driveway at the top. There is a white house, obscured by trees on the right. After crossing the driveway, avoid the path straight on. Instead take the signposted footpath half right. It leads out of the wood to a small field. It becomes an enclosed path through a little wood and out again. You can now see North Lodge through the hedge. *A plaque informs us that a Castle was built in Sedgwick Park soon after 1066 and was used as a hunting lodge. Dukes of Norfolk let it fall into disrepair at the end of 16th century and it is now a ruin.* You reach Sedgwick Lane at a corner with the private entrance to the park and the lodge on the left.

Turn right along the lane. In 200 metres just past the drive to Home Farm, take the path on the left across open fields continuing our northerly course. At Bull`s Farm pass a tennis court and twist left then right between buildings to emerge to more fields. Here we have our first view of Horsham in the distance ahead. Veer left to go through a small gate and turn right on the concrete farm track.

Keep on course to a field corner, bear left and follow the hedge on the right. In the next field our path runs parallel to a grassy track on the right with a hedge separating us from it. Horsham Church spire comes into view to act as a guide. The hedge soon has gaps and we turn right to join the grass track. Follow the field boundary, now on our left. Amiesmill Farm is ahead on the right. *A water mill, first mentioned in 1410 was closed in 1928.*Turn left through the hedge yet again. Veer left over a small field and cross a bridge over the little River Arun.

At the farm road turn left to the nearby Kerves Lane. As you cross Kerves Lane to the footpath opposite you can see Amiesmill Bridge on the left. Head west across water meadows above the tiny River Arun on the left and a hedge on the right Avoid the first gate on the right with a nearby seat. In 200 metres, when you are level with a footbridge over the river down on the left, go through a kissing gate on the right. Cross a flat field diagonally left to a tree lined track.

You join the track at a corner. Avoid turning right. Walk along the track in a northwest direction. At Chesworth Farm you reach a junction of tracks. Turn right so that you pass the farm on your left. You can now see two church spires in Horsham. That on the right shows where St Mark`s Church once stood. There is a bench on the right just past the farm. In 350 metres the track becomes Chesworth Lane.

You are on the edge of Horsham. Keep straight on, passing suburban houses and avoiding side roads. You go under the main line railway and come to a T-junction with Denne Road. Turn right towards the school then left to St Mary`s Church.

If you wish to see the old town, turn right to stroll along the Causeway and back.

From St Mary`s Horsham, walk past the west entrance below the tower. Pass on the left the modern hall that clings incongruously to the church. You are heading southwest along Barrackfield Walk. Pass through small gardens with ponds. Cross the river again. Pass cricket fields on the right. Cross the footbridge over the railway line and you reach crosspaths. Keep straight on, slightly right towards the wooded slope. Veer further to the right to skirt the woodland on your left. Climb up through the wood to the plateau at the top. This is Denne Park with scattered trees. In the distance you will see a cluster of assorted buildings, including Denne House, now residential.

Cross the plateau in a southeasterly direction so that you pass these buildings on your right. As you approach the last house, veer left towards further woodland. Enter the wood and walk down to the cycle track, Pedlar`s Way below. You find your footpath curves south to join the way. Follow Pedlars Way due south for 1 mile, first over land that has every appearance of being a common, then along a wide track between hedges.

Cross Coltstaple Road to the footpath diagonally left opposite and continue south through woodland and a field to Jackrells Farm. In the farmyard veer right to join Jackrells Lane. Here you turn left to pass the pretty farm cottage and walk along Jackrells Lane. Pass a sign 'NEWFOUNDOUT'. In 300 metres at a bend in the lane and just before a mast, turn left into a field entrance. In 75 metres you reach wide open fields.

Hug the hedge on the left as the path curves northeast. Follow the same direction in the next field to the end where you turn right then left. Pass a pond well hidden down on the left and a shack on the right. Continue northeast by the edge of two more small fields. Enter a farm track at a junction of paths turn right then immediately left to cross to Little Coltstaple Farm, a half beamed building. Pass this on your right then veer left to Coltstaple Lane. *'Coltstapole' is mentioned in early 15th century.*

Turn right at Coltstaple Lane. Pass a sign 'SEDGWICK'. Follow the lane to a road junction. Turn left below elevated houses into Sedgwick Lane and turn straightway right into a fine mowed footpath. This leads southeast to woodland. You soon leave the wood to enter a wide plain. Away to the right hidden by more woodland is the site of Sedgwick Castle. Cross the plain in a southeast direction and through shrubs to the garden of Sedgwick House. *This was the home of Emma Henderson who created famous gardens here. She was sister-in-law to Alice Liddell who as a child was the inspiration for, even supplying some of the material for 'Alice in Wonderland'. Emma lent her house for Alice`s honeymoon.in 1880.*

"I think Sedgwick will be a long time before it shelters two more foolishly happy creatures than Reginald and me" – A. Liddell.

Pass in front of Sedgwick House and you come to the driveway. Turn right here and head south. The elevated route gives glimpses across sloping farmland to the Downs. At the first opportunity turn left down the wooded slope, across a new footbridge and back to the original farm track. Pass farm buildings on the right then the footpath on the left that you took at the start of the walk. Finally, after Fox Hollow you reach Nuthurst with the pub opposite. Turn right for the church.

Sedgwick

Walk 13: West Grinstead to Cowfold

Enjoy distant views across meadows and woodland ways. From the ancient secluded church at West Grinstead you take lonely paths to the bustling village of Cowfold.

Starting Point: The grass verge opposite the Catholic Church at the south end of Park Lane, West Grinstead **GR**177212
Map: OS Explorer 134 **Distance:** 9 Miles **Terrain:** Flat
The aim is to keep St George`s Church open. For enquiries, phone 01403 710339

The Churches

West Grinstead, St George is an ancient, assured giant, 'like an old Sussex farmer in a tweed coat' according to Simon Jenkins *(England`s Thousand Best Churches).* The church grew in wood and stone through the centuries. Now this growth has stopped. Time stood still in mid 20th century and earlier ages prevailed. Medieval fairs and markets were held in the churchyard. There is a lovely 15th century porch that Simon Jenkins likens to 'a country cottage in miniature'. Go through the porch to the nave and a massive arcade of pillars. There are traces of a medieval mural of St Christopher on the north wall, east of the entrance. The front pews still bear the names of local 19th century farmers. They were reserved for the men. Many of their farms are here still. In the north wall of the nave there is some ancient herringbone masonry. Two small round headed windows are Norman. In the south aisle tall Early English arches point up to the tower. It has a quaint, shingled broach spire. There is no chancel arch. The 13th century east window has 19th century glass by Kempe. Despite its rustic appearance, the church has some handsome monuments and brasses. St. Mary`s Chapel, next to the chancel has several memorials. The most striking is a life size 18th century monument by John Michael Rysbrack. It represents in white marble William and Elizabeth Powlett in stately Roman dress.

West Grinstead

The Catholic Shrine Of Our Lady Of Consolation And St. Francis, West Grinstead has a Victorian Gothic Church. The reason such a grand church stands in this remote spot is historical. The great landowning family, the Carylls was Catholic. In Elizabethan times they lived at Benton`s Place, Shipley and owned

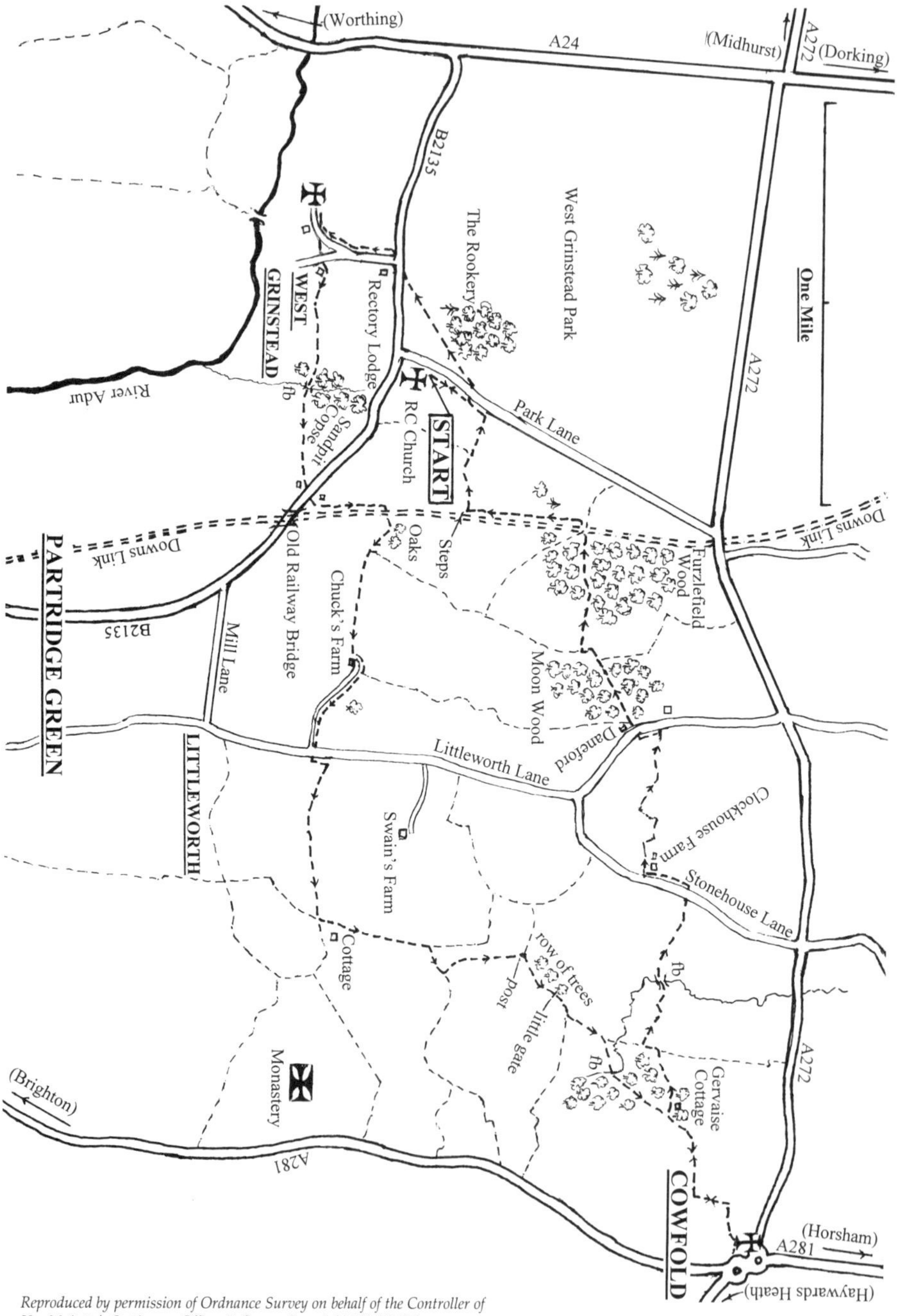
(Worthing)
A24
(Midhurst)
A272
(Dorking)
One Mile
B2135
West Grinstead Park
The Rookery
Rectory Lodge
WEST GRINSTEAD
River Adur
fb
Sandpit Copse
RC Church
START
Park Lane
Downs Link
PARTRIDGE GREEN
Old Railway Bridge
Oaks
Steps
Chuck's Farm
Mill Lane
B2135
Furzlefield Wood
Moon Wood
Daneford
LITTLEWORTH
Littleworth Lane
Swain's Farm
Clockhouse Farm
Stonehouse Lane
Cottage
row of trees
post
little gate
fb
Monastery
Gervaise Cottage
A272
(Brighton)
A281
COWFOLD
(Horsham)
A281
(Haywards Heath)

many estates in Sussex. When Catholics were persecuted in 16th and 17th centuries, the Carylls chose West Grinstead for the site of a secret Priest`s House. Mass was held in the loft and there were hiding holes for two priests in the chimney breast. Even after the Carylls had to sell their estates in 18th century, the chaplaincy at West Grinstead continued. Later, Fr. Jean-Marie Denis established a school here in 19th century and raised the money to build the church east of the Priest`s House. Inside the church the nave pillars have heraldic shields of benefactors on the spandrels. Above the High Altar the stained glass windows show saints including St George, patron saint of the Parish Church and St Bruno of the Carthusian Monastery at Cowfold. Outside, near the tower door lies the grave and memorial to Hilaire Belloc, the Sussex poet.

Cowfold Church, St Peter stands in a quiet spot near busy crossroads. Pretty cottages face away from the road to look towards the church. This is a typical wealden building with strong walls and solid tower. Lancet windows in keeping with the age of the church are Early English. One of the chancel lancets has some ancient stained glass showing the crucifixion. The four-bay south arcade was built during the reign of Henry V111. In the nave floor there is a 10 feet long brass to Thomas Neland, Prior of Lewes.

Saint Hugh`s Charterhouse, built in 1873 is the largest Carthusian monastery in Europe with 35 hermitages linked by a mile long cloister. The spire approaches 200 feet high.

Note: We view the monastery from the footpath.

The Walk

From the Catholic Church walk up Park Lane heading north for 300 metres. There is a fingerpost on the right indicating a path on the left. Turn left. The path heads southwest to the edge of a copse, 'The Rookery'. At a corner of the copse where there are pine trees, veer left down towards the road B2135. In winter you can see a little white house, 'Rectory Lodge' below. It stands at the head of the lane to West Grinstead Parish Church.

Continue south along this lane to a tiny cluster of fine old houses. Veer right for the church. Pass Glebe House on the left and enter a bygone age. Linger at the church porch to survey the rambling churchyard before delving into this fascinating building.

From West Grinstead Parish Church retrace your steps. Just past the Glebe, there is a small stile on your right. Turn right to make your way leftwards across a

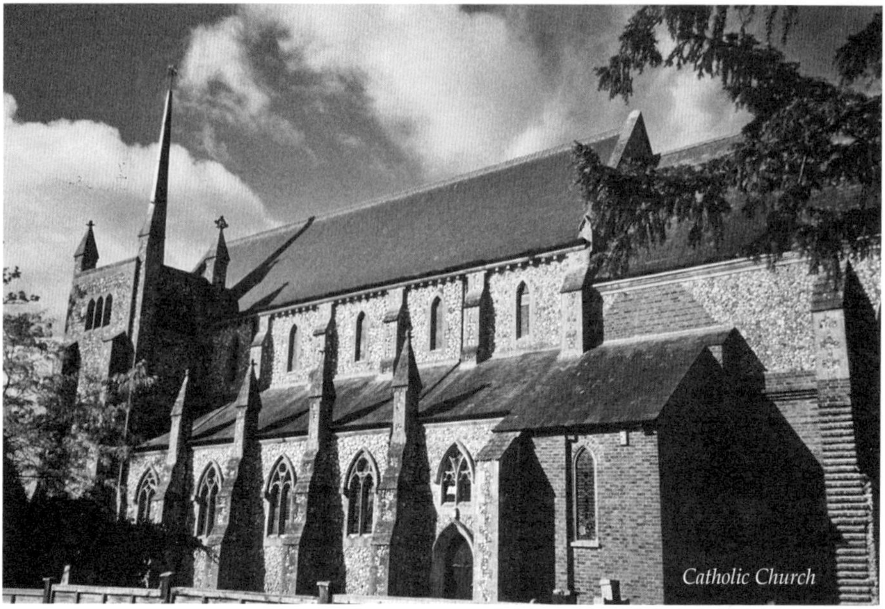

paddock. You emerge onto a driveway and take the footpath opposite. You are on an easterly course crossing a wide field towards woodland, Sandpit Copse. Go into the wood, cross a stream and scramble up a narrow path to further open fields.

Keep at a distance from the field boundary on your right and head for a renovated barn far ahead. The path brings you out near the barn and onto the B2135. Turn right, pass the barn on your right and make for the old railway bridge that spans the road here. Before the bridge, cross to a tarmac track on the left. It leads up past a house on the left to **Downs Link** on the right. At **Downs Link** turn left. *This long distance footpath and cycle way along the old railway line is described at the end of this book.*

We do not spend long on this cycle way. In 150 metres at cross paths, turn right to open fields. In 50 metres at an oak tree the path twists to the right, passes another oak and crosses a concrete track. Keep on course in the next field and up through a thick hedge.

Continue east for nearly ½ mile across the wide, open field making for Chuck`s Farm, in sight ahead. *According to O.S. map, the path goes through the farmyard then along the farm access road.* An effort has been made to divert the path to the left then turning right behind the farm to run parallel to the access road, a bumpy walk overshadowed by the hedge on your right. Both path and access road lead to Littleworth Lane.

Turn left to walk for 75 metres along the lane. Turn right into a spacious field with a long vista to the high tower and tall spire of St Hugh`s Carthusian Monastery (1873). Head straight towards the monastery. A large flock of lapwings was flapping here in the winter.

In nearly ½ mile, just before a cottage, turn left at cross paths and head north, away from the monastery. Pass the cottage on your right and cross two fields. At the second boundary you have to transfer to the footpath on the right so that you continue north on the other side of the fence. At a corner on the left with a many-armed post, turn right and walk past a row of spaced trees in the field on the left. Do not go too far! In 75 metres there is a little gate on the left into an enclosed bridle way, heading northeast to Cowfold.

You emerge to an open field, keep on course and avoid the bridle way on the right. The next field has many streams. The path forks here. Take the right fork, cross a stream, go up a bank to see Gervaise Cottage ahead Follow the hedge on the right to the corner with Gervaise Cottage. ***Note:*** *there is a path on the left for the return walk.* Turn right into an enclosed path passing the cottage on the left. This bending path leads to Cowfold Church.

From Cowfold Church retrace your steps to Gervaise Cottage and turn right on the noted path taking a mainly westerly direction for 1 kilometre to Stonehouse Lane. First, our path passes the garden of Gervaise Cottage on the right and goes through recent earth works and over a footbridge. Cross the next field diagonally left to another footbridge. Now follow the hedge on the right for two fields to Stonehouse Lane. Turn left to walk along the lane for 150 metres.

Turn right into a driveway serving several cottages, including Clockhouse Farm. Take the footpath on the left into a small field. Pass farm buildings on the right. Go through to the next field and follow the hedge on the left. At the third field you follow the hedge on the right and emerge at Littleworth Lane. *A short diversion to the right finds Camelia Botnar Homes and Gardens. Apart from garden plants and award winning craftwork, there is an excellent cafeteria! Breakfasts, real coffee, lunches and teas are served here.*

If you are not tempted to Camelia Botnar, turn left to walk along the lane for 150 metres. Turn right into a track in woodland. You are heading southwest through Moon Wood. You emerge at a sheltered space in the Weald. And cross to Furzlefield Wood opposite. The path is well-defined, heading west and downhill. Do not be tempted onto cross paths. At the bottom, cross a footbridge over a stream and climb up to **Downs Link.**

Turn left and head south on this old railway line for 500 metres to the first crosspaths. Here there are steps down to the field on the right. Take these steps and head west along the edge of a flat field. At cross paths go over a stream and continue on course back to Park Lane. Turn left for the Catholic Church, 400 metres away.

Walk 14: Slaugham, Warninglid, Bolney
with an extension to Twineham

A profusion of spring flowers adorn this walk in April. Wood anemones, primroses, wild daffodils and bluebells thrive in these small woods, fields and hills of the High Weald. Bring a compass to help find the way!

Starting Point: The triangle in front of Slaugham (pronounced 'Slaffam') Church
Map: OS Explorer 134 **GR**257282 **Terrain:** Gentle slopes
Distance: 10 Miles + optional 6 Miles to Twineham. See below for Twineham
Local Information: Slaugham, Warninglid and Bolney each has a pub. Bolney has two!
The River Ouse is believed to rise just west of Slaugham. The large Millpond served the iron industry in 16th century Slaugham.
The ruins of an Elizabethan house, Slaugham Place can be seen at the end of this walk.

The Churches

Slaugham Parish Church, St Mary`s dates back to Norman times when William de Warenne held the rape of Lewes. He and his wife encouraged the building of churches and are probably responsible for Slaugham. This large church still stands on and overlaps its Norman base. The north wall and its round headed blocked

Slaugham

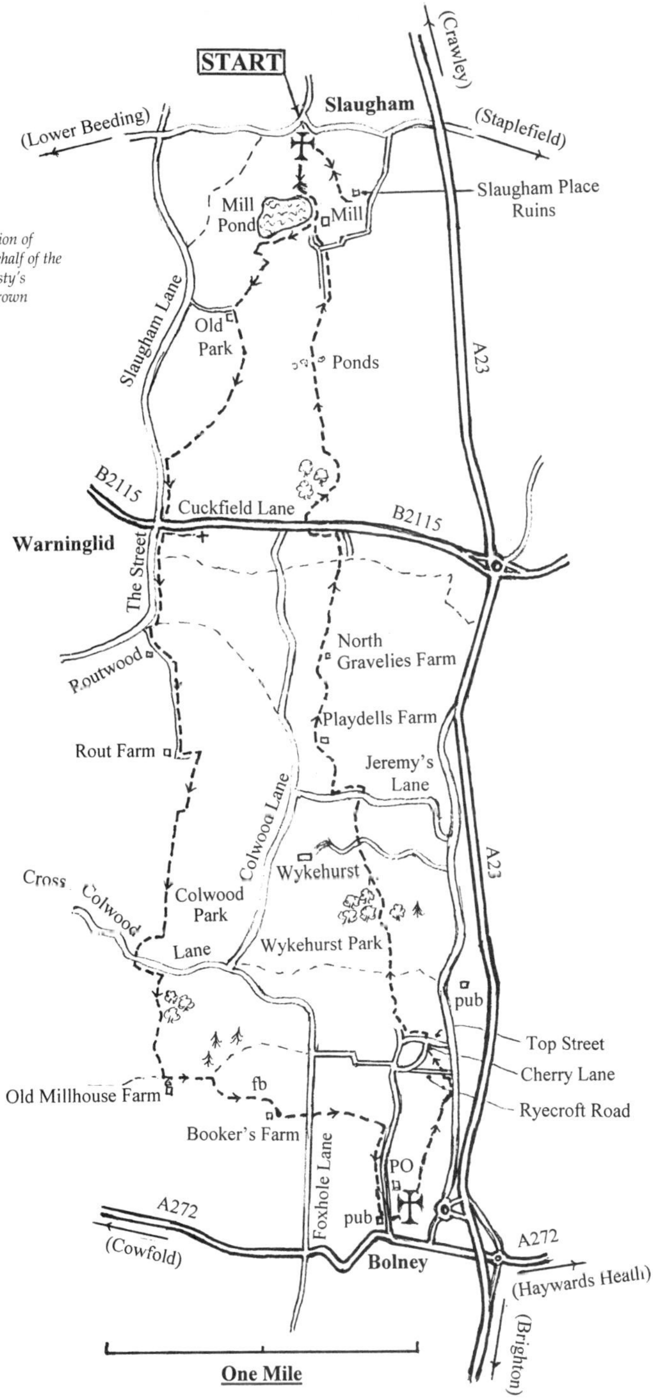
START
Slaugham
(Crawley)
(Lower Beeding)
(Staplefield)
Slaugham Place Ruins
Mill Pond
Mill
Slaugham Lane
Old Park
Ponds
A23
B2115
Cuckfield Lane
B2115
Warninglid
The Street
North Gravelies Farm
Routwood
Playdells Farm
Rout Farm
Jeremy's Lane
Colwood Lane
Wykehurst
A23
Cross Colwood Lane
Colwood Park
Wykehurst Park
pub
Top Street
Cherry Lane
Old Millhouse Farm
fb
Ryecroft Road
Booker's Farm
Foxhole Lane
PO
A272
pub
A272
(Cowfold)
Bolney
(Haywards Heath)
(Brighton)
One Mile

doorway are Norman. The square font of Sussex marble is late Norman and has an unusual carving of a fish on one side. The tower is late 13th century. The chancel east window is 14th century. The Covert Chapel was built on the south side of the chancel in 1613. In 1858 the Victorians removed the west wall and enlarged the aisle, making the church big. In the south wall of the Covert Chapel there is a monument of Richard Covert (died 1579), followed by a line of 17 kneeling figures. All are beautifully carved. The stained glass, late Victorian is in good condition. The lych-gate was built in 1903. There are no intrusive telephone wires; in 1937, Colonel Warren, Lord of the Manor paid to have them laid underground.

Warninglid, St Andrew was built of brick in 1935.

The Parish Church of St Mary Magdalen, Bolney also dates back to Norman times. The south doorway inside the porch and a little window high in the east wall of the chancel are Norman. The other chancel windows, also the recently restored piscina in the south wall are 13th century. John Bolney is responsible for the tower, built 1536-8. The tower clock of 1897 marks the Diamond Jubilee of Queen Victoria. The north aisle was added in 1853. In 1905 Edward Huth of Wykehurst presented the magnificent lych-gate to the church. There is a fine ring of eight bells with dates ranging from 1592 to 1740.

The Church of St Peter, Twineham is unlike any other. It may be the earliest brick church in Sussex. Built in 1516, it had the benefit of the recent arrival of Flemish brick builders. The roof has Horsham tiles and the broach spire has sweet chestnut shingles. The church is early Tudor with typical depressed arches. Fortunately the Victorian restoration did not spoil it. Existing material was used to rebuild the porch. The east window has the soft colours of Kempe. He depicts the Virgin Mary with a wreath of Christmas roses on her brow. Another window in the chancel is low down, possibly to allow for confessions or for lepers to participate in the service without entering the church. The reredos panels may be 13th century. The font is also 13th century. A church is mentioned here in 1291. The name, 'Betwyneham' means 'between two rivers'. In fact the hamlet lies between two arms of the River Adur. As in West Grinstead Church (Walk 12) some of the pews carry the names of local residents. The Squire`s pew has fine Elizabethan carving. The pulpit is Jacobean. As you enter the churchyard, you see on the left a square of land with no tombstones. It is the burial ground for about 60 Quakers. They were safely buried here, away from 17th century persecution.

The Walk

Pass to the south side of Slaugham Church and keep straight on, avoiding the path to the left (the fingerpost is in the churchyard). Leave the churchyard by the well-worn path, passing a large wooden hut on your right. Go through a small copse to the Mill Pond, a sizeable lake. Pass the old water mill on your left. The main building is in a hollow and the renovated mansard roof is at our level. Avoid the lane on the left and walk around the edge of the Millpond on your right. Keep on the narrow path by the lake until you can go no further and have to turn left. Follow the edge of the field then turn sharp right.

Old Park Farm is ahead and you go between two large barns to an enclosed path behind gardens. The path opens to fields with a stream down on the left. Veer slightly to the right and head southwest uphill across a wide field. Remember to look behind for the view!

You come to Slaugham Lane and turn left. The pavement on the left peters out. Take care as you walk up to crossroads at Warninglid. A short detour to the left takes you to the church. Otherwise keep straight on, passing the corner pub on the left.

Walk down the Street, Warninglid, passing old cottages and the ponds at the entrance to Lydhurst on the right. Ignore the first footpath to the left. After a steep descent, you come to a bend with a drive entrance on the left. There are two footpaths here on either side of Rifleman`s Cottage. Take the bridleway south on the High Weald Circular Walk along the private drive leading to Routwood, a handsome country house.

Here the bridleway swerves left through a copse then continues its southerly course up the track to Rout Farm. Again the path slips away to the left before resuming its way south. Keep to the field edge on the right as you walk down two fields. You then walk above a steep hollow with a large pond at the bottom. Track marks on the far side suggest that vehicles use this humpy terrain for switchback rides.

The path joins an enclosed track down to houses at Colwood Park. Here it bends right then left on a tarmac drive, coming down to Cross Colwood Lane. Turn left to walk along the lane for 150 metres.

Turn right and go down into woodland with masses of wood anemones in spring. Take a tree-lined track down to cross paths with a delightful old millhouse on the left. Turn sharp left, swinging slightly back on yourself and pass the house on the right. Keep straight on to cross a footbridge over a stream and and enter woodland. You come to a fork of ways. Turn right then curve to the left to leave the wood and enter a vineyard.

You are heading east, the field boundary on the right and vines on the left. Turn right to pass a barn and farm buildings. At a T-junction turn left on the access road of Bookers Farm. Pass the vineyard reception on the left then reach Foxhole Lane.

**An extension of this walk from Foxhole Lane to Twineham is described below for later.*

For today, cross to the footpath opposite. The narrow path leads to Bolney Street.

Turn right and walk on the pavement down past the houses of Bolney. You can see the imposing church ahead. Pass the shop and post office on the left. The village pub is on the right. ** *(The extension rejoins here).* The church is opposite the pub. Climb steps up to and through the impressive lych-gate. Note that a footpath crosses to the left through the churchyard. Before taking this path, veer right to enter the church via the south porch.

After visiting Bolney Church return behind the tower to follow the churchyard path. It leads to a track past the village school on the left and sports field on the right. The path follows the field boundary on the left where nature reserves can be spied through the hedge. Noise from the A23 is a constant companion on the right. You come up to the old road on the right and may wish to follow it to the pub ahead.

Bolney

Otherwise, turn left along Ryecroft Road then almost immediately right onto a footpath across a village field to Cherry Lane. Turn right up to Top Street. Turn left to walk along Top Street to the end. Take a track on the right here. It leads through scattered houses on the edge of Bolney.

Continue north along a footpath past a farm on the left. The path becomes a sunken way and goes under a stone bridge in Wykehurst Park. Pass staggered crosspaths and climb up to a pylon. Veer left here on the muddy path north down through woodland where wood anemones, primroses and bluebells grow. The large 19th century 'chateau', Wykehurst built by E. M. Barry can be seen on the left.

About 100 metres after the pylon, the path forks. Take the left fork to leave the wood for a sheltered glen. Climb up to and through a coppice. Pass a pond on the left and a corrugated shed. Cross the driveway to Wykehurst. In the next field, climb up to houses on Jeremy`s Lane. Turn left.

You walk along this elevated leafy lane and pass occasional affluent houses. In 150 metres turn right into a narrow path north skirting above a 'cottage' garden on the right. Cross small fields towards Playdells Farm. A water tower can be seen over to the left.

Cross a tarmac farm track. The farm is on your right. Keep heading north through bushes to a large field. Follow the field boundary on the right to a gated corner. Go through to a tree plantation to find a choice of ways. Fork left keeping the plantation on your right. This path leads down to the large garden of a sumptuous cottage, North Gravelies Farm. Follow the waymarkers through the garden. You pass close to the cottage on your right and continue north.

Keep on route across a small meadow and up to an opening in woodland ahead. Go through the laurel in a small wood. Cross a field to a farm gate. The ground in front of this gate is a morass of churned-up mud. Once you have wallowed past the gate you are at crosspaths. Keep straight on along an enclosed track past horse paddocks and stables to Cuckfield Lane, B2115.

Turn left and walk with care along this busy road. Just before a sign, 'Warninglid' turn right and escape to a footpath on the right. This leads down to a little bluebell wood. Follow the path through the wood and emerge to a sloping field with an extensive view to the ridge ahead. Keep close to woodland on the right until you come to a fingerpost. Veer left here towards a lone house. You reach three ponds. Take the path between the two lower ponds then continue on route north towards an enclosed track.

Go up through an avenue of oaks leading to the lane to Slaugham Mill and the familiar Mill Pond. Retrace your steps to Slaugham Church.

If you still have the energy, you may care to take the path you avoided at the start of this walk. It is now on your right in the churchyard. It leads to Slaugham Place, the Elizabethan house built by Sir Walter Covert, son of Sir Richard whose monument is in the church.

Foxhole Lane, Bolney to Twineham *(separate map on Page 70)*
The outward walk to Twineham is marred by a succession of overhead power cables. The terrain is peaceful meadowland with some lanes. Escape the pylons on the return walk.
Starting Point: Foxhole Lane (marked * above). There is an unofficial lay-by near A272
Map: OS Landranger 198
GR257226 **Terrain:** Flat. Some quiet road walking. **Distance:** 6 Miles

The Walk: From Foxhole Lane cross the A272 to Bolney Chapel Lane opposite. Walk along this lane for 250 metres, passing houses on the left. At Garston`s Farm on the left a footpath crosses the road. Turn right heading west into a pleasant field. At the next field fork left towards Brooklands Farm.

At this ancient building, go across the farm track to enter more fields. Veer diagonally right to go under power lines. Keep on course towards a hedge with woodland nearby. You are at cross paths on the other side of the hedge. Turn left and hug the hedge on your left. Then veer right towards Coombe House. You enter a corner of this property where 'private' notices enable you to find the footpath by a process of elimination.

When you emerge from this corner, avoid the alluring track southeast. Instead, follow the direction of the finger post southwest towards the wooded edge of the field. Follow this edge for ½ mile, passing under two sets of power lines and over a farm track. You come to Bob Lane. Twineham Court Farm is sign posted opposite.

Turn left and walk along this quiet lane with scattered cottages. At a bend after a cottage, turn right into a footpath. Walk behind the cottage and fork left. There is a wide, grassy swathe, bordered by trees and hedges and on the right the inevitable power lines. Follow this sinuous path south, crossing plank footbridges

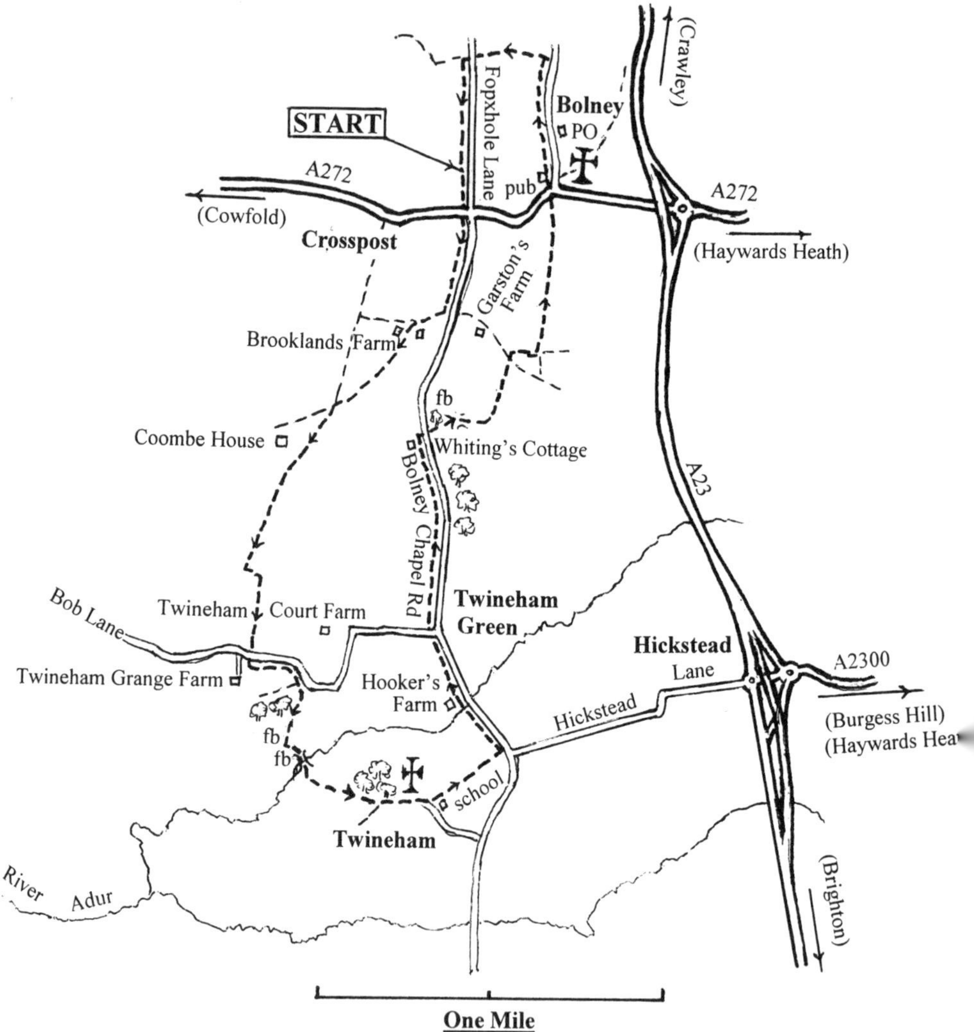
START
Fopxhole Lane
Bolney
PO
pub
A272
(Cowfold)
Crosspost
A272
(Haywards Heath)
(Crawley)
Garston's Farm
Brooklands Farm
fb
Coombe House
Whiting's Cottage
Bolney Chapel Rd
A23
Twineham Green
Bob Lane
Twineham Court Farm
Twineham Grange Farm
Hooker's Farm
Hickstead
Lane
Hickstead
A2300
(Burgess Hill)
(Haywards Hea
fb
fb
school
Twineham
River Adur
(Brighton)
One Mile

over streams and ditches. In 250 metres you reach a proper footbridge over a branch of the Adur.

Once you have crossed this little river, follow the hedge on the left for 100 metres then turn left to leave the pylons at last. Rejoice in wide fields free of power lines! Large birds of prey inhabit the trees on the left. Twineham Church is hidden behind trees ahead. At a field corner, you join a track through the hedge to the church. You can imagine yourself back 500 years to the troubled times of Henry V111, for here is a perfect Tudor church.

Twineham

From Twineham Church make for the nearby village school and take the footpath on the left heading northeast on a slightly raised causeway. At the tarmac road turn left and head north for one mile, passing a few houses then Bob Lane on the left. After a small wood on the right and the strikingly lovely Whiting`s Cottage on the left, take a footpath on the right into a field. Hug the copse at the edge of the field on the left. At the field corner turn left into the copse and over a long footbridge leading to a meadow. Veer right across the narrow meadow. In the next fields hug the boundary on the right. In 300 metres you come to cross paths and keep straight on. Garston`s Farm is away to the left. Just after these first cross paths turn right and follow a short stretch of field boundary. You reach another set of cross paths and turn left. Head north for ½ mile passing a copse and then a large field with handsome old oak trees.

Walk 15: Ashurst to Henfield

A footbridge over the River Adur links the village of Ashurst to the small town of Henfield **Note:** *when the water meadows are flooded after heavy rains, follow* **Route B.**

Starting Point: Church Lane, Ashurst, there is a verge opposite the footpath just south of the church. **GR**176163 **Map:** Explorer 122
Distance: 6 Miles (5 Miles when flooded) **Terrain:** Mainly flat
Local Information: the writer, Margaret Fairless (see under "Writers in Sussex" in the Introduction to this book) is buried northeast in Ashurst churchyard. Also local actor, Laurence Olivier.
We cross Downs Link twice in this walk. For details of this way see the end of this book

The Churches

The Parish Church Of St James, Ashurst is separate from yet near the village. The tower with broach spire stands at the southwest end. It is here that the original wooden church stood, extending westwards into the churchyard. Inside, the tower is open to the wide south aisle, both built around 1200. To create this aisle, the south wall of the church was removed and an arcade built. The original doorway was re-used. The tower arch has stiff-leaf foliage on the capitals of the uneven piers. The northwest end of the church, that is the odd little section at the back of the nave, is the oldest part of the existing building. The square, 13th century font of Purbeck marble was once built into the internal buttress. The roof spans both nave and south aisle. The chancel was rebuilt in 13th century. There is no chancel arch but the Victorians created an arch in Early English style on the south side in 1877. *Keys to church may be obtained from the nearest neighbours at the time of writing.*

Ashurst

St Peter`s Church, Henfield stands in a pleasant old part of the town. An impressive 104 clipped yew trees line the footpaths to this church. There has been a church here since 8th century. This Saxon building has vanished. In 1250 a simple

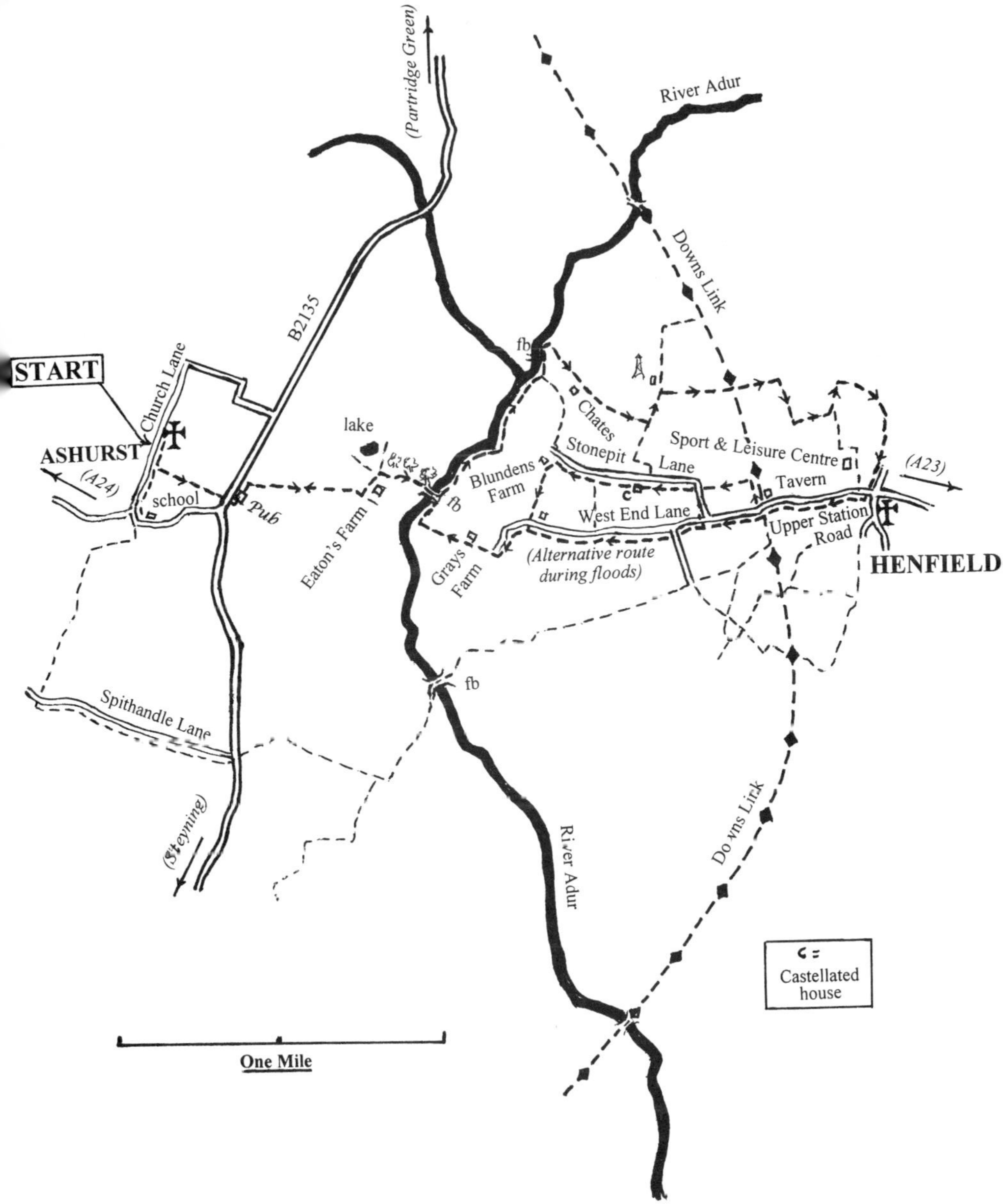
START
ASHURST
(A24)
Church Lane
school
Pub
B2135
(Partridge Green)
lake
Eaton's Farm
fb
Grays Farm
Blundens Farm
Chates
Stonepit Lane
West End Lane
(Alternative route during floods)
River Adur
Downs Link
Sport & Leisure Centre
Tavern
Upper Station Road
(A23)
HENFIELD
Spithandle Lane
(Steyning)
fb
River Adur
Downs Link
Castellated house
One Mile

church, just nave and chancel was built with Caen stone. The chancel arch and two lancet windows in the present vestry survive from this second building. The church has been gradually enlarged. The nave arcades and the porch entrance date from the 14th century. The Parham Chapel, next to the chancel and the tower were added in 15th century. Pevsner describes the Perpendicular tower as "grim as it would be in Northumberland". Still, the eight bells give one of the best rings in Sussex. In 1773, Lambert made a delightful drawing of the church, tower and all. Woodard architects carried out a drastic Victorian restoration. Most of the windows are by C. E. Kempe but Pevsner notices the contrasting windows in the chapel are by Lowndes and Drury, 1901. In 1969 engraved glass windows of agricultural scenes were inserted between chancel and Parham Chapel.

The Walk

Cross to the footpath just south of Ashurst Church. It makes a bee-line across small flat fields for the pub. At the B2135 the pub is opposite. Turn left to walk beside the road for 75 metres to a footpath on the right. This takes you along a metal farm road. After a bend to the left you are on a pleasant course due east through gently rolling countryside. In 500 metres you reach the venerable buildings of Eatons Farm with some Horsham tiles on the roof.

Fork left into a field with spaced trees and a lake ahead. Veer right away from the lake and cross to the next field to find the River Adur spanned by a sturdy old footbridge. Cross the river here.

Route B (when the meadows are flooded) *Turn right and follow the raised bank southwest for 150 metres. Turn left here on a path down through a narrow meadow with a hedge on the right. Enter a lane and rise up away from the river. At the T-junction turn left. The road soon bends to the right and takes you all the way to Henfield Church, nearly 2 kilometres east. On the way to the church, it crosses Downs Link and passes a tavern on the left. Your road changes from West End Road to Upper Station Road. Some of this route is through suburbia but you keep dry feet!* ***A and B unite for the return***

Route A After crossing the river, turn left and follow the raised bank northeast for a kilometre, passing one footpath on the right. Stay on the river bank. After a fork in the river you pass private footbridges on the left and then a second footpath on the right. Stay on the bank for another 250 metres and turn right at the third footpath. Take this path over water meadows, cross a small footbridge then an unbridged stream and climb the slope up to dry land.

You have reached an open field and hug the hedge on the right. Pass Chates, a house on your right and continue on their earth drive up to a track at a T-junction. (There is no path opposite as shown on OS map). Instead turn left on the track, go through a new metal gate and walk gently uphill towards a mast and a barn.

Turn right here and head east on a clearly marked path beside a hedge of small trees on the left. Through the trees you glimpse across fields to St Hugh`s Monastery near Coolham (See Walk 13). In 300 metres you reach the long distance cycle and walking trail, Downs Link. Cross to the path opposite and you can see Henfield ahead to the right.

Take the zigzag path southeast following the footpath signs. When you reach the backs of houses, turn left and head east along the edge of the field. You pass a sports field beyond the hedge on your right and come to a new road with no houses as yet built. Just past a large shed on the right, turn right into a small car park. In the left hand corner you can walk through to the field and into Henfield Cemetery. Follow paths on your right through the cemetery until you emerge through a lychgate to Upper Station Road. Church Lane is opposite the lychgate and the church is on the left.

Return route for A and B:

From Henfield Church return to Upper Station Road and turn left, heading back west on this suburban road. It will be familiar if you took Route B. Ignore all turnings to left and right. In 500 metres you reach the welcome Old Station Tavern on the right. It overlooks the old railway line, Downs Link. Pass the pub car park, avoid Downs Link. Turn right.

Here is a footpath on the edge of a field. Downs Link is down behind trees on your right. In 150 metres turn left for a gentle climb up through the field to enter Stonepit Lane. This elevated track heads west with a scattering of trees, few houses and extensive views north. In 400 metres pass a track on the right and a castellated white house on the left. According to a notice we are passing a haven for badgers and rodents. Pass another path on the left and continue to farm buildings at the end of the lane.

At the first barn veer left to Blundens Farm. Turn immediately left at a stile into an elevated field. Enjoy this while you may for there is a narrow, muddy, enclosed footpath ahead on the right leading downhill for 150 metres. You come with relief back onto West End Lane at a more rural end where farms abound.

Turn right to walk along West End Lane to a T-junction. Turn left to continue on the main track for 75 metres. Turn right towards Grays Farm. Pass a storage yard on the right then a chicken run on the left. Keep straight on along the hedge-lined track down to the River Adur. Turn right and follow the raised bank back to the sturdy footbridge.

Retrace your steps past Eatons Farm, along the farm road back to Ashurst, across the B3125 and finally take the footpath through small fields to the church.

5 Walks
Near Brighton

Walk 16: St Nicolas of Myra, St Michael and All Angels, St Paul`s, Brighton, Brighton Quaker Meeting House

This mini- tour of Brighton includes only four of many churches. We follow quiet ways past classical houses, a Regency Square and along the sea front. We return through ***'the Lanes'*** *and pedestrian roads. Visitors to the Royal Pavilion must find their own way.*

Starting Point: Brighton Station **GR**310049
Map: OS Explorer 122 **Terrain:** Gentle slopes, mainly pavements
Distance: 1 Mile
Local Information: The Brighton Festival is in May, a good time to visit the churches. Otherwise, St Paul`s is open daily from 10.30 a.m. to noon. It stays open until 2 p.m. on Wednesdays and until 3 p.m. at Christmas and Easter

The Churches

To check on opening of each church, phone (01273) 321399, 822284, 739639, 770258

Saint Nicolas Of Myra The first church may have stood amongst fishermen`s cottages in the Saxon settlement near the seashore. St Nicolas of Myra was the patron saint of fishermen and of children. In Domesday a church is mentioned at Brighthelmston. The present flint church stands on a pleasant green slope overlooking the south part of Brighton. It is still the oldest church in Brighton and is mainly 14th century. When the tower was repaired in 1853, Norman work was found on some of the stones. The Norman font has many headed sculptures. Some represent the Last Supper. Some may show St Nicolas making thieves restore their plunder. Human nature has not changed – thefts and break-ins occurred in the 20th century! In 1705 there was a violent storm that stripped the roof of its lead and caused repairs to be made. The main body of the church was much restored in 1853 by the architect skilled in medieval styles, Richard Cromwell Carpenter. Inside, recent modernisation has made the church comfortable and welcoming.

St Michael and All Angels Not many Victorian churches soar to such heights. St Michael`s is large, but only when you enter do you perceive its full magnificence. It was built by two architects in two separate stages. The south side was the work of G.F. Bodley (1858). It includes a chancel with a ceiling painted by William Morris. The Lady Chapel has beautiful windows by William Morris and Burne-Jones. Entrance to the church by steps on the south side, enables the visitor to view the whole dramatic interior. The first church, more restrained in style, has become the south aisle to an even more ambitious building of 1893 by William Burges. It is in French Gothic style. The nave`s Gothic arcades have coupled columns. Three large lancets form the east window. Glass in the new church is by Charles Earne Kempe.

Saint Paul`s, Brighton was designed by Richard Cromwell Carpenter and consecrated in 1849. Externally, the church tower draws attention and admiration. There is no spire which might possibly be too heavy for the tower on clay soil.

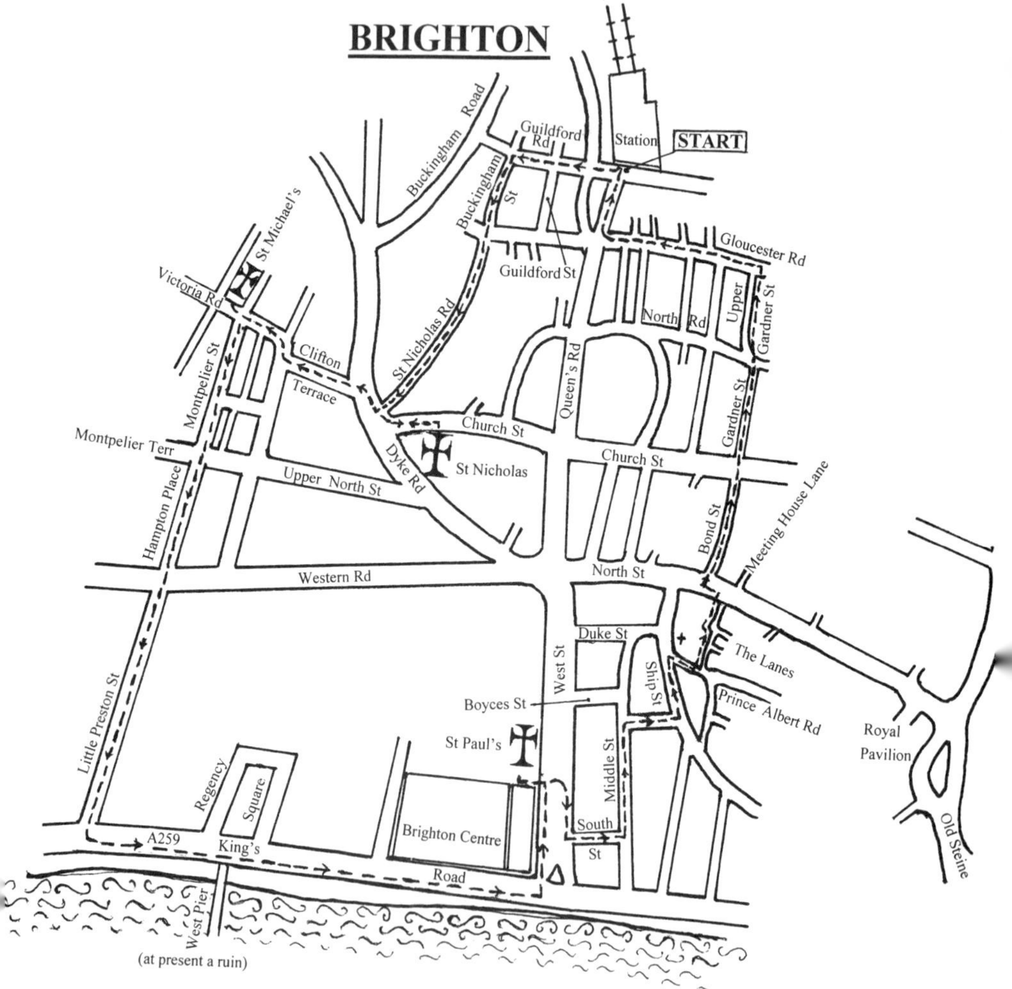
BRIGHTON
START
Station
Guildford Rd
Buckingham Road
Buckingham St
Guildford St
Gloucester Rd
St Michael's
Victoria Rd
Clifton Terrace
St Nicholas Rd
North Rd
Upper Gardner St
Queen's Rd
Gardner St
Montpelier St
Church St
Montpelier Terr
Dyke Rd
St Nicholas
Church St
Upper North St
Hampton Place
Bond St
Meeting House Lane
Western Rd
North St
Duke St
West St
Ship St
The Lanes
Boyces St
Prince Albert Rd
Royal Pavilion
St Paul's
Little Preston St
Middle St
Regency Square
Brighton Centre
South St
A259
King's Road
Old Steine
West Pier
(at present a ruin)

Instead, an unusual wooden octagon was added in 1873. It was designed by the architect`s son, R. H. Carpenter. Other unusual features include the long side passage to gain admission to the Narthex. In 1880 G. F. Bodley added the Narthex, a large vestibule in the style of some very early churches. Here people assembled before and after services. The large nave in Decorated style has a fine roof in the shape of a ship`s hull. The uncomfortable pews are original. The chancel roof is painted, the skilful work of G. F. Bodley. Perhaps the greatest treasures of this church are the windows by W. N. Pugin. Recently repaired and cleaned, they glow in all their glory. (Open weekdays 10.30 a.m. to noon)

Friends` Meeting House, built of red brick in mid-Victorian times, has a classical air. Part of the frontage has bays and pediment. This large building with lawns at the front is a hospitable refuge from the congested roads all around. You may find local produce, Fairtraide stalls and a cafeteria here on a Saturday.

The Walk

Before starting I must mention, as an aid to finding your bearings, that the entrance to Brighton Station faces south to Queen`s Road leading to West Street and the Sea.

Now step out! As you leave the station, face Queen`s Road and turn right. You cross Terminus Road at traffic lights. Go up Guildford Road as far as Buckingham Street. Turn left here. At the end of Buckingham Street, cross to a narrow road opposite and keep on course. This is St Nicholas Road and leads to Church Street. Cross diagonally left down to St Nicolas Church.

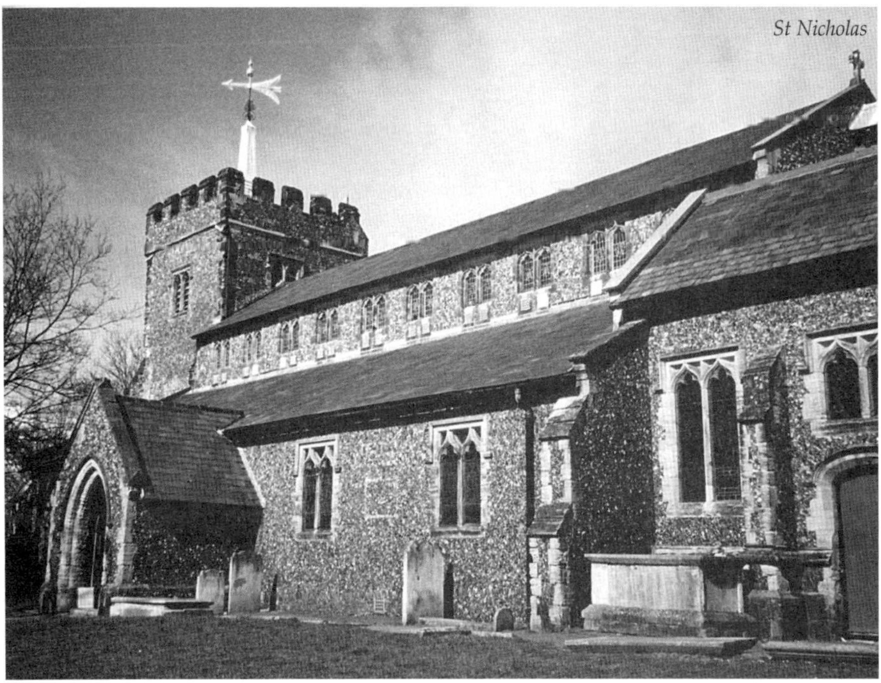

St Nicholas

From St Nicolas Church retrace your steps to pass the entrance to St Nicholas Road and cross to the elevated Clifton Terrace. The handsome houses here overlook a park, then the town and beyond that the sea. At the end of Clifton Terrace, curve to the right and cross to Victoria Road which takes you to St Michael`s Church. On your way along Victoria Road you pass Montpelier Street on the left.

St Michael

After visiting St Michael`s Church, return to Montpelier Street and go straight downhill. The sea beckons below. To reach the sea you continue down Hampton place, cross the busy shopping thoroughfare, Western Road and keep on course along Little Preston Street to the main coastal road, A259 below.

Cross the A259 to the promenade opposite and turn left. You pass Regency Square on the left and the sad remains of West Pier on the right. (This pier may have vanished or it may have been re-built by the time you arrive). After the Brighton Centre and the Odeon Cinema on the left, you leave the sea front and cross back into town at the traffic lights.

Turn up West Street to the long passage to St Paul`s Church on the left.

After visiting St Paul`s Church, retrace your steps along West Street and cross to the little side road, South Street. At the end of South Street, turn left at the T-junction. This is Middle Street. In about 100 metres you come to a twitten, Ship Street Gardens on your right. Despite the narrowness of this alley, it manages to

Regency Square

contain a shop and other business premises. At the end of the alley turn left up Ship Street and find the Friends` Meeting House at a busy road junction.

Come out of Friends` Meeting House through the little garden and turn left to walk a few yards along Prince Albert Road. There is a black pedestrian sign indicating 'The Lanes' on the left. We shall not resist the lure of the Lanes, but hang onto your rucksack!

Head north along the first lane, avoiding right turns. At the T-junction, turn left then immediately right to continue north along Meeting House Lane. Avoid left turns.

You should reach North Street and the fun is not yet over. Cross diagonally left to Bond Street where market stalls abound on a Saturday (possibly other days as far as I know). Go across Church Street (no longer the country lane of yore) and keep straight on along Gardner Street, still alive with vendors. At North Road (yes, you have already crossed North Street!), cross diagonally left to Upper Gardner Street.

At the end of Upper Gardner Street the fun ends. You have reached Gloucester Road. Turn left and walk uphill to the end of Gloucester Road. Steps lead up to Queen`s Road. Turn right and the Station looms ahead.

Walk 17: Jack and Jill Windmills, Clayton Church, Wolstonbury Hill, Pyecombe and Newtimber Church *an optional extra*

Avoiding trunk roads, railway lines and tunnels, we set off from Victorian windmills to head for an Iron Age fort, 677 feet high. We visit Saxon and Norman churches. You have to go under the A23 to see Newtimber Church, an extra 2 miles

Starting Point: Jack and Jill Windmills Car Park, Clayton, off A273. **GR**303134
Map: OS Explorer 122 **Terrain:** Hilly (very steep slopes down to Newtimber and back)
Distance: 5 miles or 7 miles if you include Newtimber
Local Information: Jill, the white mill is open to the public weekends and Bank Holidays, Easter to September. The free car park is often crowded then and so a bus 38 from Hassocks Station operates during that period. Phone 01273 292480 for details.

Clayton Tunnel, over two miles long was built in 1841 and runs under Pyecombe.

The Churches

Clayton, St John The Baptist stands on ancient cross roads, Underhill Lane and the main South Coast to London road. The simple building of nave and chancel with high walls of flint and sandstone still has the appearance of the original Saxon church. There is a bold 11th century chancel arch. The church has shed its transepts which held chapels in the 12th and 13th centuries. The nave has retained its amazing Norman wall paintings, some of the oldest in England, dated by Pevsner as early as 1140. They give a full interpretation of the Last Judgement in colours of red and yellow.

Pyecombe, The Church of the Transfiguration also stands on an ancient route, now known as the South Downs Way. The old stage coach road also crosses here. The lovely flint church with tower and porch, set on a hill among cottages presents a conventional village picture. Any illusion of old-world peace is shattered by the constant traffic on the main roads below. There is a rare Tapsel Gate at the entrance to the church. It is wide with a central pivot, allowing people to leave and enter the churchyard at the same time. Built in 1170, the nave and chancel are Norman. The main chancel arch is part of the original Norman church. The circular lead font of 1170 is similar to that of Edburton. The 13th century tiles on the sanctuary floor have been the inspiration for the modern encaustic tiles in the tower. The tower itself was added in the 13th century. The 14th century porch has Horsham slabs on the roof.

Newtimber, St John Baptist retains an aura of antiquity despite thorough Victorian restorations. The idyllic situation among trees and meadows, overhung with wooded slopes contributes to the effect. 'Niuembre' is recorded in 1086. Opposite the church, stands the moated mansion, Newtimber Place, the present

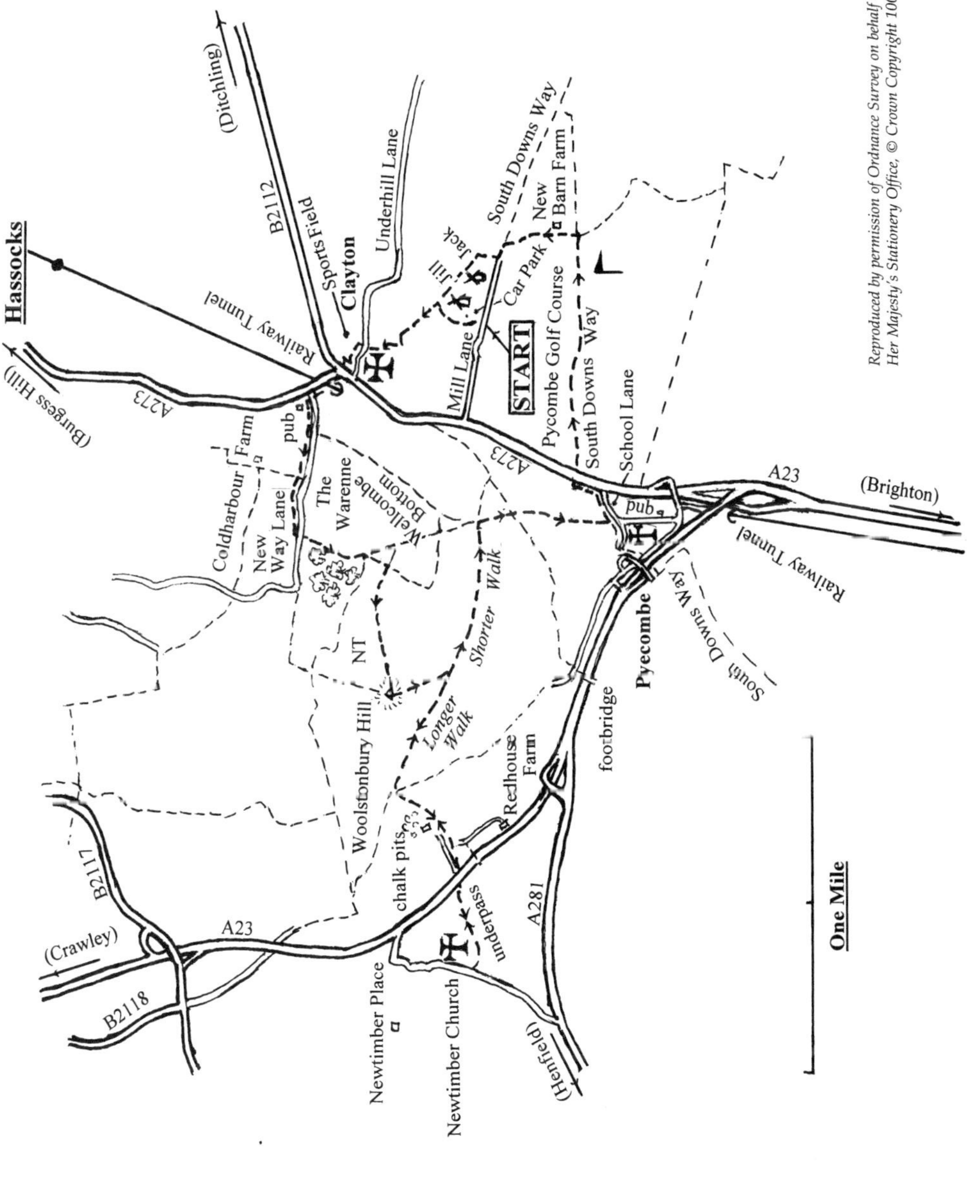
Hassocks
(Ditchling)
B2112
Sports Field
Clayton
Underhill Lane
Railway Tunnel
(Burgess Hill)
A273
Jack
Jill
South Downs Way
New Barn Farm
Car Park
Mill Lane
START
Pycombe Golf Course
South Downs Way
School Lane
A273
pub
Coldharbour Farm
New Way Lane
The Warenne
Wellcombe Bottom
A23
(Brighton)
pub
Railway Tunnel
South Downs Way
Pyecombe
NT
Shorter Walk
Longer Walk
Woolstonbury Hill
Redhouse Farm
footbridge
chalk pits
underpass
A281
B2117
A23
(Crawley)
B2118
Newtimber Place
Newtimber Church
(Henfield)
One Mile

house is 17th century. The church has Early English chancel and nave and Victorian tower in Gothic style. The rose window is Victorian. The carved oak pulpit is 16th century. Beside the main path to the church in the ground a memorial stone remembers African troops who came to help England in the First World War and sank in the ship Mendi in 1917. In particular Chief Henry Bokleni Ndamase is named.

The Walk

In the far corner of the car park, go through a gate onto open downland. Cross diagonally left downhill to join a bridleway to Clayton. In May there were orchids on these slopes. In 300 metres you join an enclosed track down to Underhill Lane, Clayton. Turn left for the church.

Newtimber

After visiting Clayton Church, continue along the lane to a T-junction with A273. (You can cut instead across the corner of the sports field). Turn right on the pavement and fork left at the road junction, keeping on the main road. In 100 metres cross with care to the single track road, New Way Lane. There is a large pub in front and the grand, castellated entrance to Clayton railway tunnel behind.

Walk along New Way Lane for half a mile passing a path on the left and one on the right leading to Coldharbour Farm. Turn left up a driveway at the Warenne. Pass a substantial house on your left and continue on the track with woodland on your right. Ignore the first track on your right and keep climbing.

In 300 metres you also avoid a path on the left leading to Wellcombe Bottom. Stay on your track and you come immediately to a post with blue arrows. Turn right to an unmarked gate into downland. This is National Trust land. You can see Wolstonbury Hill straight ahead. As you approach the hill, you skirt a steep hollow on the left and, beyond it, you see a wide valley.

As you climb the hill, You look down over the plain below on the right. Cross the ramparts of the ancient Iron Age Hill Fort. Climb to the Trig. point and admire the views all around.

Turn left and walk gently downhill on a narrow rough path. At the T-junction with a wide elevated track skirting National Trust boundary of Wolstonbury Hill, you have to make a decision.

For the shorter walk, turn left and continue as after the italics below.

Those wishing to visit Newtimber Church *turn right and walk along this elevated track for 250 metres. Enjoy views south to Newtimber Hill and east to farmland. Pass the strange shapes of grassy earthworks on the right. Look out for the huge scar of the chalk pits down on the left. Follow the first arrow and fork to the left. Leave the boundary of National Trust land and come down to an enclosed track at a T-junction. Turn left on this track then immediately right to take the path that descends steeply. It plunges southeast down the boundary of the chalk pits. Wild flowers adorn the banks in spring and summer.*

When you reach the concrete track below, turn right then left onto a wide road serving the chalk pits. Go through the underpass to the layby on the other side of the A23. Turn right then left onto a footpath leading across two fields to Newtimber Church.

From Newtimber Church retrace your steps to the underpass and up the steep slope. Near the top take care! Avoid turning right too soon. At the enclosed track turn left then immediately right to re-enter National Trust Land, Now you can turn right to rejoin the elevated track heading southeast. In 250 metres you pass the familiar footpath on the left and the decision point. Keep straight on.

Both shorter and longer walks:

Head southeast for a kilometre on the elevated track along the National Trust boundary with a wire fence on your left. Ahead you have a good view of Jack and Jill windmills. Continue until you come down to cross paths and turn right into the narrowest path. Some walkers have ventured into the field on the right to avoid the mud.

You have a sheltered, enclosed, muddy track for half a mile down to Pyecombe. It is rough in places and often muddy after rain. When you reach Pyecombe crossroads, turn left on the South Downs Way down along School Lane, after you have visited the church.

At the bottom of School Lane you reach A273 and turn left onto a track, protected from traffic by a hedge. After 200 metres cross A273 with care to Pyecombe Golf Club opposite. This is still the South Downs Way. It passes the clubhouse on your right then climbs up on the edge of the golf course. In half a mile at cross tracks, turn left. Pass New Barn Farm, now given over to pony and horse riding.

At the T-junction turn left down to the windmills.

Walk 18: Edburton, Poynings, Devil's Dyke, South Downs Way

After flat fields north of the Downs, climb up to spectacular heights at Devil`s Dyke. Return to base along a high trail looking down on our earlier selves.

Starting Point: Edburton Church on the narrow underhill road north of the Downs. Limited roadside parking just west of the church at a footpath near a frozen food centre.
Either **GR**233114 Church Car Park
or **GR**231114 roadside near Springs Salmon Shop
Map: OS Explorer 122, "South Downs Way" **Distance:** 8 Miles
Terrain: Mainly flatish but one long steep hill up and one down.
Warning: Avoid the private car park for Springs Salmon Shop. Gates may be locked!

The Churches

St Andrew`s Church, Edburton

'This pearl I came upon
Set in an emerald Chalice
Sweet Saxon Edburton'.

– Part of a poem by Charles G. Mortimer.

Princess Eadburh, granddaughter of King Alfred founded the first church here 930- 940. She had chosen the religious life and become a nun in Winchester. She converted the Saxon pagans and gave her name to Edburton. There are still Saxon footings and stones in the lower walls of this much-loved church. Four mass clocks, circular sun dials for telling the time can just be seen outside; one on the north side and 3 on the south. Inside a chained stone is believed to be the ground piscina of the Saxon altar. The present church is Early English. The nave is 13th century, the chancel and the north chapel are early 14th century and the tower is late 14th century. The early Norman font is one of few with a lead bowl. Pyecombe and Parham are the only other two in Sussex. In 13th century, fonts had to have locked covers over their bowls to prevent witches taking or cursing the water. In later history Roundheads used this font as a horse trough. Back to the 13th century and there are two interesting windows low down on either side of the chancel. On the instruction of the Pope, penitents had to kneel outside. The windows had shutters instead of glass and the Franciscan Friars opened the shutters to hear confessions. Grooves for the shutters can still be seen. The 'Resurrection' east window is Victorian. Restoration of the roof timbers in 1880 and a re-roofed tower in 1947 have preserved this church in its ancient charm, such that Pevsner wrote 'Happy county to stay in its old ways without affectation'.

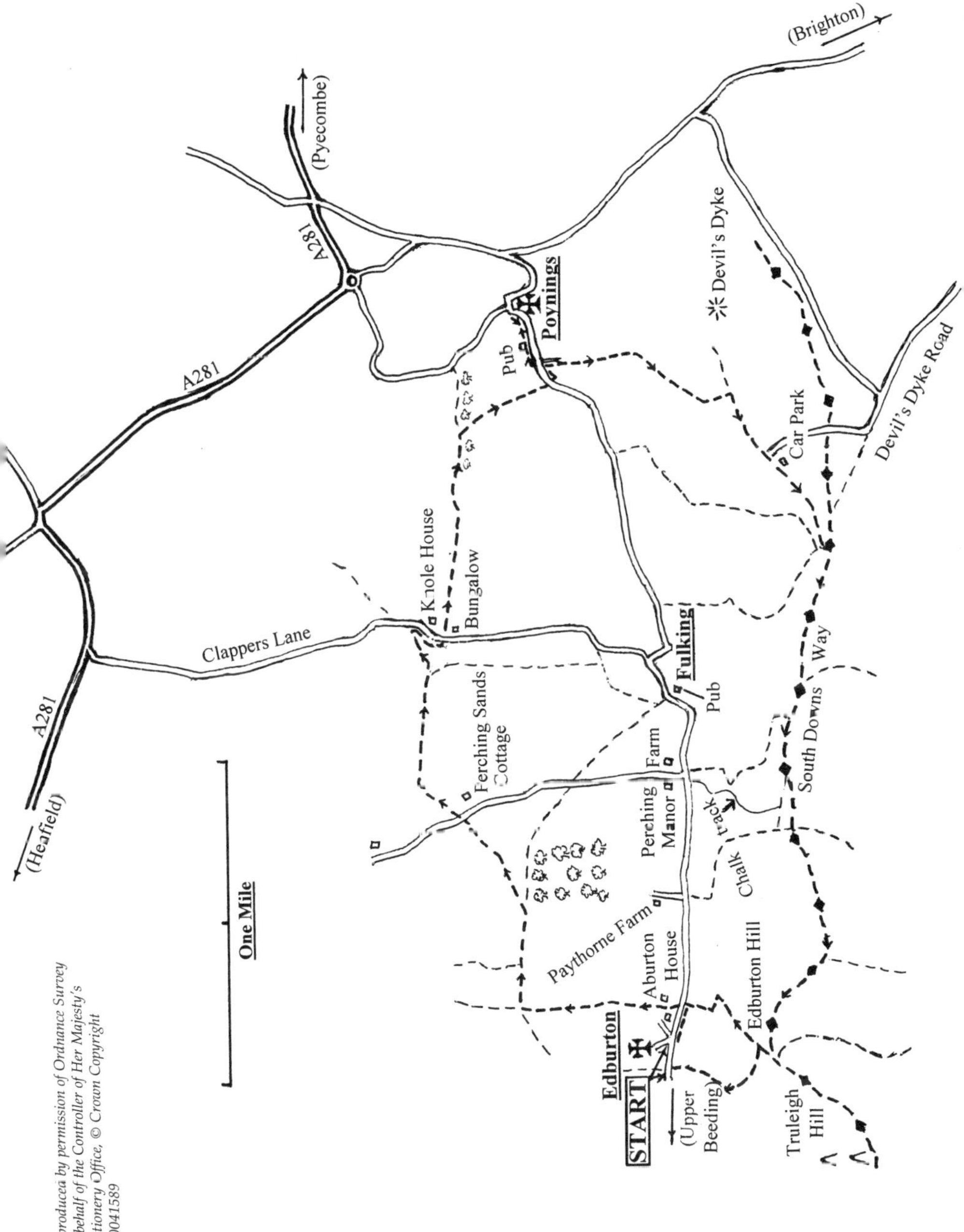
(Brighton)
(Pyecombe)
A281
A281
A281
(Henfield)
Poynings
Pub
Devil's Dyke
Car Park
Devil's Dyke Road
Knole House
Bungalow
Clappers Lane
Fulking
Pub
Ferching Sands Cottage
Farm
Perching Manor
Chalk track
South Downs Way
Paythorne Farm
Aburton House
Edburton Hill
Edburton
START
(Upper Beeding)
Truleigh Hill
One Mile

Holy Trinity Church, Poynings is a large, lofty, plain, cruciform building. In 1369 Michael Poynings, Lord of the Manor died leaving 200 marcs to replace the Norman church that had stood on this mound for 300 years. The church is mentioned in Domesday, 1087. Before then there would have been a Saxon church. Remnants from the Norman building include tiles at the base of the altar and the piscina in the chancel. Now the church is early Perpendicular with a solid turreted central tower. The outside walls are faced with flint and the roof, repaired in 1993, is mainly Horsham stone. The font is 14th century. The pulpit is Jacobean. Most of the windows have plain glass. The large 5-light east window is like those of Alfriston and Tarring. There are fragments of glass dating from 1421 in the north transept windows. You enter the church through a large porch built over the grave of Richard Poynings (died 1430), grandson of Michael. Note the ancient benches in the porch. Once inside the church, you find a large medieval mural on the south wall opposite. Over it the 10 Commandments have been painted.

Edburton

The Walk

From Edburton Church walk down to the road and, just before the sign Aburton Farmhouse, turn left. The public right of way leads along the private driveway. It then heads due north on a track between hedges. In ½ mile at cross paths, turn right into an open field, muddy in winter. Hug the field boundary on your right. At the next field you cross from West into East Sussex over a little footbridge. Head for a nearby wood. Cross a second footbridge to reach the corner of the wood. Fork left to traverse a rough field in a northeastly direction towards a farm cottage.

Walk beside the field hedge to another footbridge that brings you to a private road. The farm cottage is on your right. Cross the road to the footpath opposite and keep on course on a well-defined path. Newtimber Hill is ahead and other Downs are on our right.

Edburton

Cross a footbridge over stream in the tree-covered corner. Head due east with the hedge and the stream on your right. In 400 metres you come to a small damp valley with more footbridges. Ignore the footpath on the right. Keep the stream on your right and a grassy slope on your left. Maintain an easterly direction to a tarmac road, Clappers Lane.

Turn right to walk along Clappers Lane *(This lane takes you down to Fulking if you should wish to shorten the walk and take refuge in the village pub. You can then return to Edburton along the underhill road. Take care! Cars use these roads!).*

Those wishing to complete the walk will find a pub at Poynings. Walk past nearby Knole House and look for a concrete footpath sign in the verge on the left. Turn left into an open elevated field. Make for the left corner and continue eastwards for ½ mile. Some houses of Poynings can be seen on the right ahead. After passing alders beside a stream with some ponds, turn right just before sewage works. Climb gently sloping fields to Poynings with a backdrop of the Downs.

At the underhill road turn left, pass the pub on your left and continue on a raised footpath on the left leading down through the village and up to Cora`s Corner where you find a generous shelter holding seats. Poynings Church is across the road

Return to the pub in Poynings and continue past it for 50 metres. Turn left into Dyke Lane leading to a footpath. At the foot of the Downs, fork right. Climb steeply with the aid of wooden steps. Steps give way to a narrow path veering right diagonally up the steep slope. Below and behind are the villages and paths you have traversed. Ahead and above is the pub on the fort of Devil`s Dyke. As

you approach the top, veer right to pick your way through cars and hang gliders in season.

A trig. point and a square ruined building are ahead. Take the path southwest to pass these on your left. In 200 metres, at cross paths, you join the unmistakable South Downs Way. Follow this firm wide track heading west towards the radio station of Truleigh Hill, over a mile away. Ignore all turnings to left and right until you come to a wide fork.

Take the left fork, still the South Downs Way. There is a hedge on the left. After pylons you come to Edburton Hill with trees atop. This is National Trust land so you can walk up to the top where you find the remains of a motte and bailey castle.

Return to the South Downs Way on its curved route. Pass one footpath on the left. In another 500 metres you come to a cluster of gates at a path junction below Truleigh Hill. Turn sharp right. You are on the escarpment above Edburton and can see the hamlet below. In 50 metres you have a choice of ways down. *The wide grassy track on the right leads down to Aburton Farmhouse.* The narrow path on the left makes a wide arc above a hollow and comes down to the roadside space where you may have parked. If you choose this narrow path you descend steps at the bottom and go through the back yard of the frozen food shop to the road.

Walk 19: Shoreham Churches and Lancing College Chapel *(short walk)*, train to Fishersgate, Monarch's Way, Portslade and over the Downs to Shoreham *(long walk)*

There is enough to see in Shoreham to spend a whole day here. Come again for a more ambitious excursion by train to see Portslade Church and walk back over the Downs.This Longer Walk sets off from Fishersgate along Monarch`s Way (Details at the end of book)

Starting Point: St Nicolas Church, Old Shoreham **GR**218059
Map: OS Explorer 122, 'South Downs Way'
Distances: 3 or 4 miles (short walk) **Terrain:** Mainly flat, one hill (short walk)
7 miles (long walk) + 2 miles on the train. Hilly downland (long walk)
Local Information: Lancing College Chapel is open to visitors until 4 p.m. Admissions Secretary, phone 01273 465805
Shoreham, at the mouth of the River Adur, was a port in Roman times and earlier. A Roman road crossed the present Buckingham Park and went along the Avenue to the ford, later replaced by the toll bridge. (See map). In 1086 Domesday mentions a church at Shoreham. This is the Saxon, St Nicolas in Old Shoreham. The river began to silt up here and the Normans moved the port, building a town and church at New Shoreham. Shoreham has two very fine ancient churches.
Shoreham Airport (1910) was the first civil airport in the world.
Trains leave Shoreham at 40 minutes past the hour for Fishersgate, 2 ½ miles away
It is possible to start both walks from Shoreham Station, GR108053 if you study the map carefully and adapt the text.

The Churches

Lancing College Chapel, St Mary and St Nicolas was built of Sussex sandstone at the end of 19th and beginning of 20th centuries in Gothic style. Nathaniel Woodard who founded Lancing College was determined to have a fine chapel. He employed R.C. Carpenter as architect for the college and his son R.H. Carpenter completed the design of the chapel. It is a magnificent achievement rising to 94 feet and with foundations down 70 feet. Inside are nine bays. The crypt has an octagonal chapel at the east end. The elevated position of this imposing church has resulted in serious wear on the stones and conservation work is ongoing.

St Nicolas Church, Old Shoreham. The first church may have been built by Aella, King of the South Saxons in 481 A.D. St Nicolas, the patron saint of mariners, died in 352 A.D. The present church was built around 850 A.D. Saxon work can be found in the west part of the north wall of the nave. There is long and short work. Nearby, the arch over the blocked door is also Saxon. The fine Norman tower replaced the Saxon one. Normans adapted the long Saxon building and formed a cruciform church by adding transepts. There is rich carving on all Norman tower arches. According to Simon Jenkins, "the crossing arches form an archaeological

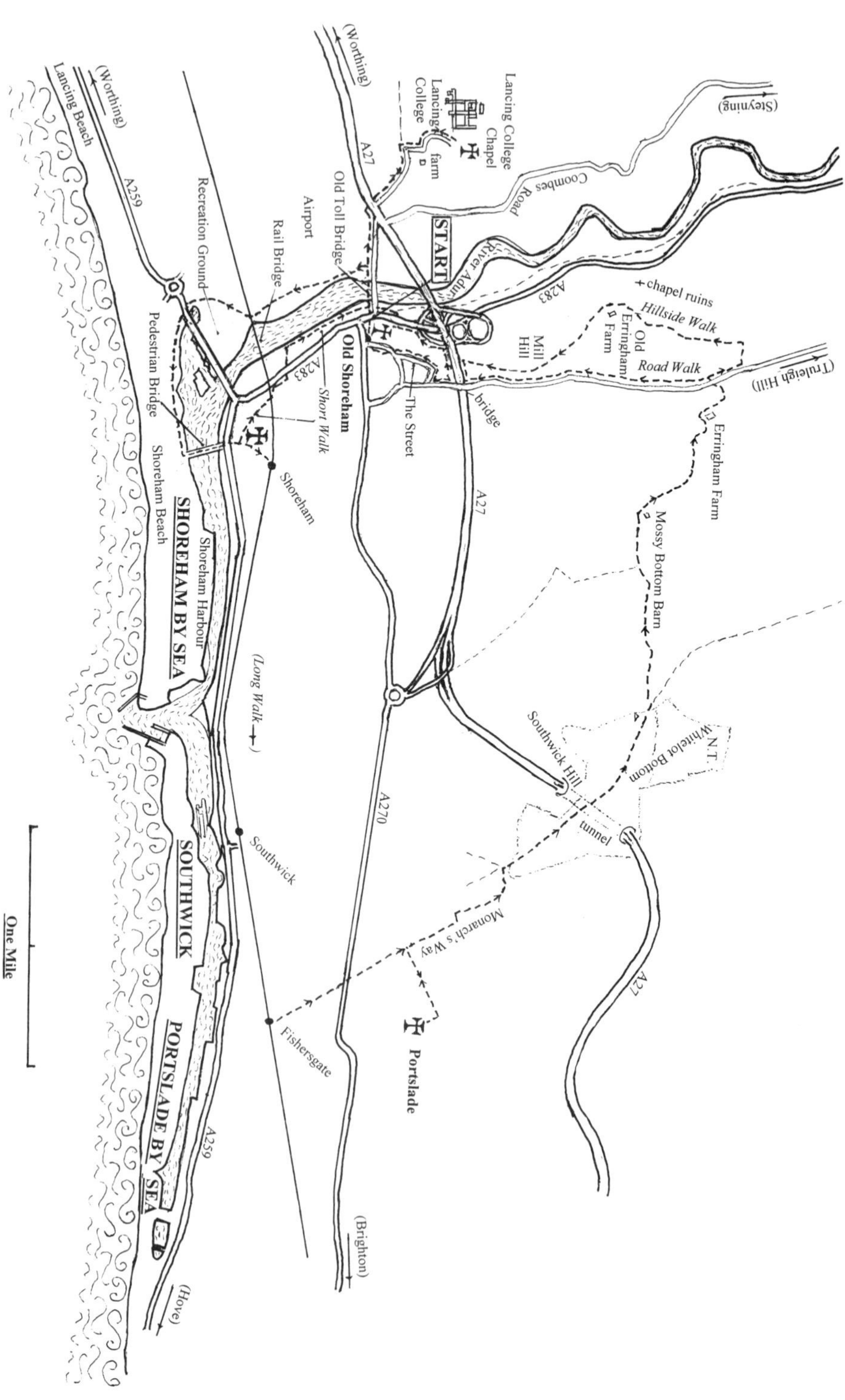
(Steyning)
Lancing College Chapel
Lancing College
farm
Coombes Road
(Worthing)
A27
Old Toll Bridge
START
River Adur
A283
chapel ruins
Hillside Walk
Old Erringham Farm
Mill Hill
Road Walk
(Truleigh Hill)
Airport
Rail Bridge
Recreation Ground
(Worthing)
Lancing Beach
A259
Old Shoreham
A283
Short Walk
The Street
bridge
Erringham Farm
Pedestrian Bridge
Shoreham
Shoreham Beach
SHOREHAM BY SEA
Shoreham Harbour
A27
Mossy Bottom Barn
(Long Walk)
Southwick Hill
Whitelot Bottom
N.T.
tunnel
A270
Southwick
SOUTHWICK
Monarch's Way
A27
Portslade
Fishersgate
PORTSLADE BY SEA
A259
(Brighton)
(Hove)
One Mile

sanctuary at the heart of the restored church". Chevron, shells, rosettes, human faces and also a cat's face and an elf are all genuine original carving. The chancel is Early English and replaced the earlier apsidal one. The list of vicars in the south transept has a mysterious gap. In 1685 the vicar disappeared. After 143 years, he was presumed dead in 1828 and a new vicar appointed.

The Church of St Mary de Haura, New Shoreham. Normans built the church here 1100 to 1130 to be nearer the harbour – 'de Haura'. According to legend, William de Braose (see the Introduction to the book under 'The Normans') intended creating a monastery. He extended the choir then escaped to France to avoid the wrath of King John. The transepts, the first stage of the tower and the tower arches are early Norman. Between 1180 and 1225 the second stage of the tower, the aisles, choir and vaulting were built in Transitional style. The two large flying buttresses are Early English. The nave collapsed in 1699, perhaps as a result of a fierce storm. With such magnificent arcades in the choir, there is no sense of loss today. The arcades themselves present a puzzle. They were built at the same time in different styles. The north side may be the work of masons from Canterbury importing the latest style from France in 1170. The Norman influence is in the alternate round and octagonal columns. The contrasting south side has gothic columns that rise to fine vaulting in the ceiling. In the expert opinion of John Harvey, St Mary's is one of the fifty great non-cathedral churches of England.

Portslade Church, St Nicholas does not rest peacefully in its neighbourhood. When I was here in the summer, a distraught vicar was waiting for the police to investigate yet another break-in. Flint walls around it offer some protection and remind us of a time when the church was less jostled. In the 12th century a Transition-Norman church stood on a quiet downland slope, facing the unspoilt coast. The round columns and mildly pointed arches are from this period. The tower and chancel are Early English. The windows were changed to lancets in 13th century.

The Shorter Walk

***From St Nicolas in Old Shoreham**, with a possible diversion to Lancing College, then on to St Mary, New Shoreham. Much of the return walk is in a built-up part of the town..*

Walk to the closed end of the cul-de-sac, St Nicholas Lane. Take care as you cross A283 to the path opposite. Go over a cycle track then linger on the timber Old Shoreham Bridge, built in 1781 and still used by traffic on the A27 until 1970 when the by-pass opened. Look for a footpath sign on the left.

***If you wish to visit Lancing College Chapel**, keep on course along Old Shoreham Lane to cross the A27 at traffic lights. Take the drive up to the college. Return the same way.*

To walk beside the river to Shoreham town centre, follow the footpath along the raised bank of the river with the field of Shoreham Airport on your right. At the time of writing this path has a succession of uneven concrete slabs, so be careful when planes take off and land not to be distracted and trip into the ditch or the River Adur! A further distraction may be the river and shorebirds. In one kilometre go under the rail bridge.

Go past a children's play area and the buildings on the left housing canoes. Veer right across a large flat open field for recreation. (You will be aware of the A259 ahead). Keep a stretch of water on the left then cross the road at an island. On the other side of the road there is a footpath beside the river.

You have an interesting walk beside varied houseboats and the river on the left and conventional houses on the right. (Beyond the houses lies Shoreham Beach. Here once stood individual wooden beach huts giving the area the name 'Bungalow Town'. Many were demolished in 1940 in case of invasion. 6th June 1944 troops left Shoreham Harbour for D-Day landings).

In 500 metres turn left to cross the river at Shoreham Harbour on a long pedestrian bridge opened in 1921. On the north bank you reach the High Street. *Marlipins Museum is nearby. It was originally built around 1130, it became a museum in 1926.*

Cross the High Street and walk up East Street to St Mary de Haura Church on the left*.

From St Mary de Haura Church take the footpath crossing the spacious churchyard diagonally to Church Street. Pass the Library on the right and the Community Centre on the left. Go under the railway line and turn left and walk along Hebe Road. Cross to Swiss Gardens leading to Connaught Ave. This residential road leads up to St Nicolas Church, seen ahead.

For the riverside walk*, go along Swiss Gardens. After a lake on the left and a school on the right, turn left into Freehold Street. Turn right at the main road A283 and in about 200 metres you can cross with care to join the cycle route, Downs Link. Turn right here. In 350 metres it brings you back to Old Shoreham Bridge on the left. Turn right and cross to St Nicolas Church.*

The Longer Walk

Starting as for the shorter walk, then taking a little train journey from Shoreham to Fishersgate, a possible visit to Portslade Church and a scenic walk back over the Downs.

Follow the instructions for the shorter walk as far as *. Pass St Mary's Church on the left. Keep on route along Brunswick Road to **Shoreham Station**. Take a train to Fishersgate, two stations east.

At Fishersgate Station, stay on the north side, climb the footbridge and turn left. You join a straight route, **Monarch's Way** up to the Downs. On the way you have to negociate crossings at Shelldale Road to an alley with allotments on the left then in 350 metres the A270 and lastly Mile Oak Road. Continue up the alley to a nearby pylon and Mile Oak Gardens on the right.

If you wish to make a diversion to Portslade Church, *turn right at Mile Oak Gardens and walk along to the main road. Cross diagonally right to a track leading down to Drove Road. Cross Valley Road and follow Drove Road, taking the second turning right. A walled lane leads up to the church.* ***Do not be beguiled by the road names! This is an urban landscape*** *and you have to wend your way back down to the valley and up to Mile Oak Gardens to rejoin Monarch's Way at the pylon. Turn right.*

Continue up the enclosed path, Monarch's Way to fields crossed by pylons. Go

Shoreham Churches

Another photo of the church on the right (St Mary De Haura) is shown on page 97

under the cables and follow the path northwest towards a clump of trees on the crest of the hill. You reach a gate and a sign 'Access Land'. Do not enter. Turn left and walk along the edge of the access land passing a gorse hedge on the right. You come down to crosspaths and turn right on the side of Southwick Hill.

You come to a wide, definite path climbing gently to pass over a motorway tunnel. (You may hear the traffic below). Once across, there are three tracks facing you in National Trust land. Take the middle track half left and head northwest through scrubland in the Downs. Do not be tempted to any side tracks. In 500 metres of gentle climb, pass a trig. point hidden in the scrub. You then reach a wide, curved space with paths at three points all leading to the open Downs. Turn sharp left.

Go through a gate into a fenced footpath heading west for nearly one mile. In summer there is a colourful fringe of mignonette, knapweed, yellow bedstraw, scabious and mallow. In one kilometre after a steep downward slope, ignore the path on the left. Continue straight on down to Mossy Bottom Barn. Here the path, now a track bears right and climbs northwest

Eventually, the welcome trees around Erringham Farm come into view. Join the tarmac road on its circuitous course past the farm and up to a T-junction on **Mill Hill**.

For the short, simple road walk, *turn left and walk with care along the elevated lane for over one mile then follow instructions below* .*

For the longer scenic hillside walk, turn right at Mill Hill and walk along the road for 200 metres. Turn left at a footpath sign and in 150 metres turn left again. You are now walking downhill for ½ mile on a track with a hedgerow on your left. Lancing College can be seen across the river below. The track leads to Old Erringham Farm, a cluster of houses that include the remains of a tiny Norman chapel. It stands in the grounds of a brick cottage and is hidden behind an ash tree. This is private land.

Whilst still outside this hamlet, fork left, cross a small field to spacious meadows. Follow the field boundary on your left. You are on a slope above meadows and the river on the right. At the top left hand corner, you enter Mill Hill Nature Reserve through a wooden gate. Avoid steps. Keep straight on to climb the narrow path through woodland then along an open slope of Mill Hill. Pass an enclosed reservoir on your left and keep on course, gradually approaching the road also on your left.

* When you reach the road, keep on course. You have joined the short road walk. Cross the bridge high above the A27 with its intricate junctions to the Adur Fly-over. When you have crossed the bridge you have a choice of ways:

Either

Turn right on the footpath descending the hill slope, veer left and continue downhill. Ignore a path to the left and descend to the A283. Turn left for St Nicolas Church.

Or

Keep straight on along Mill Hill to a T-junction. Turn right. Avoid all side roads and follow The Street. It curves left and passes a high flint wall. This is Old Shoreham where there were once farms. At the bottom, St Nicolas Lane, turn right for the church.

Shoreham

Portslade

Walk 20: Bramber to Upper Beeding and Botolphs

This riverside walk includes three medieval churches, a castle ruin overlooking the River Adur and a 15th century house for monks who guarded an ancient bridge.

Starting Point: Bramber Castle Car Park off the roundabout on A283 southeast Steyning
Map: OS Explorer 122 **GR**186106 **Terrain:** Flat with occasional slopes
Distance: 6 Miles or 5 Miles for the shorter walk
Note: The shorter walk offers a second opportunity to visit St Mary`s House (Walk 10). It is open in the afternoon on Thursday, Sunday and Bank Holiday Monday. South Downs Way and Downs Link feature in this walk. Details are at the end of book.

The Churches

St Nicholas`s Church, Bramber stands near the castle on a hill above the Adur. It was a Saxon stronghold. 'Bremer' is Saxon for 'thicket of broom'. The Normans under William de Braose built a castle here. The river then flowed close to the hill with a landing stage near the church. Bramber was a river port, probably Portus Adurni. There was already a nearby bridge spanning the Adur so Bramber had plenty of traffic. Bramber Church served the aristocratic residents of the castle and the medieval Knights Templar. The Norman cruciform church was built in 1073, possibly the first complete Norman Church in Sussex. In the Civil War (1642-6) Cromwell`s men destroyed the castle and damaged the church. A restoration took place 100 years later when the chancel was dismantled and parts of it used to repair the tower. Today`s church retains its Norman nave and tower. The old chancel and transepts have gone. In 1930 the tower was strengthened by the creation of a ceiling for the chancel below. In 1931 the vestry was added. The tower arch has rare Norman sculpture of crude figures. High on the south side of the chancel arch, there is also a fine carving of a staff below a Maltese Cross, believed to signify the connection with the Knights Templar. (See Introduction).

Upper Beeding, St Peter is an Early English church with a 16th century chancel. In 1080 the Benedictine Priory of Sele stood just north of the church. The monks worshipped in the chancel and the parishioners in the nave. In 1536 Henry V111 dissolved the Priory. Stones from the priory are in the churchyard wall. Another acquisition from the priory is the two-light window in the south wall of the chancel. The wide nave has been over restored in 19th century. The south aisle, added in 19th century has a strong arcade with foliage carving on the capitals. To contact the rector, phone 01903 815474.

St Botolph is the oldest church in this parish of Beeding and Bramber with Botolphs. It served the Manor of Annington, also known at one time as Vetere Ponte (old bridge). The church was then St Peter de Vetere Ponte. The nearby bridge, probably built by the Romans carried traffic, including tin from Cornwall, over the River Adur. In Tudor times the river receded and tides destroyed the

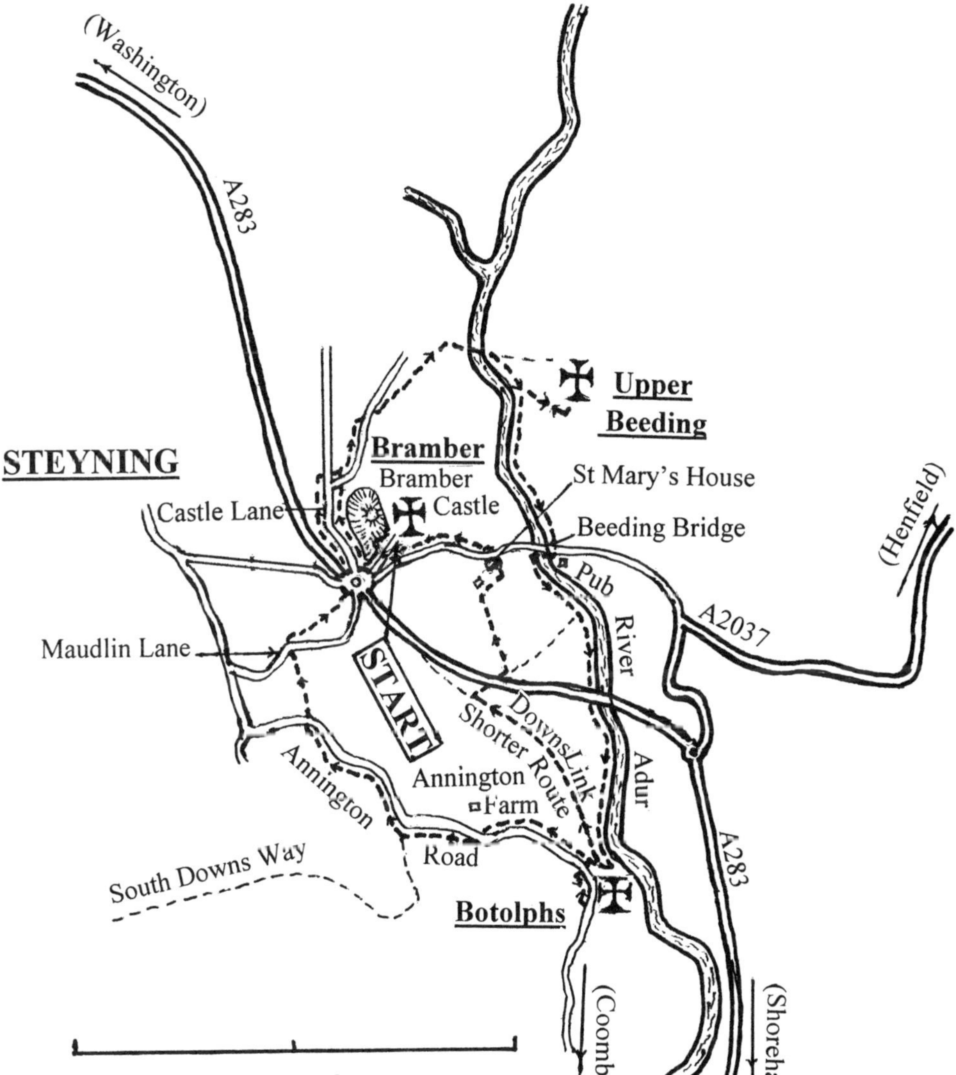
(Washington)
A283
Upper Beeding
Bramber
STEYNING
Bramber Castle
St Mary's House
Castle Lane
Beeding Bridge
(Henfield)
Pub
River
A2037
Maudlin Lane
START
Downs Link
Shorter Route
Adur
Annington Road
Annington Farm
A283
South Downs Way
Botolphs
(Coombes)
(Shoreham)
One Mile

Beeding

River Adur

bridge. Botolphs suffered more than Bramber from this catastrophe. People left the village and the size of the church was reduced. This abandonment has the advantage today that we can enjoy the building in its ancient simplicity. The south wall of the nave and one small window in this wall are Saxon. Above the Saxon chancel arch are remnants of murals such as may once have covered all the walls. The small tower and the chancel are 13th century. The north wall of the nave has a blocked arcade, evidence of the north aisle, built in 1250 and removed when the people left. There are low windows in the chancel to allow lepers to watch the mass. There was a hospital for lepers at Bramber in 13th century. They had to walk to St Peter`s, now St Botolphs for the church services. Bramber Church was for gentry!

The Walk

After visiting the Bramber Church and Castle, you have a choice of ways:

To avoid the road, *look for a recess in the car park. Here is a narrow unmarked footpath, overhung with trees and leading down the side of the hill. At the bottom you can cross a small field from one stile to another. At the track turn right and continue at * below.*

Go down to the main road at the entrance to the car park and turn sharp right.

Enter Castle Lane and walk round the base of the hill on your right. At the first opportunity, turn right into a track.

* This enclosed track leads behind houses on the edge of Bramber and down to water meadows with a view to the Downs. Make for the footbridge over the fast flowing River Adur.

Cross the river, turn right and walk along the bank. Upper Beeding Church and the handsome house that stands on the site of the Priory can be seen nearby. Turn left at the footpath towards the church and climb up steps.

Retrace your steps to the river and turn left to continue on course for ½ mile to Beeding Bridge. There are shops here and a pub overlooking the river.

From the shops and pub, cross back over the river and go down to the west bank where you have an easy riverside stroll, marred only by the ever present noise of traffic. Try to ignore it and admire the views over meadowlands to the Downs. Go under the A283 and keep going beside the river for another ½ mile. The noise of traffic recedes. Far ahead to the right you can see the chapel of Lancing College (See Walk 19).

Nearer to hand on the left you can see a footbridge over the river. Do not go as far as the footbridge. Instead turn right at the waymarker and head west on the South Downs Way. In 100 metres you first ignore the Downs Link turning on the right. You then cross a farm bridge over a rill in a copse and come to the tarmac lane, Coombes Road. Turn left here for nearby Botolphs Church.

From Botolphs Church return to Coombes Road and retrace your steps to the copse. You then have a choice.

For the shorter route *back to Bramber including St Mary`s House, described in Walk 10, enter the copse and return to the Downs Link, now on your left. This takes you northwest along the old railway line. In ½ a mile, as you approach the A283, turn sharp right to walk up to the road. Cross with care to the footpath opposite. As you join this path, you fork left almost immediately to resume a northwest course. At the back of some* *bungalows turn right then left on a track to St Mary`s House. From St Mary`s House continue to the Street and turn left. In 300 metres you are back at the familiar roundabout outside Steyning. Turn right for Bramber Church.*

For the longer route back to Bramber, avoid the copse and stay on Coombes Road taking the westerly route of the South Downs Way. A short narrow footpath follows the edge of the lane then returns to it. Pass the buildings of Annington Farm and start climbing. The South Downs Way departs to the left. We continue on our lane. It soon dips and in 200 metres passes Annington Mere Farm on the left. In 50 metres turn right into a field and take the footpath uphill hugging the hedge on the left.

In 300 metres cross Maudlin Lane to the footpath opposite. You enter a gently sloping field, turn right to pass a charming house on the right and saunter down to the left corner. The sound of traffic ahead warns you that you that you are returning to the roundabout below Bramber Castle. Cross with care to this familiar track to the castle and church.

Bramber

Botolphs

Bramber

5 Walks
Near Hayward's Heath

Walks 23, 24, 26, 27,28 and 30 take us by the River Ouse and a new Ouse Valley Way
(See the end of this book for more details of Sussex Ouse Valley Way)

Walk 21: Ardingly to West Hoathley

We pass by a world famous show ground, a Millenium Seed Bank in Kew`s country estate and a huge Sussex reservoir in order to look at the distant past when pious Saxons and ambitious Normans founded churches in remote clearings in the Weald.

Starting Point: Car Park at the Toilets and Recycling Point off High Street, Ardingly **GR**347297 **Distance:** 8 Miles **Map:** OS Explorer 135
Terrain: Some country lanes, some steep wooded slopes, some flat land.

Churches

The Parish Church of St Peter`s, Ardingly stood in a 'leah' or Saxon clearing in the forest at a strategic point above a tributary of the River Ouse. There was probably a simple church here then. As usual the Normans supplanted it with their own solid stone building. Lewes Priory held this church. The Norman church

Ardingly

was completely destroyed and replaced with a new church in the Decorated style in the early 14th century. This consisted of nave, chancel and south aisle. The chancel tomb with an effigy of a priest dates from this period. Some windows in the chancel have hood mouldings of oak. The tower was added in the early 15th

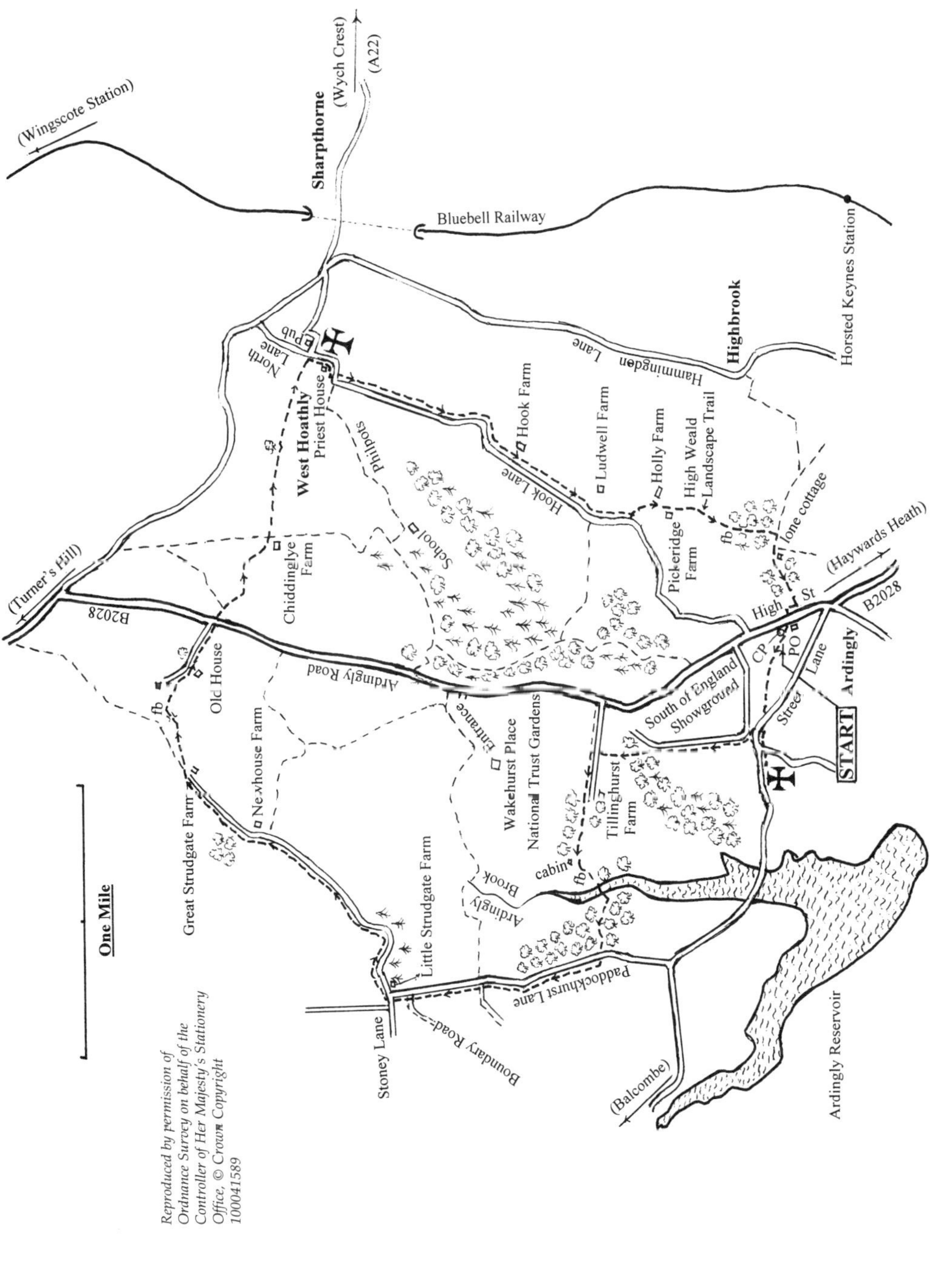
(Wingscote Station)
Sharpthorne
(Wych Crest)
(A22)
Bluebell Railway
Horsted Keynes Station
Highbrook
Hammingden Lane
North Lane
Pub
West Hoathly
Priest House
Philpots
Hook Farm
Hook Lane
Ludwell Farm
Holly Farm
High Weald Landscape Trail
Pickeridge Farm
fb
lone cottage
(Haywards Heath)
(Turner's Hill)
B2028
Chiddinglye Farm
School
High St
B2028
CP
PO
Lane
Ardingly
Street
START
Ardingly Road
Old House
fb
Newhouse Farm
Entrance
Wakehurst Place
National Trust Gardens
South of England Showground
Tillinghurst Farm
Great Strudgate Farm
cabin
fb
Ardingly Brook
Little Strudgate Farm
Paddockhurst Lane
Stoney Lane
Boundary Road
(Balcombe)
Ardingly Reservoir
One Mile

century. It is quite short with very thick walls, probably a defense against a possible French invasion. The rustic porch was added around 1500 and the north aisle in 1887. The whole building presents a perfect picture in stone. Horsham tiles complete the picture. If, sadly the church is locked when you arrive, it may be some consolation to view the lovely exterior.

St Margaret`s Church, West Hoathly stood in a 'leah' or Saxon clearing in heathland. The church has an open, elevated aspect and I recommend a wander down the churchyard where seats have been placed to offer a lovely view south. A small rectangular Norman church was built here in 1090. The Priory of St Pancras, Lewes held this church. It was enlarged 100 years later and the round Norman pillars on the north side are of this period. Also the font of Sussex marble was made around 1180. The chancel was extended in the 13th century. Two windows have painted designs on their rere arches. The Victorians painted over the original design here. A large 13th century oak chest was made to collect money for the Crusaders. The south aisle was widened in 14th century. Early in 15th century a tower was added in Perpendicular style. It has a broached spire and six bells. Swifts nest in the tower in the Spring.

The Priest House, West Hoathly is a 15th century timber framed house, probably built for Lewes Priory. It is open as a museum, 1st March to 30th October.

(Phone 01342 810479)

The Walk

From the Car Park in Ardingly, head west away from the High Street. The Sports Ground is on your right and back gardens on your left. You pass a play area with tennis courts. Keep straight on to follow the enclosed tarmac path. It passes a school on the left and brings you out at Street Lane. Turn right and walk along this quiet lane for 200 metres. Just past a waymarked footpath on the right, you come to St Peter`s Church at a road junction.

Return to the waymarked footpath, now on your left. It leads to the South Of England Showground. Go through the gate into the wide road on the edge of the showground. Turn left to the bend in the road. Turn right here and head due north on the road for 500 metres with the showground on your right. The road forks veering slightly to the right. You take the left fork into woodland. Come out of the wood on an enclosed path through fields for horses. In 250 metres at a T-junction, turn left onto a tarmac farm track.

Follow the track west for a first glimpse of Ardingly Reservoir on the left. Pass Tillinghurst Farm and wild fowl pond on your left. Keep straight on hugging woodland on the right. Descend sloping fields with another view over the Reservoir at the bottom. Go down into the wood. You are on the edge of Wakehurst Place National Trust Gardens with rhododendrons in the hedge on the right. Come down next to their cosy cabin from which you are excluded by a locked gate. Never mind! –There are joys in store.

Turn left away from the gate and descend further a wooded slope. Avoid the Nature Reserve on the left and follow the path down to the right to the calm waters at the northern end of the huge reservoir, fed by Ardingly Brook. Here you cross surely the longest footbridge in Sussex and certainly the loveliest. It takes you high above the water where trees are reflected.

Water Mill at Horsted

Once across the water, do not be tempted to the Nature Reserve again on the left. Instead, follow the narrow winding path up the hill. You have to climb through woodland for 350 metres. You come out at Paddockhurst Lane.

Turn right and walk along the lane for a mile. Avoid all turnings until you reach crossroads eventually. The way ahead is marked 'Back Lane'. Avoid this and turn right into a farm road, passing Little Strudgate Farm.

Head east then northeast on this farm road for over a mile. Pass a pond down on the left then Newhouse Farm. Avoid the path to the right. When you finally climb to the scattered buildings of Great Strudgate Farm, the road narrows and becomes a track. Keep straight on to pass cottages on your right.

You leave the track to cross to an elevated field. Avoid the path straight on and fork right towards woodland, guided by the line of telegraph posts. Enter the wood and follow the sloping path down through the fringe of trees into a secluded valley. Turn left at the bottom. You pass a pond on the right.

In the next field turn right and cross a footbridge. Hug the hedge on the right then go up a dark enclosed path with steps for part of the way. Pass Old House. Turn right and walk along the driveway. Towards the end of the drive you will see more ponds.

In 400 metres you reach Ardingly Road, B2028. Cross diagonally right towards Stonelands West Lodge. **Note:** there is a pub in sight further along to the right.

Take the path down beside the lodge (a concrete waymarker is fixed in the ground). In 200 metres you come to a glen with a tiny brick parapet over a bridge. Turn right to walk through woods. You come out of the woods to a field with a house perched on top of a hillock. Do not climb up to the house.

Follow the edge of the wood on the right. Re-enter the wood and turn left immediately. A path along a platform leads up through woodland to a farm track. Turn left and walk up the track to Chiddinglye Farm. At cross tracks keep straight on heading east along the concrete road. This leads to a field path continuing east for ½ mile. Hug the hedge on the left, pass a pond in a dip and you reach West Hoathly, conveniently opposite the pub.

In West Hoathly, turn right and south for the church in North Street. Continue south along North Street passing the nearby Priest House. If you have resisted other temptations, you may eat sandwiches in the garden here for a small entry fee.

Continue on course past a bowling green on the left at a bend in the road. Avoid the High Weald Landscape Trail towards Philpots Manor School on the right.

It is easier and in my opinion pleasanter to stick to the road which soon becomes Hook Lane. Pass Langridge Farm on the left and in a mile, the High Weald Landscape Trail rejoins the road at Ludwell Farm. Continue on the road south with the trail in tow. In 200 metres fork left towards Holly Farm. The lane sinks. Avoid the path on the left and keep on down to Pickeridge.

A view opens across the Weald to the Downs. You can enjoy this view as you stride down through the fields. First, hug the boundary on the right then the hedge on the left. At the bottom go through a narrow strip of woodland, crossing a footbridge over a stream.

Climb up beside the wood on the right and you come to sloping parkland with copper beeches scattered around. Make for the lone cottage ahead and keep straight on, avoiding the path to the left. Pass beside the cottage on your left. Enter more woodland to climb the steep slope back up to Ardingly. The last lap leaves the wood for a sloping field.

Cross another small field to a side road leading to High Street. Turn right, pass the post office opposite, then in another 150 metres you are back at the car park on the left.

Walk 22: Worth Abbey to Worth Church

Gently sloping woodland reminds us that we are walking in the once impenetrable Sussex Weald. Our reward comes in two outstanding and contrasting churches.

Starting Point: Main Car Park, Worth Abbey, just east of Worth School
(Only the church is open to the public. Avoid straying into the school area, monastery grounds marked 'Private', and all other buildings).
GR318343 **Distance:** 5 Miles **Terrain:** Flat, wooded **Map:** OS Explorer 135

Warning: *Nearly ½ mile of this walk is along pavements beside busy roads on the edge of Crawley Also there are two roundabouts to negotiate – not too daunting. Take care and return with relief to the bliss and sanity of the forest.*

The Churches

Worth Abbey Church is the most important building at Worth and possibly the finest example of 1960`s church architecture in Britain. It stands in the grounds of a 550 acre estate belonging to Worth Abbey. The main house was called Paddockhurst House until the monks bought it in 1933 after the death of the previous owner, Lord Cowdray. The surrounding land is still called Paddockhurst Estates. The Benedictine community of Downside, near Bath established a Priory

Worth Abbey Church

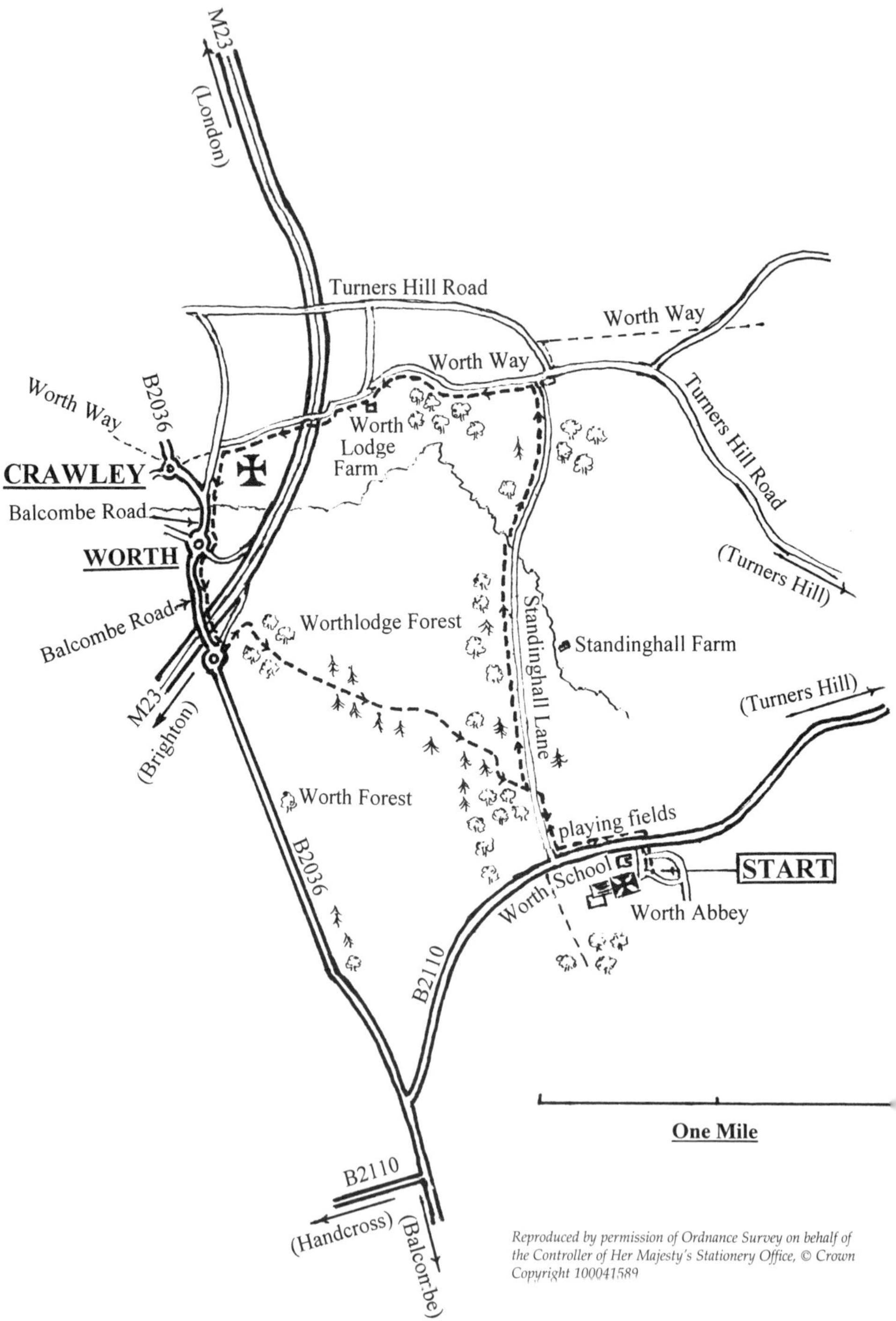
M23
(London)
Turners Hill Road
Worth Way
Worth Way
Worth Way
B2036
CRAWLEY
Worth Lodge Farm
Balcombe Road
WORTH
Turners Hill Road
(Turners Hill)
Balcombe Road
Worthlodge Forest
Standinghall Lane
Standinghall Farm
M23
(Brighton)
(Turners Hill)
Worth Forest
playing fields
START
Worth School
Worth Abbey
B2036
B2110
One Mile
B2110
(Handcross)
(Balcombe)

in the then rose garden, now south of the church. The Tudor-style Victorian mansion and other buildings were converted to open a school for boys, run by the monastery. In 1965 the Priory became an Abbey. Starting in 1966, the magnificent modern abbey church, designed by Francis Pollen, was built in stages over the years. He used a bridge building tecnique to gain space. It is a square base with a conical roof. The clerestory windows are cunningly placed high up under the conical roof. You enter the narthex to face the information centre. Behind you, steps lead down into the church. This normally holds 700 to 800 people and can be re-arranged to take double those numbers. This monastic church has prayer services throughout the day.

Times of Services can be found on the website, http://www.worthabbey.net

Worth Church, St Nicholas is a large Saxon cruciform building. In 10th century the church occupied an important place in the Forest of the Weald. It was a minster or principal church, possibly attached to a college. Today the church is on the edge of Crawley and has been separated from the forest by the teaming traffic of the M23. It has retained many original Saxon features. The solid arches of the crossing are Saxon; the chancel arch is one of the largest of its kind. There are 3 unique Saxon windows, two on the north side of the nave and one on the south, above and to the left of the Victorian porch. In each a stone baluster separates the twin windows. Pilaster strips on the outside stonework are another Saxon feature. The Victorians have rebuilt the large semi –circular apse of the chancel using the original stone. The square font is 13th century. The west door, now the entrance is 14th century. The carved pulpit is dated 1577. The lychgate is also 16th century. The tower and broach spire are Victorian. In 1986 the roof was damaged in a fire. The architect took this opportunity to strengthen the top of the Saxon walls. A new lighter weight roof was then added. This beautiful, spacious Saxon church deserves to have its place in the forest restored to it.

The Walk

From Worth Abbey Church walk back along the driveway to the road, B2110. Cross to the verge opposite. Pass Worth School on the left and the playing fields on the right. In 350 metres, turn right at a footpath sign and enter woodland at a 'Paddockhurst Estate' notice board. A wide straight track, known as Standinghall Lane leads due north through Worth Forest for 1½ miles. Do not be tempted on any side paths but make a mental note the public right of way on the left in ¼ mile. Our track goes gently downhill for 1 mile, crosses a stream and climbs gently uphill for ½ a mile.

At the northern end of the forest you reach Turners Hill Road. Do not leave the forest but turn left and join Worth Way, a cycle track. This takes you on another straight path heading west. It runs along the edge of the forest. In 500 metres at Worth Lodge Farm, veer left to cross the farm road and continue southwest for 200 metres.

There is a generous bridge over the M23 for cycles and horses. We avail ourselves of this bridge to reach houses on the edge of Crawley. We see Worth Church ahead on the left. Turn left to pass through the lych gate and a narrow avenue of trees known as the '10 Apostles'.

After visiting Worth Church, continue southwest along Worth Way to a road junction. Take the grassy footpath on the left beside the road leading south into Balcombe Road. Cross at pedestrian traffic lights to the right hand pavement. Negotiate a roundabout and keep on course to pass Europa Hotel on the left. This is still Balcombe Road. It takes you across the M23 on a road bridge with pavements. Once across, walk on the left hand verge of the road as you approach another roundabout. Cross the M23 slip road with care to a gated track and a welcome footpath sign. As pedestrians we are privileged to re-enter Worth Forest here.

The well signposted track leads northeast for 100 metres then curves to the right. Avoid the track straight on. After this right fork, follow the track climbing gently southeast. In 1 mile you rejoin the outward track, Standinghall Lane. Turn right and retrace your steps to the Car Park.

Worth Church

Walk 23: Staplefield to Cuckfield

Cuckfield Church once served the community from Staplefield to Haywards Heath. Churchgoers had to walk or ride across the Weald. We follow in their footsteps across a landscape still rich in wood and heathland. Staplefield now has its own church Come here in May for the early purple orchids that take over the churchyard.

Starting Point: Staplefield Church **GR**278282 **Distance:** 9-10 Miles
Terrain: Gentle slopes and ridges **Maps:** OS Explorer 134 and 135
One path crosses a Golf Course. OS Landranger 198 for the whole walk
Local Information: Ouse Valley Viaduct, built in 1812 is over ¼ mile long with 37 arches that still carry mainline trains.

The Churches

St Mark`s, Staplefield is a charming example of a Victorian church, built all of a piece. The architect, Benjamin Ferrey was content with a simple stone building, nave and chancel, lancet windows and a bellcote at the west end. Inside, the tall, pointed chancel arch frames delightful and colourful walls. A cheerful glow comes from the high wall paintings of angels and the three lancets with stained glass, all by Kempe. At a lower level, wood panels hide more wall paintings. One day these panels will be removed to reveal the treasure behind. Stained glass is in all the narrow lancets.

Staplefield

The Parish Church of Holy Trinity, Cuckfield is a large church on the edge of a market town. It has a fine position with a quiet close on the north and an open aspect across fields to the south. This imposing church encloses an invisible Norman chapel. The site of the first chapel is inside the nave of the existing building. In 1250 Bishop of Chichester, Saint Richard arranged with the Prior of St Pancras Priory, Lewes for the chapel to be enlarged. The Priory owned 39 churches, including 'Kukefeld' with charters granted 1088 by William de Warenne (See Introduction under Normans). His son confirmed the charters in 1092. In 13th century the square tower and the south chapel were added. Three arches with round columns in the south aisle belong to this period. In 14th century the north aisle

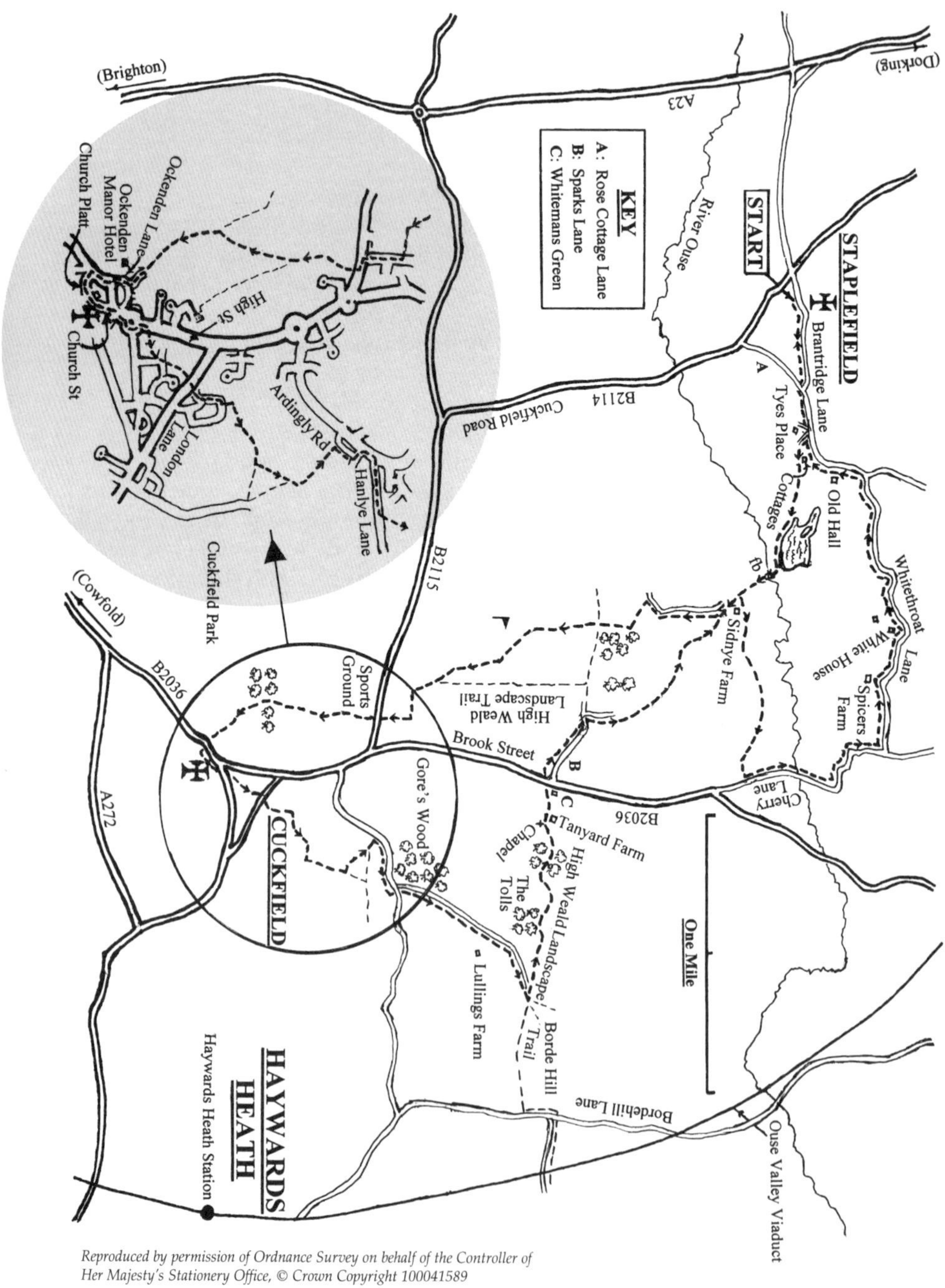
(Brighton)
(Dorking)
A23
KEY
A: Rose Cottage Lane
B: Sparks Lane
C: Whitemans Green
START
STAPLEFIELD
River Ouse
Brantridge Lane
A
Tyes Place
Cottages
Old Hall
Whitethroat Lane
White House
Spicers Farm
fb
Sidnye Farm
B2114
Cuckfield Road
B2115
High Weald Landscape Trail
Sports Ground
Cuckfield Park
(Cowfold)
B2036
A272
Brook Street
B
C
Cherry Lane
B2036
Tanyard Farm
Chapel
The Tolls
High Weald Landscape Trail
Gore's Wood
CUCKFIELD
One Mile
Lullings Farm
Borde Hill
Bordehill Lane
Ouse Valley Viaduct
HAYWARDS HEATH
Haywards Heath Station
Ockenden Lane
Ockenden Manor Hotel
Church Platt
Church St
High St
London Lane
Ardingly Rd
Hanlye Lane

with hexagonal columns and the shingled broach spire were added. The spire is big and tall. In 15th century the outside walls of the aisles were raised and this blinded the clerestory windows. The 15th century ceiling with tie beams was plain then. In 1865 to 1886 the ceiling was transformed with delightful paintings. The design by Kempe is a colourful pattern with red and white roses. Ten carved, winged angels stand at the base of the hammer beams. Kempe also designed the windows in the northwest of the church. His are quite distinctive and the colours are soft compared with the other Victorian stained glass windows.

The Walk

Staplefield Church stands on Brantridge Lane near the widespread village green. Walk east along the lane and away from the green. Pass a pond on the left, houses and Rose Cottage Lane on the right. Continue another 200 metres. Just past a signpost to Tyes Place on the right, turn right towards Old Hall Cottages. The path goes between the cottages and emerges onto a gently sloping field with views south.

Follow the path on the left hugging the hedge. It divides you from the opulence of the grounds of Old Hall, owned by one of the Saatchi brothers so I am told We catch a glimpse of a huge ornate greenhouse and then a portico and a statue.

Enter woodland to go down a damp path, deprived of a view of the lake by the bank and high trees. A footbridge over the little River Ouse finally releases you. Take the clear path up the slope to nearby Sidnye Farm, now a hub of environmental improvements.

In the farmyard avoid the left turn and go straight on passing a cottage on the right. When you overlook a horse exercise enclosure, turn left then right to leave the farm along a **wide track** heading south. You pass a cleared pond and go up between newly planted hedges. The track leads to the top of a low ridge where you can see another larger, newly cleared pond down among trees on the left. You leave the track after it turns to the right.

Find a new access gate into the field ahead. Veer left downhill across this field and towards a small gate into a double hedgerow of trees. Cross a footbridge to the next field then resume a southerly course uphill, hugging woodland on your left.

In 300 metres you reach crosspaths and go straight on. Cross a short plank to arrive on the edge of a golf course. Stay on the edge and continue south for 400 metres. As you approach a new plantation, look out for a path on the left to take you across the golf course. Cross a small stream and keep on course up through golfers to enjoy their view north over the Weald and the distant Ouse Valley Viaduct.

You leave the golf course at woodland where you join the High Weald Landscape Trail. This leads through the wood, a short climb. Turn left to cross a field and then right when you reach houses. A lane leads to the B2115 at Whitemans Green. Cross diagonally left.

The High Weald Landscape Trail continues south along a driveway. At the end you can see a sports field on the right but you follow the path on the left. You step into a grassy haven, a sweeping descent sheltered by trees. The tall spire of

Cuckfield Church can be seen ahead. Follow the trail south, avoiding turnings to left and right. Go down to cross a footbridge then bear left and up a slope.

Take a quiet lane into Cuckfield. A high wall hides the ground to the right. Turn right at Ockenden Lane and pass the entrance to Ockenden Manor Hotel. *Lunches and teas are served in this handsome stone house with a lovely black and white timbered section.* You come into the village at South Street. Turn right onto this main street. Pass a pub on the left then turn left for the church.

Cuckfield

Leave Cuckfield Church by the lychgate and walk along Church Street. You are then back in South Street and turn right. Go up past shops and carry straight on at the roundabout. You are now in High Street. Opposite the Museum, turn right into Mytton Twitton, an enclosed way. It bends to the left, crosses a residential road, then reaches London Lane.

Cross diagonally right to Glebe Twitton. This leads to another residential road on the edge of Cuckfield. Keep on course and you find you are in a cul-de-sac with a footpath at the end. Take this path for 50 metres then turn right into fields. Head northeast gently uphill for ½ mile. At the top turn left across a field back to residential roads. Go through Ardingly Road and turn right. Pass the old hospital on the left. Curve right to the main road, Hanlye Lane. There is a pavement here, separated from traffic by a hedge.

In 100 metres at the first gap, cross with care to the private road opposite. It is a wide, tarmac drive with Gore`s wood where bluebells grow on the left. Keep on this drive for one kilometre. On the way you pass Lullings Farm then a lodge on the left. After the lodge the drive enters parkland and you can just spy ahead to the right some buildings of Borde Hill, famous for its tree collection.

Our route takes us away from Borde Hill. As you approach crossways, turn left into a footpath across an elevated field. You are once again on High Weald and

Landscape Trail. It has a fine aspect over the Ouse Valley on the right. In the next field make for a small wood, 'the Tolls'. Pass it on your left. Then go down fields to find the corner entrance to another wood. Here you take a wide path through bluebells in the Spring.

After 150 metres of woodland walk, turn right to emerge into fields. Hug the hedge on the right. In 300 metres turn right to slip down a short steep slope and into another field. Make for Tanyard Farm ahead and go through deserted buildings to pass a large detached house on the left. There is a small black corrugated chapel on the right. This has been converted into a centre for art and picture frames.

You reach the B2036, Brook Street. Cross diagonally right to the track opposite, Spark`s Lane. Pass a car workshop and some bungalows. In 350 metres at crossways, avoid the track and path ahead. Keep on the lane as it bends right towards Collins Farm.

Pass the cottage on the right and continue northwest to walk gently down a sloping field. Look towards Sidnye Farm in the distance left. Hug the hedge on the right. At the bottom, cross a stream into the next field. Hug the hedge on the left and climb towards Sidnye Farm for we are going back there. Before you reach the farm, turn left across the narrow field to join the familiar **wide track**. Go through the farmyard and turn right.

This is Ouse Valley Way and follows the access lane. Pass a cottage on the left and continue east on this quiet tarmac lane for one kilometre. Wild flowers grow on the banks. Towards the end of the lane you have a distant view ahead to Ouse Valley Viaduct

You come to Cherry Lane and turn left. (Ouse Valley Way turns right). Go down to cross the little River Ouse then turn left into a footpath. This gently rising path cuts off a corner of Cherry Lane. In 200 metres rejoin the lane and turn left. Carry on uphill on the lane which curves to the right and heads due north. In another 200 metres there is a pond on the right and a cottage on the left.

Turn left before the cottage and head west along a private, concrete lane. This is Whitethroat Lane, one mile long and as delightful as the name suggests. There are views over the River Ouse on the left. Pass the handsome house and garden of Spicers Farm on the left. Then follow the lane as it bends right and heads for White House. Pass the house on the left and a pond on the right. Do not be tempted up the driveway to the right.

Keep on the lane as it curves to the back of White House and offers a lovely view of the gardens on the left and the lake below ahead. Avoid the footpath off to the right. Go down the lane past the lake on the left, over a stream and uphill through woodland. Wood anenomes grow here. At the end the lane swings to the right and you go straight on along a short footpath with some steps down to Brantridge Lane.

Turn left for a mile walk along Brantridge Lane back to Staplefield Church. On the way you pass Old Hall on the left then the familiar path to Old Hall Cottages. Finally pass Rose Cottage Lane and you will have had a sample of lovely lanes!

Walk 24: Lindfield to Horsted Keynes

Time is essential on this walk to savour the Weald, the River Ouse and admire two pretty villages with ancient buildings. We cross the Bluebell Railway and hear the steam trains.

Starting Point: Wilderness Car Park, Lindfield **GR**349257
Note: There is a 4 hour restriction on parking, Sundays. Other days parking is allowed for 23 hours.
Map: OS Explorer 135 **Distance:** 9 Miles **Terrain:** Gently undulating
One of the oldest water mill sites in Sussex is at Horsted Keynes.

The Churches

Lindfield

All Saints' Lindfield stands at the northern end of the "finest village street in East Sussex" * – (Pevsner). Among the amazing ancient houses near the church, the grandest is Old Place (1590) and the oldest are two 15th century cottages. The church of course goes back much further. In 765 King Aldwolf mentions 'Lindefeldia', the space of linden trees. It was a minster church, linked to the College of Canons of South Malling near Lewes. When the college was dissolved in 1545, Lindfield went into decline. The fabric suffered for churchwardens sold 'stones, little old timber, old carved work, the rood loft'. Despite this neglect, it emerges as a large church and has kept its 13th century basic shape. From this same century, the tower is probably the oldest part of the building. It has a broach spire and wooden shingles. The arcades of the transepts are Decorated. The chancel arcade is Perpendicular. In 1991, the

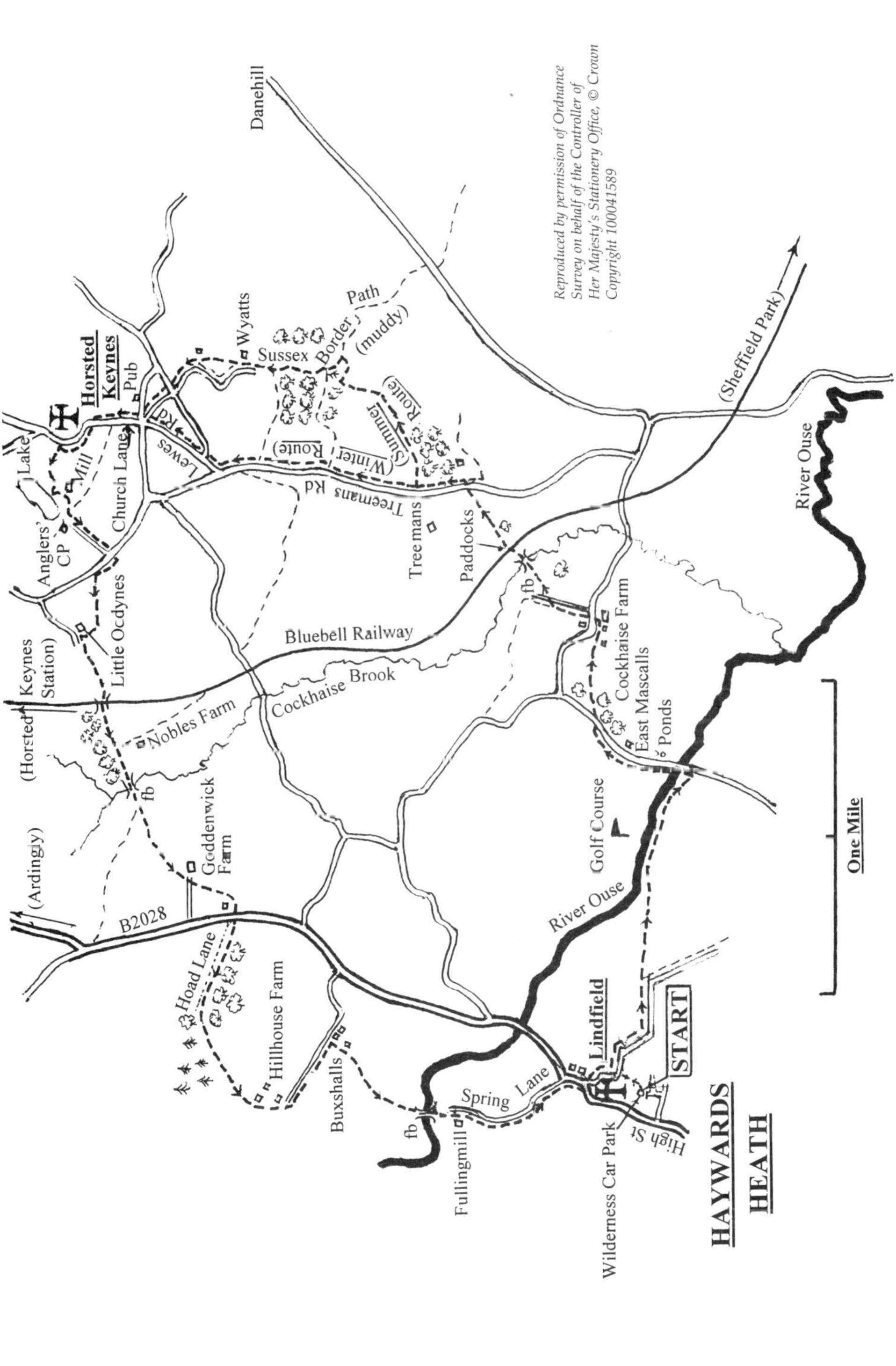
Danehill
Reproduced by permission of Ordnance Survey on behalf of the Controller of Her Majesty's Stationery Office, © Crown Copyright 100041589
Horsted Keynes
Pub
Wyatts
Sussex Border Path
(muddy)
Lake
Mill
Church Lane
Lewes Rd
Winter Route
Summer Route
Treemans Rd
(Sheffield Park)
Anglers' CP
Little Ocdynes
Treemans
Paddocks
River Ouse
(Horsted Keynes Station)
Bluebell Railway
fb
Cockhaise Farm
Cockhaise Brook
Nobles Farm
East Mascalls
Ponds
fb
Goddenwick Farm
Golf Course
One Mile
(Ardingly)
B2028
River Ouse
Hoad Lane
Hillhouse Farm
Lindfield
START
Buxshalls
Spring Lane
fb
Fullingmill
Wilderness Car Park
High St
HAYWARDS HEATH

former chancel arch was moved nearly to the back of the nave. From here you have a good view to the chancel, the early 17th century embossed ceiling and the five-light Decorated east window. Two angel corbels have been moved from the south chapel and are now on either side of the east window. The stained glass in this church is modern and the influence of Charles Kempe who lived at Old Place in 19th century, is apparent in some. (See the 'Guide to the History of the Church'). There have been two Victorian restorations of the church. In 1848 the architect, John H. Taylor has left us a church in mainly Decorated style. During this restoration three wall paintings were destroyed but a Miss Slater did a very good drawing of one from the south transept (see the Guide). In 1882 restorers compared the earlier restoration with the parent who 'cured the child of squinting by cutting its head off'!

St Giles' Church, Horsted Keynes lies northeast to southwest where it catches the rising sun and may stand on the site of a Pagan temple. 'Horsted' is Saxon for 'a horse place'. 'Keynes', pronounced 'kanes' comes from the Norman 'Cahaignes'. William the Conqueror presented Ralf de Cahaignes with this manor as a battle reward. The present church reveals its Norman origin with its central tower. The tall, slender broached spire is shingled. The round tower arch is Norman. The door in the north aisle behind the font may be even older. It is known as the 'Saxon doorway' and was moved here from the nave in1885. The chancel arch is Decorated. The lancet windows in the chancel are Early English. The small square-topped one in the south wall of the chancel is Perpendicular. The large window in the west of the nave is also Perpendicular. All the stained glass is modern. There is a small, 13th century effigy of a crusader, possibly Richard de Cahaignes, in the north wall of the chancel. There is a headless lady on the south wall of the nave. This 14th century elegant brass has sadly been damaged.

The Walk

Some paths on the return walk were overgrown. I am told they have been cleared.

In the corner of Wilderness Car Park, furthest away from the entrance, there is a walkway to Lindfield Parish Church.

With the church on your left, turn right along a narrow cul de sac, passing under the high windows of the extraordinary wooden pavilion. Hug the huge wall on the left, pass the road with a row of cottages on the right.

In the corner opposite enter the dark alleyway. It leads to an enclosed path heading east with fields on either side. In ½ mile the main track, Ouse Valley Way goes off to the right. You turn left into a field and continue east. Go down to a wooded field boundary and cross to a flat meadow. The River Ouse is ahead.

Walk beside the river on your left. It is quite narrow here. A golf course can be spied on the other side. In 1 kilometre you reach East Mascalls Road. Turn left and cross the river. Walk carefully beside the road for 500 metres. You pass a farm with goldfish ponds and a model house on your right then the handsome house of East Mascalls. The golf course is on your left. Just after the entrance to the golf course turn right at the finger post and follow the footpath through woodland.

Climb up 75 metres through the wood to an open field. Make for a building in the centre of the field, then Cockhaise Farm ahead. When you reach the tarmac road, turn right. A few cottages line the road. On the left there is a detached cottage with a distinctive overhang below the roof. Turn left just after the cottage into an earth track, heading northeast. You go through a copse with a hidden pond on the right. In 300 metres from the road, fork right.

You enter an elevated field and look across to the copse opposite. Avoid this copse and keep to the left side of the field. You come to a slope overlooking the Bluebell Railway Line. Go down, heading northeast towards a flat footbridge over Cockhaise Brook and

Pause! The footpath ahead is well hidden. Just to the left, opposite there is a wooded causeway. Well concealed in here – at least in summer – is a footpath sign.

Climb up to the causeway and walk along it to the railway line. Make sure no train is coming and cross the line. Descend to the footpath on the other side. It turns immediately right and follows the fringe field beside a horse paddock. Above the paddock, at some distance is a large house. Follow the curves of the paddock boundary on the left. Avoid the wooded slope down to the right.

When you reach Treemans Road, you have a choice: (The checker of this walk prefers to follow the summer walk, the Sussex Border Path he asserts is not too muddy!)

In winter or wet weather here is a short, simple road route: *turn left and walk with care along the road for one mile to Horsted Keynes. Enter the village on the Lewes Road. Walk to the post office and village green then proceed at instructions below, marked *.*

In summer or dry weather, avoid the path opposite. Cross Treemans Road diagonally left. Go through the hedge to a strip of land used as an off-road footpath. Turn left and head north. Follow the hedge on the left for 350 metres. You reach a driveway to a nearby brick house on the right. Cross the drive to a large field and turn right so that you walk behind the house. Go down to a corner on the right where the field joins East Wood.

Walk northeast along the edge of the wood and continue on course when you reach a gap. In 500 metres, at another field corner cross to a little mound on the other side and bear slightly left. Follow the hedge on your right to enter woodland ahead. The path goes downhill through the wood and swerves to the right. It leaves the wood, curves left. Shortly after crossing a footbridge, turn left to re-enter the wood. In 20 metres you join the Sussex Border Path.

When you reach the Sussex Border Path turn left and follow this wide, rutted, muddy track through Sandpits Wood, avoiding paths on the left. It heads north for 1 kilometre to Horsted Keynes. Only the first part of the way is through woodland. In 400 metres it opens to a dry track. Keep straight on and pass a handsome black and white house, Wyatts on the right. Avoid walking along a manicured, pebbly drive as the automatic gates at the end are liable to block your way. Instead, take the parallel path behind the hedge. It leads to a bungalow where you turn left and join Wyatts Road. Turn right for Horsted Keynes. In 250 metres you reach crossroads. Go straight on along the narrow Chapel Lane to emerge at the centre of Horsted Keynes. Turn right to an apparent T-junction but you will see some bollards opposite guarding Church Lane.

* *Before heading down to the church, you may wish to take this last opportunity to buy refreshment. There is a pub across the village green on the right.*

Return to the bollards opposite Lewes Rd and walk downhill between delightful cottages in Church Lane. Sussex Border Path also follows this route. The church steeple beckons as you proceed. Welcoming roses in summer line the path to the church porch.

From Horsted Keynes Church return along the rose garden path and turn right. You have rejoined the Sussex Border Path – but not for long. In 50 metres turn left into an enclosed path down through woodland. When it seems you can sink no more, the path leaves the wood for a sheltered field and curves left then right, passing an ancient water mill.

Go past the water mill and follow its access lane. There is an extensive lake on the right and a seat has been provided for those who wish to gaze on it. Do not be tempted to left or right. Continue along the lane past an anglers` car park on the right where the lane bends to the left.

In 300 metres you reach a tarmac road, Waterbury Hill. Turn right and cross the road to the footpath opposite at the base of a sloping field. Climb diagonally right towards Little Oddynes Farm. Turn round to admire the view. You may just see the spire of the church we have left well behind us. Take the track to the farm then turn left through the mucky farmyard. Once out of the yard, keep on course southwest across an elevated field. In 300 metres you come to a sturdy bridge over the Bluebell Line.

After crossing the Bluebell Line you follow the edge of the wood on the right. This, I think, is the prettiest part of the walk. A little white cottage on the left, Nobles Farm overlooks rolling fields with remnants of forestland and Cockhaise Brook away below on the right wends its way through sheep country.

Avoid turning left to Nobles Farm. Keep straight on downhill, hugging the wood on the right. In the valley turn right at a footbridge over the brook.

Continue on course, southwest on the other side and you come to another sloping field. Fork left and climb to Goddenwick Farm. The narrow footpath past the farm is up on the right. It follows the boundary round the farmhouse then goes through a small wood. You emerge to an immaculate little sports` field.

Enjoy the walk along the farm drive for a short way and turn left into a footpath across more fields. Cross the first little field to a gap then climb diagonally right through the next one, heading for a brick garage. Pass the garage and the cottages it serves and you reach the main road to Lindfield, B2028.

Cross with care to the footpath opposite. It heads southwest through dense woods. The first kilometre is along Hoad Lane. After that the lane narrows to an enclosed path that comes out along the side of a private garden near Hillhouse Farm. Pass the house and keep straight on along the road for 150 metres. Follow the road as it curves left.

Keep on this road for 500 metres as it heads southeast. Just before the hamlet of

Buxhalls, turn right into rough fields. You are still on the edge of Buxhalls and join a track past an elevated bungalow on the left. The spire of Lindfield Church can be seen away to the left. **Pause here**. The footpath sign and the track do not coincide. You have to leave the track to find a footpath on the right leading downhill with the hedge on the left. At the bottom of the field you battle through rough scrubland.

In 300 metres you escape onto a fine wooden footbridge over the River Ouse. Cross the soggy field to Fullingmill Farm ahead. Pass the house on your right and continue south on the farm road.

In one kilometre you reach a row of cottages in Spring Lane. Go up the lane to the main road, Lindfield High Street. Turn right and walk along the pavement for 150 metres. Cross to the picturesque old houses opposite (See under the heading above 'All Saints, Lindfield'). Turn left into the lane before the church and retrace your steps to the Car Park.

Horsted Keynes

Walk 25: Wivelsfield, Chailey, Plumpton Green And Wivelsfield Bethel Baptist Chapel

A Wealden Walk through gently rolling fields and fragments of ancient forest with 4 churches, 4 pubs and innumerable stiles!

Starting Point: Church Lane Car Park, Wivelsfield off B2112, south of Haywards Heath **GR**339208
Or Plumpton Station **GR**364162 (See the heading, Plumpton Green to Wivelsfield)
Map: OS Explorer 122 **Terrain:** Undulating **Distance:** 12 Miles
Advice: A Compass for easy orientation would be useful on this walk.

The Churches

The Parish Church of St Peter and St John the Baptist, Wivelsfield. 'Wifelsfelda' is mentioned in AD 765. The name means the 'feld' or enclosed land, owned by Wivel. Apparently, he also owned a 'denn' or swine pasture 2 miles east, Wivelsden Farm. Ownership changed after 1066. William de Warenne, acquired much of Sussex, founded the Cluniac Priory of St Pancras in Lewes and donated several churches to the Priory, including Plumpton, Ditchling and Wivelsfield. The church has a Saxon core. The oldest part of the present church is the north doorway. It has been moved from its original position in the Saxon nave to the north aisle. It is tall to accommodate Saxon banners, narrow and has a multi-reeded arch. Although they saved this doorway, the Victorians demolished the Saxon wall when they built the north aisle in 1869. They also destroyed the Hebrew texts found on the walls of the nave and dismantled and re-modelled the fine Jacobean pulpit. They removed the east window from the chancel and placed it in the north aisle. The 13th century chancel was given a new east window. The chantry chapel is also 13th century. It was built so that masses could be held for the souls of the landowners, the Mores. There is a small lancet window high in the east gable. The south aisle and the tower were built in 15th century. Outside, the belfry window has carvings of an owl and a musician. All the stained glass in the windows dates from the 19th century apart from a modern window in the north aisle of St Francis with bird and flowers. This is an appropriate memorial to Montagu Allwood 1880 – 1958. He perfected Alwoodii dianthus and one is called 'Sweet Wivelsfield'.

The Parish Church of St Peter, Chailey. There was a place called 'Chagel' in 1091 but no mention of a church until 1269. The 13th century tower is the oldest part of the present building. It is short with a shingled spire. The weather vane in the shape of a cockerel, added in 1772, reminds us of St Peter. The chancel is also 13th century with three original lancet windows on the north side. The Victorians blocked the priest`s door in the south wall and rebuilt three windows to match those on the north side. The chancel windows have shafts on either side with capitals in floral design with two exceptions. One has serpents biting each other

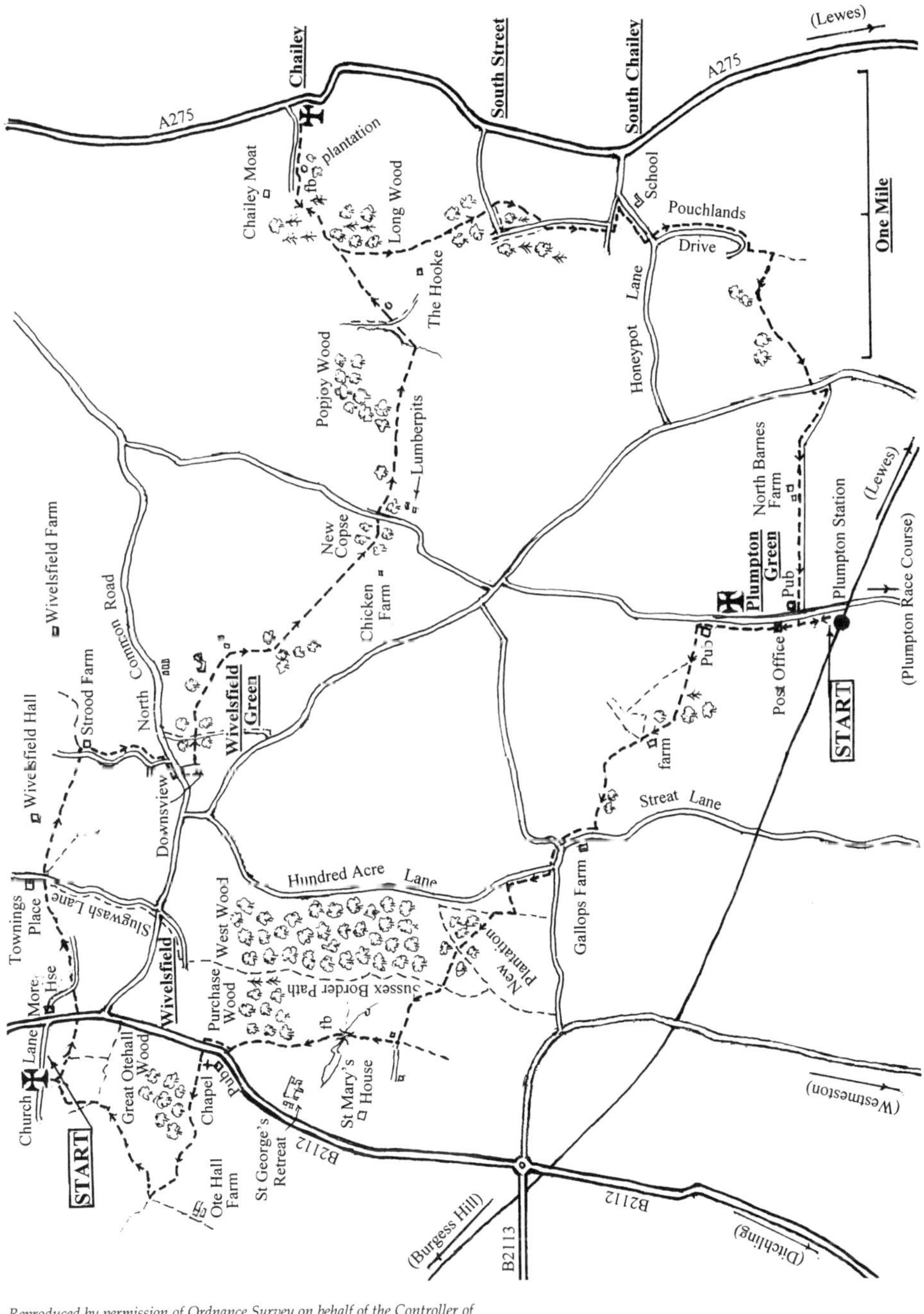

Chailey
South Street
South Chailey
A275
(Lewes)
One Mile
Chailey Moat
plantation
fb
Long Wood
The Hooke
School
Pouchlands
Drive
Honeypot Lane
Popjoy Wood
Lumberpits
New Copse
Chicken Farm
North Barnes Farm
Plumpton Green
Plumpton Station
(Lewes)
(Plumpton Race Course)
Pub
Post Office
START
Wivelsfield Farm
Strood Farm
North Common Road
Wivelsfield Green
Wivelsfield Hall
Downsview
Townings Place
Slugwash Lane
More Hse
Wivelsfield
Hundred Acre Lane
West Wood
Purchase Wood
Sussex Border Path
New Plantation
Gallops Farm
Streat Lane
farm
Church Lane
Church
START
Great Otehall Wood
Chapel
Pub
Ote Hall Farm
St George's Retreat
St Mary's House
B2112
B2113
(Burgess Hill)
(Ditchling)
(Westmeston)

and one has a 'green man', a pagan symbol of fertility. The south aisle was added around 1350. The north aisle was enlarged in 1846 and again in 1878. As a result there is a huge space around the nave whilst the chancel seems to be in a small corner. The handsome church on a village green makes a delightful picture.

Plumpton Green, All Saints is a little Victorian church with unusual octagonal tower. The outside is flint. Inside a generous wooden roof curves over the low brick walls.

Wivelsfield Bethel Baptist Chapel is an attractive brick building. In 1762 Henry Booker left the Ditchling Baptists to set up a stricter branch in Wivelsfield.

The Walk

There is a long straight path behind Wivelsfield Church, leading through the churchyard to a gate into open fields with the Downs behind. Go through the gate and turn left. The footpath is clear to the next field. You are heading mainly east, parallel to Church Lane.

Keep on course when you cross B2112 to the footpath opposite. Go through the farm gate and turn right on the track. This leads down to a mucky patch, enclosed by trees. On the other side of this patch you emerge to a wide sloping field. The track goes straight on. The path is just to the left of the track and goes northeast, gently uphill for 500 metres towards a large house, Townings Place. Go through a grassy enclosure to Slugwash Lane.

Avoid the Sussex Border Path along this lane. Cross to the entrance road to Wivelsfield Hall. Pass a bungalow on the right and go straight on to the footpath. Follow the left finger pointing east across a little elevated field. Go through the boundary of trees and keep on course across two more fields, taking time to admire the view south.

The fourth field sweeps down to open country, dotted with trees and woods. Tear yourself away from this fine view and veer slightly to the right, **NOT** sharp right. Keep to the left of an irregular, overgrown hedge down towards the buildings of Strood Farm. Now turn right through the hedge and follow the access road southwards, passing a large duck pond on the right. In 500 metres at the bottom, pass new houses and Strood Close on the right Turn left down to the main road, North Common Road.

Cross diagonally right to Downsview, a straight residential road. In about 75 metres turn left into an alley, leading to fields behind houses. Keep straight on. In the right hand corner of the second field you come to a wooded track. Cross the track to the footpath opposite and up to farmland. Continue to a farm track. Again, cross the track.

The field ahead rises to woodland. Cross diagonally right towards the field corner. Officially, the path goes through the wood. At the time of writing the woodland route is impassable and walkers have gone through a field gap just below the corner. They then skirt the wood to rejoin the path in 50 metres.

Head southeast towards nearby buildings. There are some wonky stiles here, I shall report! Pass the south-facing rooms of a rest home on your left and continue on course downhill. Pass a garden on your left and come to open country.

Follow the line of the footpath south towards the far field corner where two woods meet. Go through this wooded corner and you are in a wide flat plain. Head southeast for ½ mile, passing a free range chicken farm away to the right. The last part of this path goes through a newly planted copse and brings you to the byway at Lumberpits.

Cross this lane diagonally left to continue southeast through the plain. Hug the hedge on the right and keep on course passing two woods. Emerge from the second wood, Popjoy to a wide sequestered space in the ancient forest. In 200 metres, at a watercourse there is a welcome finger post. Turn left here to head northeast with the straight watercourse on your left. In 150 metres, turn into a strip of trees on the right. They hide a cross track.

Do not be tempted along this track. Look for the concealed path opposite. It will take you northeast across a narrow field. Pass a sedge pond on the right and find the way, marked with arrows, through to the next field. Keep on course for 300 metres. You come to another tree-lined track and turn left.

You take this track in reverse on the return walk. Remember the way back to it!

Meanwhile, head north on the track, avoiding a rickety footbridge on the right and a private trail on the left. Make for the wood ahead. Just inside the wood, arrows point the way. Take the right fork, heading northeast through the wood. In 300 metres you emerge at a lake in front of a large house, 'Chailey Moat'. Turn right. Pass the lake on your left and enter a new plantation of trees. At the end of the plantation, turn left to the entrance to Chailey Moat. The driveway on the right leads to Chailey Church.

From Chailey to Plumpton Green, retrace your steps to the tree-lined track mentioned in italics above. Continue south on this track. It skirts Long Wood on the left and goes through peaceful meadows where sheep graze. Pass the house, 'the Hooke' away to the right. Veer left and southeast to go through a rough, enclosed field and out across more meadowland towards a wood.

Keep on course through the wood and you reach a wide drive. Go straight across to a path, not shown on the Ordnance Survey map. It follows inside the eastern edge of the wood for 300 metres and comes to another drive. Turn left here and walk southwards along the drive for 500 metres then turn left to the main road.

Turn right and cross to Chailey Comprehensive School opposite. Walk on the pavement past the school, then past some houses on the left. After a residential close, turn left into the concrete of Pouchlands Drive. It leads to the farm buildings of Yokehurst. Ignore footpaths to the left and follow the Drive to the end where it bends to the right. Just after the bend, turn down the track on the left and enjoy the wide view to the Downs.

At the same time, keep an eye open for an inconspicuous footpath on the right in about 75 metres. Turn right and cross the field diagonally left towards woodland. Hug the wood on your right and keep on course, southwest crossing fields for ½ mile.

You come to a byway and turn left. Cross to a concrete farm drive, Barnes Lane. This leads west for over one mile and offers open views on all sides. The Downs are on your left. As on Walk 29, you can see a large 'V' made by trees planted on the slope in 1897 to commemorate Queen Victoria`s Diamond Jubilee. You reach Station Road, Plumpton Green at a welcome pub. There is a post office opposite. Turn right, heading north.

Walkers from Plumpton Station start here after they have walked up Station Road.

From Plumpton Green to Wivelsfield, continue north along Station Road, passing Plumpton Green Church on the right and a second pub on the left. Immediately after the second pub, turn left into an alley. You soon escape to open country with wooded hedges.

Keep to the edge of the field on your left and head mainly west. After crossing a footbridge between two precipitous stiles, avoid a path to the right. Keep on course hugging a hedge on the left. Go through a copse and turn right. A farmhouse dominates a small field. Cross this field diagonally right. A small pond is in the corner of the field. Go through the double hedge. Avoid the track between the two hedges on the right.

Turn left into a wide sloping field. Head northwest, again hugging the hedge on the left for ½ mile of gentle uphill walking. Turn to the right to admire the view over to Chailey Windmill in the distance. You finally go through a strip of woodland to Streat Lane. (Visit the hamlet of Streat in Walk 29).

Turn right and head north along Streat Lane. The delightful black and white cottage on the left is Gallops Farm. At the top you reach Middleton Common Lane, B2113. Turn left and cross this main road with care to Hundred Acre Lane, leading to Wivelsfield Green. Walk up this lane for 300 metres as far as a finger post on the right and a concrete sign in the ground on the left.

Turn left into a field and pass a house on your right. Hug the boundary on the right. In the next field, turn right to a new enclosed plantation. Follow it on your left until you come to a small stile. Turn left and cross the plantation on a narrow path, just discernible by the imprint of other footsteps. It leads to another small stile. Ahead is a wooded cross track, a bridleway.

Go straight across the bridleway to the footpath opposite. Cross a field to enter another wooded track, the Sussex Border Path. Turn right then immediately left into a long narrow field. Cross diagonally right, avoiding the disused stile in the wood on the left. Pass a gap to the next field then take the excellent 'Monday Group' stiles through the wood. Head towards farm buildings and turn right after a barn.

Plumpton Green

You now have an open, straightforward path north for one kilometre, passing at a distance St Mary`s House then St George`s Retreat, both on the left. When you have passed Purchase Wood on the right you reach a sloping field. Fork left and go down to the far corner. Go through a strip of trees to the B2112.

Turn right and walk past the pub. Then cross to the Bethel Baptist Chapel. The public footpath goes beside the chapel entrance. Pass the chapel on your left and follow the footpath west across fields and up to Great Otehall Wood. Go round the edge of the wood on your right. Ote Hall Farm can be seen away to the left. At the end of the wood turn right into a large sloping field. Hug the boundary on the right as you go up to the field corner.

Turn right into a wide, grassy, hedge-lined track, heading northeast. In 500 metres the track ends at a field with a choice of paths. Go straight on uphill with a ditch and hedge on your right. At the top turn right and you enter the field just below Wivelsfield Church. Go through the metal gate into the churchyard, up the long path and around the church to the road. Church Lane Car Park is down to the right.

5 Walks
Near Lewes

Walk 26: Lewes to Glynde

From Lewes` ancient High Street go past the castle and descend to walk over the picturesque bridge into Cliffe Village then climb up through the golf course and onto the sweeping heights and bottoms of the Downs to Glynde. Return over more downland.

Starting Point: the County Car Park behind St Anne`s Church, there is a small charge at weekends. On weekdays you should find street parking nearby. **GR**409099

Alternative Starting Point: Glynde Car Park, north of the station. **GR**458088

Distance: 7 Miles **Map:** OS Explorer 122

Terrain: Hilly one path crosses a golf course

Local Information: You pass the Tourist Information Office on your way down the High Street. It is on the left about 75 metres past St Michael`s Church.

The Churches

**St Anne`s Church Lewes** stands outside the old west gate at the top end of High Street. Originally the dedication was to St Mary the Virgin. Before the Reformation St Anne`s image in the church was much venerated and may have caused the change of name. Much late Norman influence can be seen in this church. The tower with its lancet windows, the nave, south transept and south arcade are all 12th century. The north doorway and font are also Norman. The south arcade has round pillars and carved foliage on the capitals. The arches are pointed, apart from the east arch. In 13th century the chancel was extended eastwards. The chancel arch is Victorian. In1927, during the building of the vestry, the anchorite`s cell was discovered between the south transept and the chancel. She lived a life of solitary prayer and is mentioned in the will of St Richard, Bishop of Chichester in 13th century. The chancel also contains a 14th century altar tomb, possibly from the church of St Peter Westout that once stood nearby. St Anne`s still has a fine crown post roof; the original medieval tie beams survive in the chancel.

St Michael in Lewes, a bit lower down the High Street, stands below the castle. It has a remarkable round tower, one of three near the River Ouse (See Walk 28, Southease and Piddinghoe). The adjoining west wall is 13th century. There is also a 13th century lancet window in the south aisle, at the western end. The south arcade of octagonal piers is 14th century. In 16th century St Michael`s was the mother church of Lewes. The benefice was among those seized by Henry V111 and the church began to decay. Rebuilding took place in 18th century. The north arcade was built of wood in 1748. The street front was also rebuilt in Georgian style with neat doors at either end. It is a fine example of knapped and squared flint. The Victorians altered the windows to Gothic style. Near the organ recess on the north wall the Pelham monument has the figures of husband, wife and 10 children, 1559. Sir Nicholas Pelham led the defence of Seaford against the French.

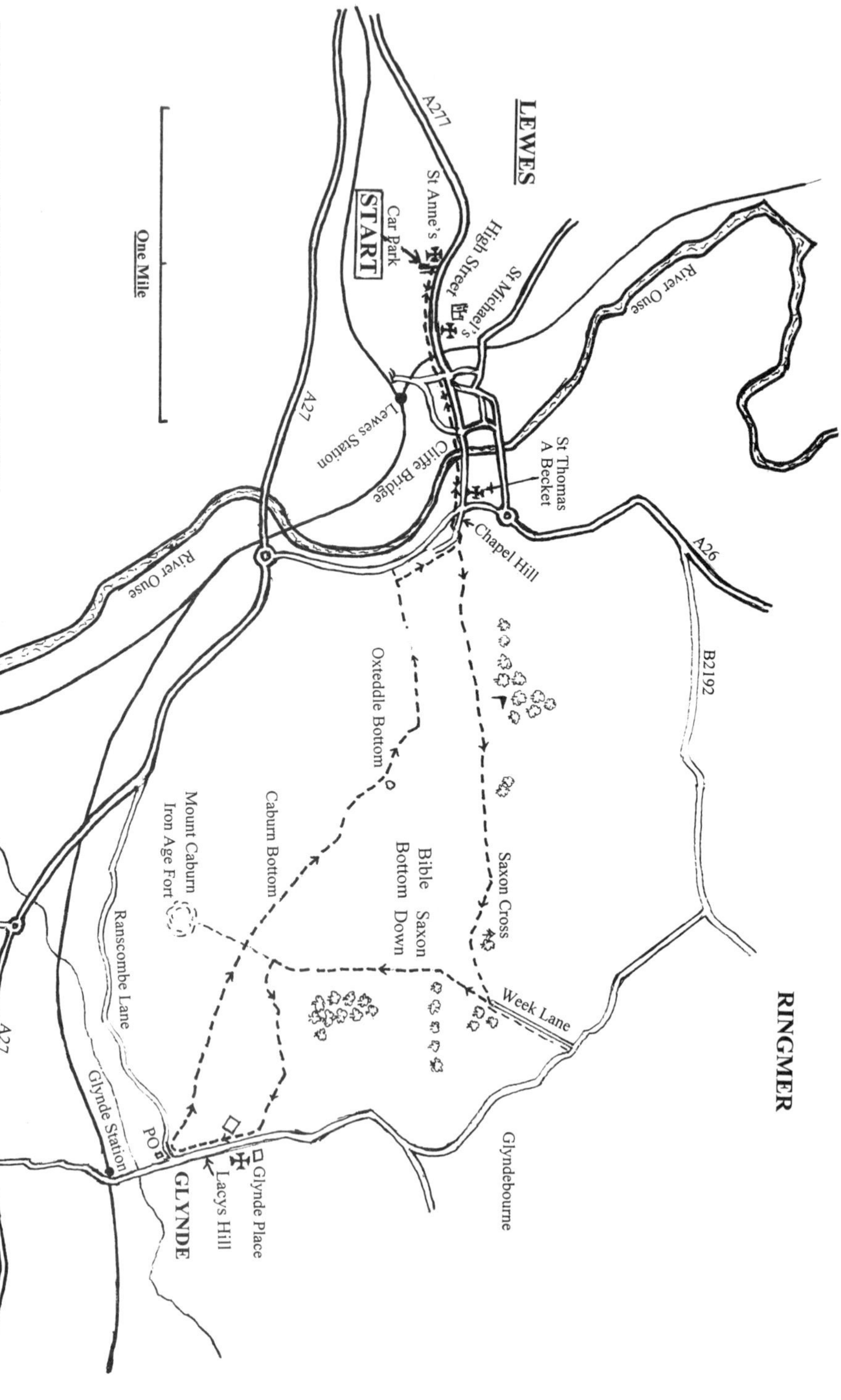
LEWES
A277
St Anne's
Car Park
START
High Street
St Michael's
River Ouse
One Mile
A27
Lewes Station
Cliffe Bridge
St Thomas A Becket
Chapel Hill
A26
River Ouse
B2192
Oxteddle Bottom
Caburn Bottom
Mount Caburn Iron Age Fort
Bible Bottom
Saxon Down
Saxon Cross
Week Lane
RINGMER
Ranscombe Lane
A27
Glynde Station
PO
GLYNDE
Lacys Hill
Glynde Place
Glyndebourne

St Thomas A Becket at Cliffe was originally built by the canons of Malling Benedictine College. It was a chapel of ease in the village of Cliffe. When you enter the chancel, you are in that 12th century chapel. There is a double squint to enable lepers to see mass. The addition in 14th century of a south aisle has put the squint inside the church. The flint tower is Perpendicular. In 1670 James Looker made the clock, possibly the second oldest in Sussex. There is a fine Victorian glass in the east window. The present organ is the successor of several earlier ones. In 1960 and again in 2000 the church suffered flooding which covered the font on the second occasion.

St Mary the Virgin, Glynde was also built by the canons of Malling in 12th century. Their building has not survived. In 1763-5 the owner of Glynde Place, Richard Trevor, Bishop of Durham had the present church built in Palladian design. Thomas Robinson was the architect. The church has a classical symmetry. Even the Victorians could not take that away. In 1895 William Kemp designed stained glass for the windows. He included some of the original Flemish glass. In my opinion plain glass would have better suited the church.

The Walk

Glynde

From St Anne`s Church walk down the High Street, passing St Michael`s Church with its round tower then the entrance to the castle, both on the left. Keep heading east on the High Street then School Hill. If you keep on the right hand side of the road in a continuous descent, you cannot go wrong. Cross the pretty arched bridge over the River Ouse into Cliffe. Continue along Cliffe Street to pass St Thomas A Becket Church on the left. At the end of Cliffe Street, cross South Street to Chapel Hill opposite.

Climb up Chapel Hill, passing cottages perched above the River Ouse. Remember to look back over Lewes. After the last house you leave the lane which is heading for the golf course. There is a signpost on the right, hidden in the hedge, indicating that the footpath on your left leads to Ringmer. Turn

Lewes

left here into a footpath that starts on a short tarmac track to a private gate and the sign 'RESIDENTS ONLY'. Follow the narrow path as it bends to the right up through scrub to the golf course.

Keep straight on heading east-northeast. You have to pass through the middle of this extensive golf course overlooking the Downs, stark and shapely on the right. You may be distracted from admiring the view. There are several warnings on route of the danger of golf balls and you have to seek the occasional way marker. In 600 metres towards the end of this ordeal, avoid stiles on the right. Instead, keep straight on to a stile into ACCESS LAND. You can now relax and look down over the treeless slope of Bible Bottom to more downs.

Keep on course to go through a farmgate then finally a kissing gate. Here at Saxon Cross you have a new aspect across the Downs to the Weald in the north. A boundary stone is at your feet. Head for a nearby small wood clinging to a northern slope. Follow this wood, keeping it on your left. Go down to Week Lane, a track over to the right. It leads down to Ringmer.

Turn right on this track and go uphill away from Ringmer. At bumpy ground, you come to a fork in the track. Fork left and head towards a farm gate. Here is a permissive path heading south with a view to Lewes on the right. In about ½ mile you can see the distinctive shape of Mount Caburn ahead. We explore this hill later.

At the moment follow a fence on the right until you come to a farm gate. Turn left here. *There is no waymarker at the time of writing.* Descend on open downland to find an enclosed track with a few trees. Here is a waymarker to another permissive path leading down to Glynde.

Turn right when you reach the road, Lacy`s Hill. The stately house, Glynde Place and the church are side by side. Pass them on your left as you go downhill to the post office in Ranscombe Lane below on the right.

Further south is **Glynde Station** for those wishing to start the walk here. There are toilets and a car park just north of the station.

Pass the post office in Ranscombe Lane and turn right onto a footpath up a steep hill towards Mount Caburn, an Iron Age fort and now a nature reserve. There is a fence around the nature reserve. The entry point is at the fence corner.

To return to Lewes from the fence corner, head north for 250 metres following the line of the fence to a stile. Turn left here to follow the well trod path back to Lewes.

First the path sinks gradually into Oxteddle Bottom. Walk along the bottom until you come to a large empty round pond on the right. There is a choice of 4 gates here. Avoid two gates on the left and one on the right. Instead, go through the gate straight on and veer left uphill with waymarkers to show the route.

Veer further left to walk along the hillside. The golf course is up on the right. When you reach the end of the path turn right. From the entrance to the golf course go back down Chapel Hill. Retrace your steps through Lewes.

Walk 27: Kingston Near Lewes to Rodmell and Iford

Leave the Conservation Area of 'The Street', Kingston for a downland walk to the charming hamlet of Rodmell, once home of Virginia Woolf. Return across the alluvial plain of the River Ouse calling in at the near perfect Norman church of Iford.

Starting Point: The Parish Church, The Street, Kingston **GR**391081
Map: OS Explorer 122 **Terrain:** Two climbs, one descent, otherwise mainly flat
Distance: 7 Miles

The Churches

Kingston-Near-Lewes, St Pancras Church stands at the top end of the village, near the Downs. From the year 1100 until the Dissolution in 1538, the Priory Of St Pancras, Lewes held the church. Kingston joined the parish of Iford in 1666 and the parish of Rodmell in 1976. The church, even the Victorian restoration, is in early 14th century style with symmetrical Decorated windows. Lightning damage in 1865 led to much restoration. The tower is small for this church and may be part of an earlier building. The early campaigner for justice and human rights, Michael Scott (1907- 1983) is remembered in this church. A window in the north side of the chancel has much blue stained glass. It is the design in 4 parts of Maud Cotter, inspired by his poem, "Spirit of the Lord". A very different window is in the south side of the chancel. It is a sunny picture of nature by M.C. Farrar. There is a rare Tapsel Gate

Kingston

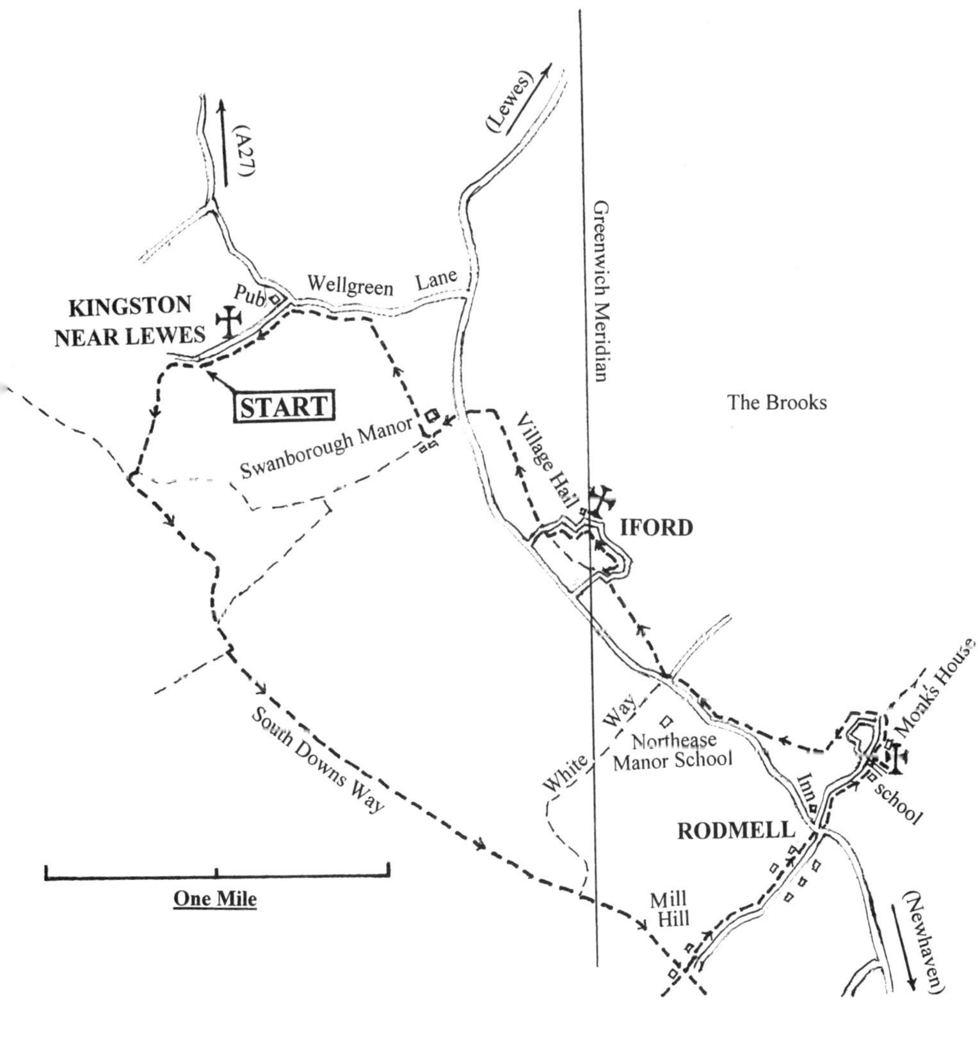
(A27)
(Lewes)
Greenwich Meridian
Wellgreen Lane
Pub
KINGSTON NEAR LEWES
START
Swanborough Manor
Village Hall
IFORD
The Brooks
South Downs Way
White Way
Northease Manor School
Inn
Monk's House
school
RODMELL
Mill Hill
(Newhaven)
One Mile

at the entrance to the church (See Walk 17, Pyecombe Church).

Rodmell, St Peter`s Church is in a Saxon village near the River Ouse. Known as 'Redmelle' meaning 'red soil', it is mentioned in Domesday, 1086. The view from the church across the River Ouse to Beddingham and Mount Caburn is almost unchanged. On the other side of Glynde Reach Valley you see Firle Beacon. Early in 12th century, monks from Lewes Priory may have helped build a Norman church. The nave, chancel and south chapel are of this early building. The south aisle has a 12th century pillar with a square capital and carving of foliage. It is similar to pillars in St Anne`s Church, Lewes (See Walk 26). A small Norman window is in the north wall of the chancel. The east window was rebuilt in 15th century. The little Trinity window above the pulpit has some medieval glass. The font is 12th century. The cottages of Rodmell are described in the Guide. Among them, Monk`s House, once the home of Leonard and Virginia Woolf 1882 – 1941, is now a National Trust property.

Iford, St Nicholas Church is a near perfect Norman building in a peaceful part of the Ouse Valley where trees and flowers abound. It serves a rural community. The nave is 11th century and still has the round Norman arch with roll and chevron carving. This arch led to the original chancel under the tower. The second chancel, built by monks of Lewes Priory around 1100, is still in use today. Tall round arches support the central tower. It contains ancient bells dating from 1426. The shingled pyramid roof of the tower is a later addition. There is an impressive triplet of rounded-headed Norman windows at the east end. They were uncovered in 1868.

The Walk

Head up to the top of the Street, making for the Downs. When the Street becomes a track after a gate, you turn almost immediately left at a stile. Follow the steep winding path uphill. Turn to admire the view back down to Kingston.

As you reach the top, there is a track on the left. It leads down to Swanborough Manor. Avoid this track and turn right. You come straight up to the South Downs Way as it rides the Downs from northwest to southeast. Turn left to walk over Swanborough Hill. In ½ mile, ignore another track to the left.

In another 200 metres turn sharp right. Avoid the path straight on heading south. Keep to the South Downs Way which becomes a concrete track. There are views south to the coast and north to Mount Caburn. Just below on your left you can see Iford Church and ahead the hamlet of Rodmell.

At crossways keep straight on. White Way on the left leads down to Northease Manor. Our way is the South Downs Way that leads straight on along a footpath and crosses the invisible Greenwich Meridian line in 100 metres. Start climbing Mill Hill where fences make you wonder if you are still on the Downs.

At crosspaths turn left down the tarmac road of Mill Hill. You have now left SDW. Pass houses all the way down to the main road. Cross with care diagonally left to the old inn opposite.

Go down the picturesque village road of Rodmell, passing farms and cottages. *In 450 metres the footpath on the left leads to Iford, we join it a bit further on.* Just past this path but before you reach Monk`s House, turn right into School Lane. The school and the church are on either side of this lane. They both look east to the Downs.

From Rodmell Church return to the village road, and continue your trek through Rodmell passing Monk`s House on the right and other cottages on the left. Avoid the footpath straight on and follow the road as it curves to the left. In 100 metres the road bends left. Take the footpath on the right. In 100 metres you join the noted footpath leading to Iford. Turn right here and cross the wide field with views to the Downs you crossed earlier. Make for the left corner of the field where you rejoin the main road.

Turn right to walk for 250 metres along this road. Pass Northease Manor, now a school on the left. When you reach a lane, turn right then immediately left into a field.

Follow the path northwest across the field to Iford. You come to the village road. Avoid the path straight on towards Sutton House. Turn right on the road that makes a loop round the hamlet. On your tour you pass a lane on the left to Iford Manor and a farm road ahead. Here you curve left. Before completing the loop you come to Iford Church on the right, then the village hall which is on the Meridian line and finally, after another bend, you find a footpath on the right

Turn right. You have in fact rejoined your footpath northwest. It enters a track then veers left over fields. You are walking parallel to the main road. In 500 metres aim for the waymark post in the centre of the field. Turn left here to rejoin the main road.

Cross with care to the road opposite. Pass Swanborough Manor on the right. It dates back to 1200 and was renovated in 15th century. I understand it is now home to the vice chairman of Sussex University. Go through farm buildings and fork immediately right to pass stables and emerge onto a straight stretch of footpath back to Kingston.

In 500 metres turn left at Well Green Lane and walk on the pavement as far as the telephone booth. Turn left here into the Street and the welcome sight of the pub. Continue along the Street to Kingston Parish Church.

Walk 28: Southease, Telscombe, Piddinghoe

Above the River Ouse stand three churches, unique for their round towers. We visit two on this walk. The third is in Lewes (See Walk 26). We also climb up to a more conventional church in a sheltered spot in the Downs and return along the riverbank.

Starting Point: Southease either **Start 1** Southease Halt **GR**432055
Or **Start 2** Southease Village Green **GR**424053
Map: OS Explorer 122 **Terrain:** Gentle hills and flat land.
Distance: 7 Miles (can be shortened to 5 ½ miles by omitting Piddinghoe)
Note: "The Main Road" we cross four times is the Lewes to Newhaven back way. Some cars still come hurtling along it – so, Take care!

The Churches

Simon Jenkins has chosen Southease Church to include in his book, "England`s Thousand Best Churches". Southease has an unrestored simplicity and charm. Another church with a round tower and much inside beauty, Piddinghoe should also be included.

The Parish Church Of Southease overlooks the village green of this tiny hamlet near the River Ouse. In 966 King Edgar granted the church and manor of *Sueise* to Hyde Abbey, Winchester. The name of the little fishing village has evolved over the centuries. *Suo Hese* originally meant 'South Brushwood'. By 1268 the name was *Suthese.* The Normans built a cruciform church. Norman windows, one blocked, still survive. Contrary to the usual practice, this church has since grown smaller, shedding its aisles. Blocked arches show where the aisles were. The present simple building consists of a Norman nave, a round tower added before 1150, a 16th century porch and a 14th century chancel. There is a curious wooden chancel arch. The 13th century wall paintings are faint; they probably once covered the whole church. Christ in Majesty is on the west wall and symbols of St John and St Luke. Two bells, one dated 1280, were re-hung in 2000.

Telscombe Church, St Lawrence is a traditional flint church with a square tower, Norman nave and chancel. A north aisle and chapel were added in the late 12th century. Round arches throughout the church are Norman. The name, 'Titelescumb', meaning 'Titel`s Valley` is mentioned in 966. *Unless you time your*

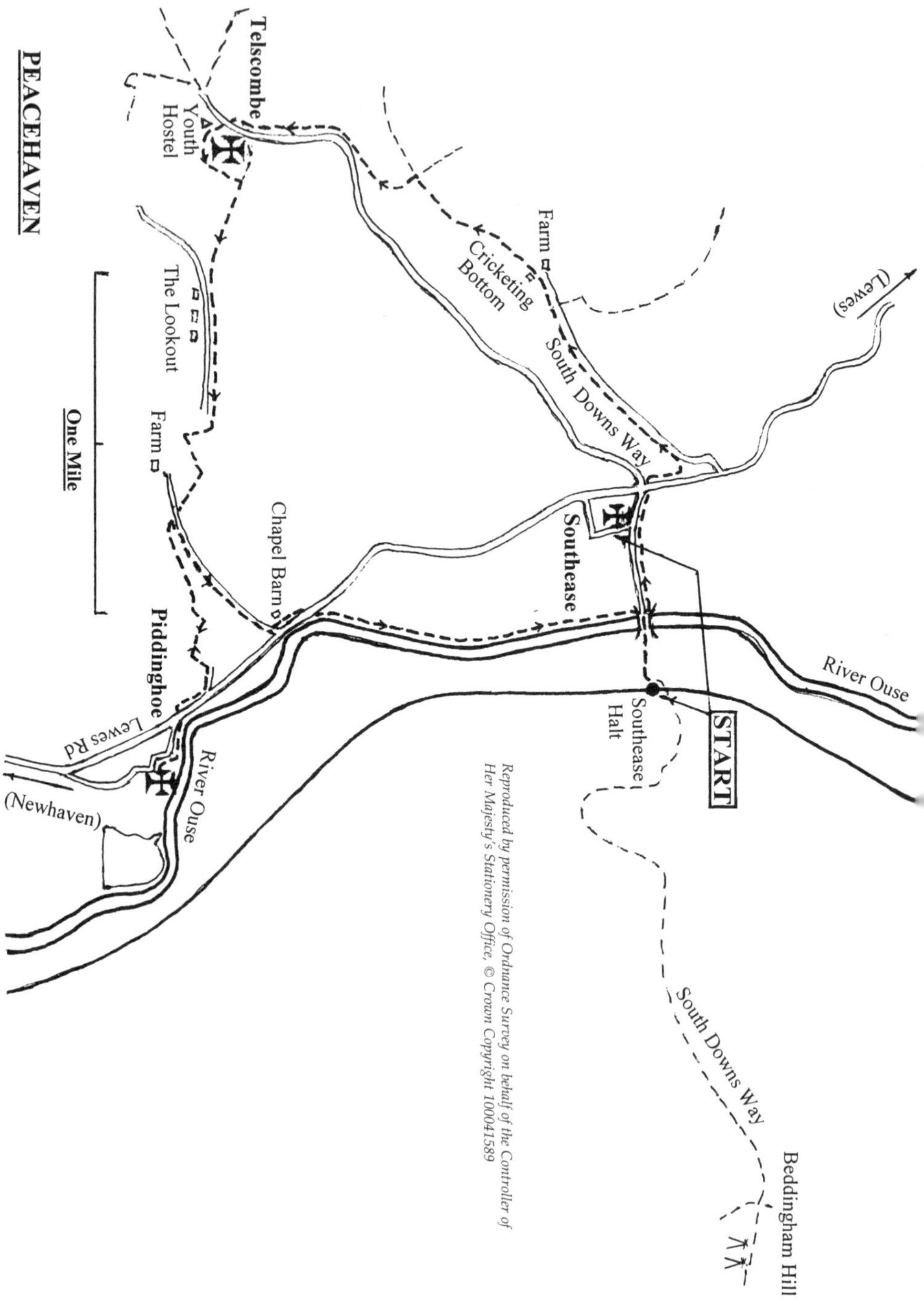
PEACEHAVEN
Telscombe
Youth Hostel
Farm
Cricketing Bottom
(Lewes)
South Downs Way
The Lookout
One Mile
Farm
Chapel Barn
Southease
Piddinghoe
River Ouse
START
Southease Halt
Lewes Rd
(Newhaven)
River Ouse
South Downs Way
Beddingham Hill

visit to coincide with Sunday Morning service or Saturday morning cleaning, it is difficult to enter this church.

Piddinghoe Church, St John the Evangelist overlooks the River Ouse in a wide, shallow valley, much flooded in the past. The Saxon, 'Pyddinga hoh' means 'the spur of the Pyddingas'. The original church was smaller; just a flint round tower and a nave. An early precipitous wooden ladder still stands inside the tower. It is marvellous that the centuries old wood should be in such good condition. Round, 12th century Norman arches in the north aisle contrast with pointed or Gothic arches in the south aisle. The chancel in Early English style was added in 13th century. It has three delightful lancets and a round window in the east end. In 1882 the Victorians made a thorough restoration of the aisles. They also re-roofed the chancel, re-shingled the tower and added the porch. Sadly they covered the old stone flagging of the floor with tiles. Apart from this last outrage, the valiant Victorians brought the building from a state of decay to one of near perfection.

Telscombe

The Walk

Start 1: From Southease Station head west along the South Downs Way to the nearby River Ouse. The SDW crosses a bridge over the river and becomes a track through meadows with reeds and water courses. We come up to the unspoilt hamlet of Southease. Pass the village green. Continue as on Start 2.

Start 2: Face the church and turn right and take the leafy lane, still the South Downs Way up to the main road. Follow the verge on the right then cross to the byroad to Telscombe. Immediately turn right off this road onto the indicated South Downs Way footpath across fields. There is a zigzag path down to the farm track below. Turn left and follow this track southwest through a bare downland valley. In about one kilometre you say farewell to the South Downs Way as it branches off to the right.

Continue southeast through farm buildings, ascending gradually above Cricketing Bottom on the left. In half a mile take the footpath to the left. It climbs the slope and curves right for

Telscombe

a steeper climb back to the road to Telscombe. Turn right, walking towards, then down through to the centre of the little village. The church is above on the left. A YHA hostel is nearby.

From Telscombe Church go up through the churchyard to the extra burial ground and turn left. On the boundary there is a gate leading to a hedge-lined footpath along a track. Turn right to walk east along the footpath. You reach a ridge with pleasant downland views to the left. Ahead and northeast the two masts of Beddingham Hill are in sight for much of the way. You reach a line of bungalows, apparent strays from neighbouring Peacehaven on your right.

You soon leave the bungalows behind and cross the right corner of a grassy field. Continue on course on the other side of the boundary then turn right into a narrow footpath that takes you down a short steep slope and abandons you in the flat field below. The path crosses diagonally left but it is safer to go straight down to the hedge-lined driveway ahead. Turn left on the driveway, you will then find a footpath sign in about 100 metres on the right. Lewes is indicated straight on and Newhaven to the right.

Shorter Walk *(omitting Piddinghoe)*

*The driveway leads back to Southease (it is indicated to 'Lewes'). If you wish to shorten the walk, omitting Piddinghoe, take this route northeast and continue at * below.*

Longer Walk (to include Piddinghoe)

The walk to Piddinghoe, a distance of 1 kilometre, is up sloping downland on the right. (You will have to retrace your steps from Piddinghoe to avoid road walking).

Piddinghoe

Follow the 'Newhaven' sign and curve to the left. In May time cowslips cover this bank. The path gets wider as you climb, culminating in a private drive down to Piddinghoe. At the bottom cross the main road diagonally right and pass a house on the left with a brick kiln in its garden. Here is a preserved reminder of one industry in this village. Walk up the village street to Piddinghoe`s famous gold fish, described by Kipling as a dolphin. The church on the left probably stands on the original village road, now a mere track.

From Piddinghoe retrace your steps over the cowslip hill and down to the conspicuous finger post. Here turn right. *Follow the driveway northeast in the Lewes direction. Pass Chapel Barn on the left and go beside grand gates to the main road. Cross to the footpath opposite and turn left to walk on the flood bank beside the River Ouse as far as the bridge at Southease. Turn left for the village and right for the station.

Walk 29: Ditchling Beacon Car Park, South Downs Way, Plumpton, Streat, Ditchling, Westmeston

After a spectacular stroll along the top of the Downs, you descend for a rewarding crawl between five very varied churches then climb back up to Ditchling Beacon

Starting Point: Ditchling Beacon Car Park **GR**333130
(The National Trust levies a small charge that should be paid into the cash box.)
Map: OS Explorer 122, 'South Downs Way' **Distance:** 8 – 9 miles
Terrain: Gently undulating high ground, an easy slope down, fairly flat low ground, a steep climb at the end of the walk
Warning: ***The South Downs Way crosses a busy road on a blind bend. We make this crossing at the start and at the end of the walk after a steep final climb!***

The Churches

The Parish Church of St Michael, Plumpton, wedged between college buildings, still retains its rustic simplicity. The Saxon name, 'Plum Tun' gives a picture of plum orchards, even wild plums. The Saxon church among plum trees has gone. The Norman church was built in 1077. The variety of stones in the present building include flint, rubble, Sussex marble and sandstone. Parts of the tiled roof have a skirting of Horsham slabs. The nave with a partly unblocked window in the north wall is Norman. The frescoes on that wall and in the edge of the window were made on plaster when it was still damp. There are 16th – 17th century wall paintings on the south wall. The font base is Norman. The bowl is

Plumpton

Plumpton

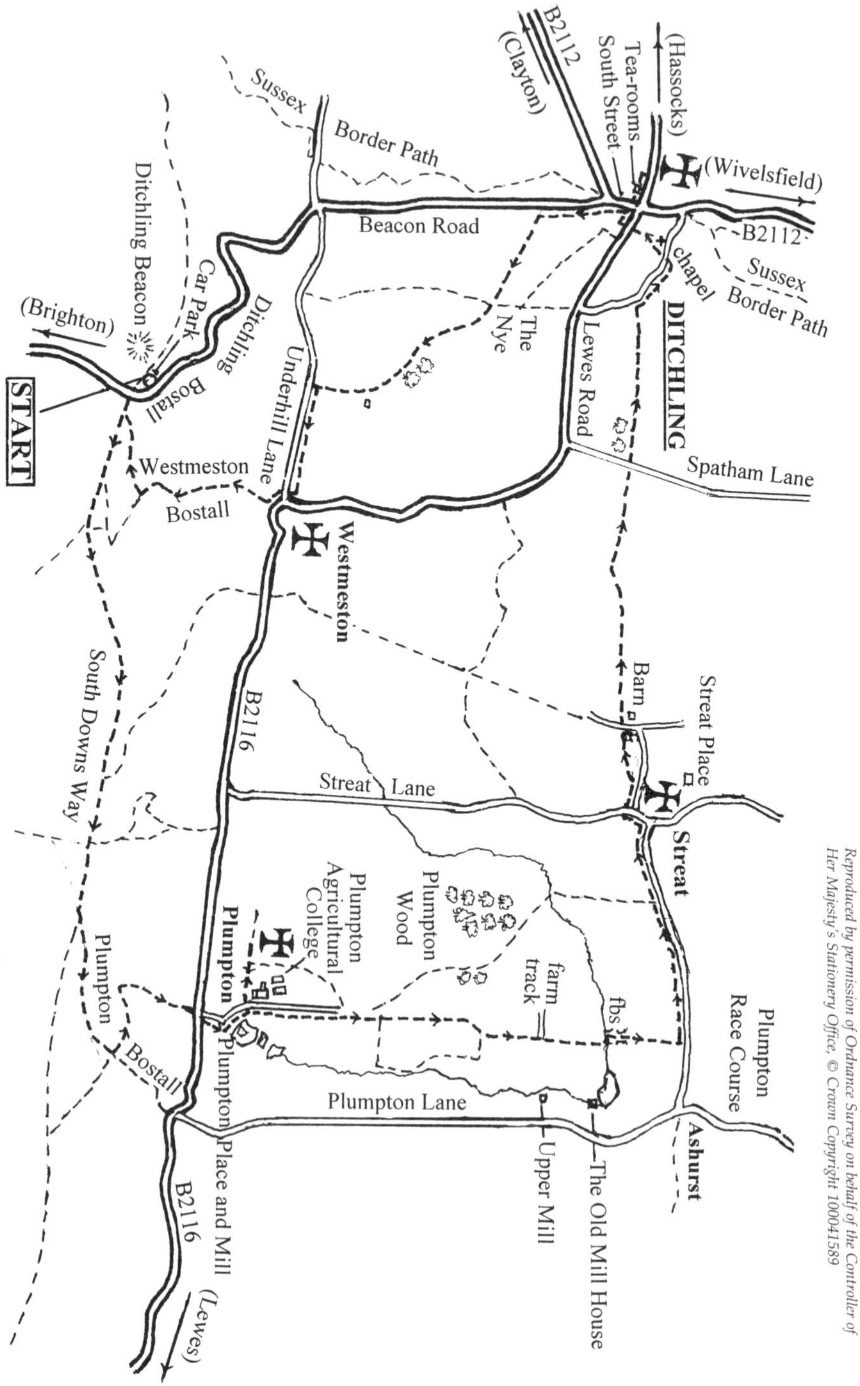
(Hassocks)
(Wivelsfield)
B2112
(Clayton)
Tea-rooms
South Street
Sussex Border Path
Beacon Road
B2112
Sussex Border Path
chapel
DITCHLING
Ditchling Beacon
Car Park
Ditchling
Bostall
(Brighton)
START
The Nye
Lewes Road
Underhill Lane
Spatham Lane
Westmeston
Bostall
Westmeston
One Mile
South Downs Way
B2116
Barn
Streat Place
Streat Lane
Streat
Plumpton Wood
Plumpton Agricultural College
Plumpton
farm track
fbs
Plumpton Race Course
Plumpton Bostall
Plumpton Place and Mill
Plumpton Lane
Upper Mill
The Old Mill House
Ashurst
B2116
(Lewes)
Reproduced by permission of Ordnance Survey on behalf of the Controller of Her Majesty's Stationery Office, © Crown Copyright 100041589

Ditchling Beacon

much repaired and may also be Norman. The chancel was rebuilt in 13th century. It has retained its Early English character despite more rebuilding in 1854. A buttress to the south wall has two carved stones. One is a consecration stone. The other has the cinquefoils of the arms of the Bardolf family who held the manor in the late 13th century. The tower has a 13th century bell frame with some even older timber. The choir stalls are Jacobean. An ingenious use has been made of the old box pews: they have been used to line the roof!

Streat Church was founded in Saxon times and stands at the northern end of the Roman, 'Via Strata' – hence the name. In fact there were two Saxon churches in Streat. The Normans built their church on the site of one of them. The north and west walls of the nave have Norman work. The present church has been so restored as to seem completely Victorian. It has a delightful position with a view south to the Downs and north to the idyllic mansion Streat Place. The whole hamlet is now a Conservation Area.

The Old Meeting House, Ditchling, is registered as 'The Unitarian and Free Christian Church', Ditchling. Before building the present 18th century meeting house next to an ancient cottage, Sussex dissenters used to meet in barns and farmhouses. They started in Oliver Cromwell`s time. They have an enlightened policy of not imposing their beliefs on others. In 1933, Sir Adrian Bolt was married here and remained a life member. Other famous people have lectured here. Services are on Sundays at 11 a.m.

St Margaret`s Church, Ditchling is a large cruciform building with a low central tower. It stands on a rise in the land, probably the site of a pre-Christian centre of worship. A sandstone rock in the west wall of the churchyard may have been a pagan altar. In 10th century the first stone church, probably rectangular replaced earlier Saxon building. During 13th century the church grew to its present form

Ditchling

Ditchling

and Caen stone was used. Tower, transepts and the long chancel are of this period. Arches are lofty and ornate with much carving of chalk stone.

St Martin`s Church, Westmeston is just under the Downs. The actual parish extends from the top of the Downs northwards for six miles. In 765AD in 'Cartarium Saxonicum', 'Westmaeston' is mentioned. The name means the westernmost 'tun' or farm. The church was founded in 12th century. Some walls in the nave, the north doorway and the font are of this period. The font is cup shaped and made of chalk clunch. The south aisle was added in 14th century. The 13th century chancel has an arch and walls rebuilt in 19th century. Medieval wall paintings were lost when the arch was enlarged. The porch has 14th century timbers on a 17th century base. The neat turret is 14th century. Today the churchyard is a Conservation Area.

The Walk

Cross the Ditchling Road and take the easterly course along the South Downs Way. There is a dew pond on your right at the start of this walk. You are riding the Downs on a high ridge with distant views to Birling Gap on the right and over the Weald on the left.

Ignore paths to left and right (they are not well signposted and you may not know you have ignored them!) In one mile you cross a narrow tarmac driveway. Avoid following it up to Streathill Farm on the right. Instead keep on course and carry on uphill for another 250 metres then turn left down a stony downland track, heading northeast with Plumpton Agricultural College seen below. Go down this track, Plumpton Bostal for 350 metres, pass a path on the right then turn left almost immediately.

This is a pleasant path with light tree cover. It descends southwest and offers views along the downland slope. The path curves down to a lane between tall hedges. It brings you gently down to the B2116, Ditchling to Lewes Road.

Cross diagonally right to the driveway of Plumpton College. Follow the driveway as it veers left. Just before the main brick buildings, turn left on a narrow enclosed path to the Church.

From Plumpton Church, retrace your steps to the main building and turn left on the driveway. *(There is an alternative path behind the church and avoiding the College but it is hard to find. The way markers are hidden and there is even a swampy patch).*

As you leave the college on a track heading north, you pass horse trial fields on either side then sewage works and beehives on the left. Here you may have a choice of routes:

The safe route is to continue due north on the track for over a mile to Old Mill House, in trees on the right. Here are two new footbridges over streams. Keep on course up towards houses and an unmade road used as a bridleway, a long east-west track. Turn left here. You are near Plumpton Race Course.

The undirected field route: *at the time of writing there is no signposted access to this path on the left. Some walkers have taken the track past the beehives on the left.*

If the path is properly opened, cross the field on the left to a footbridge and stile. In the next field follow the footpath towards a gap in the woodland. Go through and turn right to follow the field boundary on the right. Go through a copse and emerge to a field on the left. Cross diagonally right to Plumpton Wood. Cut inside the corner of the wood. Keep on course over a field then turn right and up to the long east–west track.

Westmeston

Turn left onto the hard track and look south over farmland to the magnificent Downs. Trees in the shape of a V on the side of the Downs were planted In 1897 to commemorate Queen Victoria`s Diamond Jubilee. In 150 metres or (1 kilometre if you took the safe route) heading west, you reach the hamlet of Streat. Turn left along Streat Lane. Pass the handsome stately home, Streat Place. The church is next door.

Streat

From Streat Church take the track west. It runs just below the church. In 100 metres turn left on a footpath to cross the corner of a field and come out behind a barn. There are cross tracks in front of the barn and a farm on the right. Opposite is a private tarmac road. Follow this open road, still heading west with fields all around. In one kilometre when you are tiring of tarmac, you cross Spatham Lane to steps up to an enclosed path.

This path leads to sports fields on the edge of Ditchling. Keep heading west until you come to East End Lane. Turn right to follow this lane through pleasant houses. In 250 metres turn left at a sign to the Old Meeting House (Unitarian). You have entered a twitten that passes the chapel on the right then continues to bring you down to Lewes Road, B2116. There are two pubs to the right.

Streat

Turn right to pubs and busy crossroads in the centre of Ditchling. Cross to West Street opposite. There are tearooms on the left and the church up on the right.

From Ditchling Church return to the crossroads and turn right down South Street. In 200 metres fork left into Beacon Road. In 300 metres turn left into a lane where Gospel Farm is advertised. In 450 metres along this track you come to a junction in an area known as 'the Nye'. Turn right then left heading southeast on the lane under a canopy of trees. In half a mile you pass a large house on the left and come up to a T-junction with Underhill Lane. Turn left on this long single-track road below the Downs. In 500 metres at crossways at Westmeston, the church is on the corner opposite.

Before you cross to the church, the way up to Ditchling Beacon is on your right along Westmeston Bostall. This starts gently along a hedge-lined track then climbs more steeply on a downland path. The path veers left. In another 50 metres you turn right onto a narrow waymarked public footpath steeply uphill. To admire the fantastic views, make sure to stand still on this precipitous slope. All too soon you reach the familiar South Downs Way. Take care crossing the treacherous road!

Walk 30: Offham to Hamsey and Barcombe

Just north of Lewes, near the River Ouse, little villages have survived through the centuries. We visit three of their churches and enjoy distant views of the Downs.

Start 1 (longer walk)**:** Offham Church near the A275 **GR**401121
Start 2 (shorter walk, omitting Offham Church)**:** Ivors Lane, Hamsey **GR**412124
Map: OS Explorer 122
Terrain: Mainly flat, one climb at the end of longer walk
Distances: Longer Walk, 6 Miles Shorter Walk, 4½ Miles
Start 3: ***Rail travellers from Cooksbridge Station can join the shorter walk. See end.***

The Churches

Offham Church, St Peter was built in 1860 as a replacement for Hamsey Church. The population had shifted from the River to the main road to Lewes. It is a large flint building in Decorated style, designed by Ewan Christian. It stands on elevated ground between the Downs and the River. The tower is above the chancel. The stained glass in the windows is by respected Victorian designers: Capronnier, Kempe and Tower.

St Peter`s Church, Hamsey is in a lonely spot on a bend of the River Ouse. It opens for occasional summer services and a Christmas Carol service. There is no electricity. Fortunately this deserted church has escaped both demolition and Victorian restoration. Once the door key has been traced (see the Walk below), you can enjoy the pure Norman character of this church. White-washed walls contrast beautifully with creamy stones. Apart from the east end, all the walls are Norman. The chancel arch and the window in the north wall of the chancel are also Norman. A medieval piscina is in the south wall of the chancel. A large squint and a 16th century aumbry are next to the chancel arch. A blocked arch in the north wall of the nave suggests that this led to a north transept in 13th century. There is a small Norman window in the south wall of the nave. 24 fragments of 14th century glass were discovered in 1928. They have been combined and installed in a little Norman window in the south wall of the nave. They make an attractive stained glass design. The three-light east window and the tower window are 14th century. The tower and the octagonal font are Perpendicular.

Parish Church of St Mary the Virgin, Barcombe. There was a church here in 11th century, possibly sanctioned by William de Warenne (see Wivelsfield, Walk 25 and also the Introduction under 'The Normans'). Much flint from a nearby Roman villa went into building the church. The village, then known as 'Bercham' is mentioned in Domesday as having three and a half mills and a church. The nave is basically early 12th century. It has a medieval window rescued from Bolitho Church, Lincoln and inserted in the north wall. The tower and transept chapel were added in 13th century. The spire was re-shingled in chestnut in 2001. The Victorians have marred

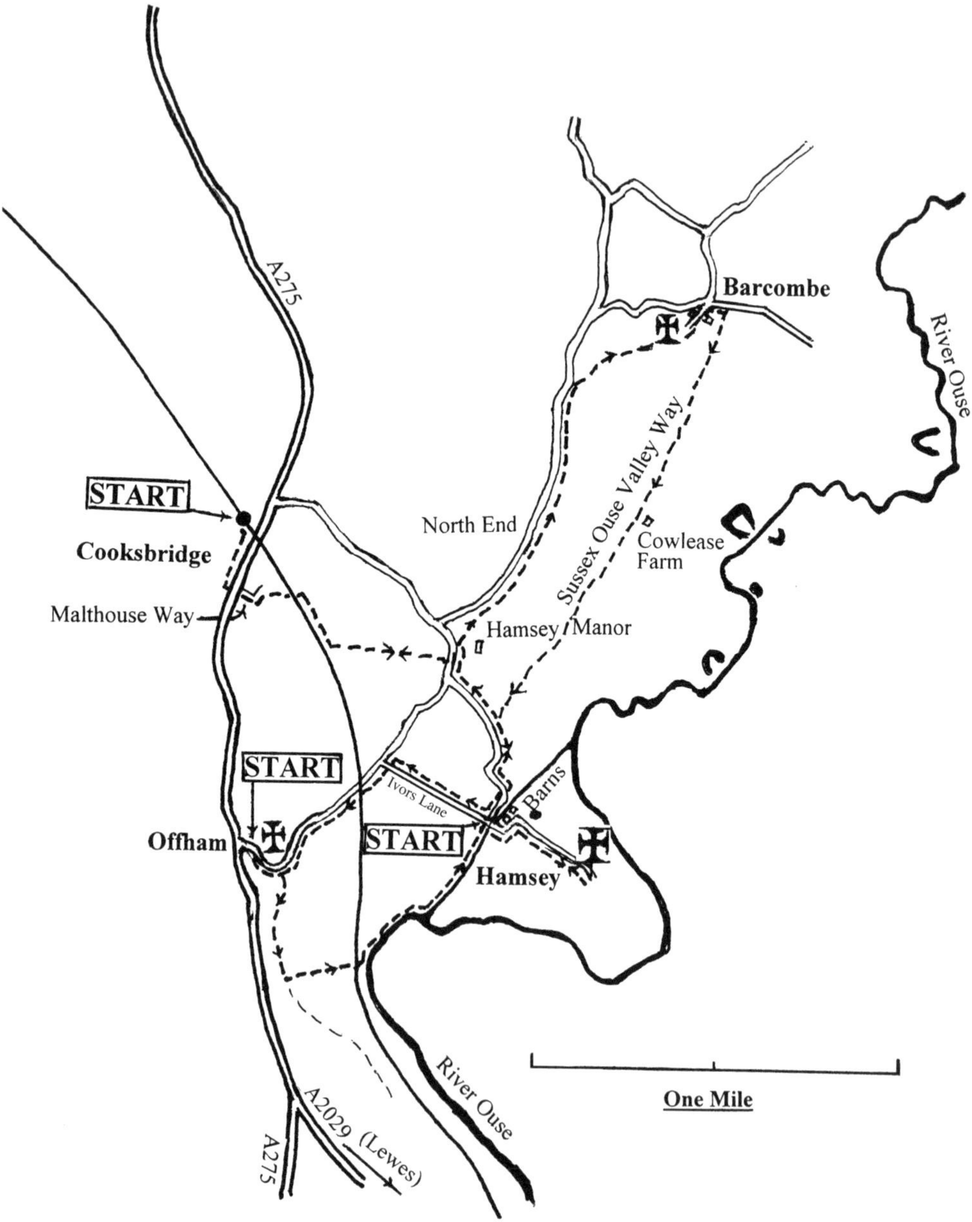
A275
Barcombe
River Ouse
Sussex Ouse Valley Way
START
Cooksbridge
North End
Cowlease Farm
Malthouse Way
Hamsey Manor
START
Ivors Lane
Barns
Offham
START
Hamsey
River Ouse
One Mile
A2029 (Lewes)
A275

the ancient character of the church with their 1878 restoration. One redeeming feature of their effort has been attractive stained glass windows in the south wall. One is by Kempe; the others are from his school. Fitted into the medieval tower arch, is glass engraved by Jennifer Conway. She depicts human forms ascending and helping one another.

Offham

The Walk

The Longer Walk: From Offham Church go down the lane, 'the Drove' to the nearby track on the right at a bend in the road. Follow this tree-covered track for nearly ½ mile. Ignore the first path to the left. Go down to an opening in the trees on the left with a farm gate and stile in sight. Turn left here, passing above a backwater of the river. Head due east across a field and go under the railway bridge to the River Ouse.

Turn left and walk on the bank beside the river. Here the Ouse is unfettered, flowing and winding through meadows. Too soon we leave the river which has come from the right. Go straight on passing a wartime shelter on the right. In 500 metres you reach crossroads and buildings.

The Shorter Walk *starts from the verge on Ivors Lane on the left.*

Both Walks: Head southeast towards Hamsey Church. Pass two barns on the left. (We obtained the key to the church from the first barn). The second barn has a lake behind and below. The road curves to the right and crosses the old railway line then leads up to the lone church.

From Hamsey Church retrace your steps to Ivors Lane. Avoid Ivors Lane and turn sharp right along the Sussex Ouse Valley Way. This is Whitfield Lane. Pass a cluster of cottages. Sussex Ouse Valley Way follows a footpath on the right. *Do not be tempted onto this path; we reserve this for the return walk.* Continue to the end of the lane. At the T-junction turn right and pass the handsome garden and house of Hamsey Manor.

* At a bend in the lane, just before a stable, turn right at a footpath. Veer left across a small field, go over a footbridge and continue towards the hedge on the left. Beyond the hedge is the road. The path runs beside the hedge and parallel to the road. *You may prefer to go through the gap to the road and continue north.*

Both routes lead to the few houses of North End. Continue north on the road for nearly ½ mile, passing over a small, white-posted bridge. Turn right at a footpath sign into a field. At the time of writing, there is rough ground on your left,

Baecombe

apparently the result of demolition. Go past this ground, making a curve to the left. Then cross the narrow field to a small copse. To the left of this copse you will find a gap in the hedge. Go through to a field and you have a glimpse of Barcombe Church behind trees ahead. As you approach the church, you pass earthworks where excavations have revealed a 4th or 5th century Roman villa.

Barcombe Church is the perfect place for a picnic. Benches are strategically placed in the churchyard to enjoy the rural views and a circular threshing shed in the lane may be open to the winds but has a thatched roof. Behind the shed stood the assize court.

From Barcombe Church go up the access lane, passing a pond on the left and the threshing shed on your right. At the T-junction turn right and walk along the quiet road where the fortunate few houses bask in peace. Their numbers were depleted in 17th century when residents fled north to Barcombe Cross to escape the Plague.

In 200 metres you leave the road as it curves to the left. Do not follow it. Instead take the farm road straight ahead. In only 50 metres turn right into a green track, Sussex Ouse Valley Way and head southwest in almost a straight line for 2 kilometres. You have fine views across fields to Malling Hill in the Downs. On the way you pass a long garden and then a footpath back to the church both on the right. About halfway you pass Cowlease Farm on the left. William de Warrenne and his wife Gundreda, who founded Lewes Priory, may have had a summer house at Cowlease. (See Introduction, 'The Normans').

After Cowlease Farm the track peters out but the way ahead over the field is marked by arrows fixed to telegraph posts. Towards the end of the 2 kilometres, the path again becomes a track and here it is overhung with trees. You then emerge to the familiar Whitfield Lane. Turn left and retrace your step to Ivors Lane, now on your right.

The shorter walk ends here but rail travellers turn left to visit Hamsey Church.

For the longer walk, turn right and walk to the end of Ivors Lane. At the T-junction turn left and walk back to Offham Church along the Drove. This is less than ½ mile and on the way you go over the level crossing and gently climb the only hill on the walk.

Travellers from Cooksbridge Station, GR401135, *can join the shorter walk. Head south along A275, passing on your right the lane to Chiltington and ignoring the footpath through an* ***alley*** *on the left. In another 50 metres, you pass the old malthouse, now the*

Hamsey

*village hall. Turn left into Malthouse Way. This residential road curves left and in 50 metres you come to the despised alley. Turn right and enter the second part of the alley. You soon reach a field with a crossing over the railway on the left. Take care no trains are coming. Cross to a larger field. Turn right and follow the hedge above the railway on the right. In 250 metres turn left and hug another hedge on the left. You pass Copyhold Farm on the left, crossing a grass track. Walk across the field to the left of the houses in Hamsey. You come out on the lane opposite Hamsey Manor. Turn left, walk along the lane and follow the above walk at *.*

After visiting Hamsey Church, return to Ivors Lane. Turn right, and return to Hamsey Manor. Cross to the familiar footpath and retrace your steps to the station.

Long Distance Paths or Ways encountered on these walks:

South Downs Way 100 miles, Eastbourne to Winchester, east – west over downland. This is the oldest way in our book. Ancient nomads took the high ground above the swamps and thick forests. (Walks 5, 10, 17, 18, 20, 27, 28 and 29).

Monarch`s Way 610 miles, the longest walk in this book. We only visit a fraction of it. It aims to follow the route taken by the young King Charles 11 after defeat in the Battle of Worcester. In 1642 he crossed to safety in France from Shoreham. (Walks 8, 9, 19, 20)

Sussex Border Path 150 miles, keeps close to the County Boundary, Emsworth to Mile Oak near Brighton. (Walks 11, 22, 24, 25 and 29).

High Weald and Landscape Trail 90 miles, Horsham to Rye. Our section winds about through small fields and woodland. (Walks 14, 21, 23 and 24).

Sussex Ouse Valley Way 42 miles, possibly the youngest way in this book. From Lower Beeding near Horsham through Lewes to Seaford. The River Ouse has been an important navigation route in past centuries. Some of the walks listed here follow the riverside but are not yet written into the Way. (Walks 14, 23, 24, 26, 28 and 30).

Downs Link 37 miles, Guildford to Shoreham, opened in 1984 as a bridleway along a disused railway line. (Walks 10, 11, 13, 15, 19, and 20).

Wey-South Path 36 miles from the River Wey, Guildford to the River Arun and crossing the Arun Valley Flood Plain to Amberley. A canal connected the two rivers 1816 – 1868. (Walk 2).

Worth Way 7 Miles, opened in 1979, another old railway route from Three Bridges, Crawley to East Grinstead. (Walk 22).

For more details, ask at Tourist Information Centres for brochures and books. Local libraries are another useful source.

Bibliography

The Buildings of England by Ian Nairn and Nikolaus Pevsner (1996) *Penguin Books*

England`s Thousand Best Churches by Simon Jenkins (1999) *The Penguin Press*

Historic Sussex by Chris Hare (1998) *Southern Heritage Books, Worthing*

In Saxon Sussex by Alec Barr-Hamilton *Arundel Press, Bognor Regis*

The Roadmender by M. Fairless (1981) *Wildwood House, Hamstead Road, NW1 3EE*

Sussex by Esther Meynell (1950) *The County Books Series, Robert Hale, Bedford Square, London, W.C.1*

Twelfth Century Church Architecture In Sussex by Richard Roberts (1988) *The Book Guild Ltd, Lewes, Sussex*

Diana Pe has provided a guide to enable walkers to uncover the hidden paths of the ancient Weald where some communities and churches escaped detection by the Normans and are not mentioned in Domesday. She and her companion, Doreen Peskett have followed riverside paths and delved into the history of the rivers Arun, Adur and Ouse. Near the banks of the Ouse they have found unique round towers on the Norman churches. In Sussex towns they have wondered at the beauty of some magnificent old churches. The architecture and history of the churches comes under scrutiny. They have climbed into the Downs to enjoy the views over coast and plain and to link the village churches. They have followed long distance paths and cycle ways to link other churches. They have traced the churches where the Knights Templar held sway. They have found the secret rooms where Catholic priests could hide from their oppressors. They have visited the charming Quaker meeting house with the intriguing name, 'The Blue Idol'. And they have delighted in following the paths to the simple village church where folk long ago expressed their artistic and religious powers. Moreover they have not forgotten the village inn!